Number 148 of 250 si

THE MONTPELIER CRICKET CLUB

Published by Mischief Makers
17 Norfolk Road, Tunbridge Wells, Kent, TN1 1TD.

British Library Cataloguing in Publication Data.
A catalogue record for this volume is available from the British Library.

ISBN 978-0-9555433-8-8

Photos: (this page) Montpelier Tea Gardens plate
Front Cover: Montpelier Gardens cricket ground in 1796

Printed and bound by Catford Print Centre (020 8695 0101)

Introduction

Over the years there have been a variety of books outlining the history of Surrey County Cricket Club and The Oval. I have read most of them, and have generally been impressed with the research and content that have furthered my knowledge of the club and ground.

I was aware that the club evolved from the remnants of the Montpelier Club, but the authors seemed unable to give any detailed analysis, or history of this local club.

The club hardly gets a mention in Gordon Ross's *History of County Cricket Surrey*, or in Nick Yapp's *A History of The Oval*, although this is perhaps more understandable, and I found nothing extra in the centenary history of the club published in 1945 entitled *Surrey County Cricket Club 1845-1945*. In the latter book the brief comments relating to the club in 1845 written by H.D.G. Leveson-Gower a century later appear to have been copied verbatim from Henry Montgomery's *The History of Kennington and its Neighbourhood.* As old maps seemed hard to find I began to worry that other researchers may have been down this route and given up!

Despite the publication of a few club histories in latter years the book that has held its place as the authority on early cricket in Surrey is Charles Alcock and Lord Alverstone's *Surrey Cricket - Its History and Associations* published in 1902. Despite more recent books doing an admirable job on the history of Surrey County Cricket Club and The Oval, nobody has attempted to re-write or add any more history to these early years. So, over a century later it remains the book that one should refer to for a lead into the early years of cricket in the county.

When I read these club histories some fifteen to twenty years ago I was unaware of *Scores and Biographies* by Arthur Haygarth, I knew nothing of the road changes in the Walworth area, and of course the Internet was not available.

It was only when friend and Surrey C.C.C. committee member Gary Sutton told me in 2004 that his home was close to where the Montpelier Club was once based, that my interest was rekindled. I quickly found a level area about the size of a cricket ground now partially built on, behind *The Beehive* pub, Walworth and believed that I had found its location.

When I sought out older cricket books and maps of the area in local libraries doubts crept into my mind. There were conflicting dates of formation for the club, *Scores and Biographies* appeared to show the existence of two different grounds in Walworth - the Montpelier Gardens ground and the Beehive ground - and I could not find any sign of a cricket ground where I initially assumed it to be.

At this time I had not found *Annals of Cricket* by W.W. Read, in which on page 79 he writes in relation to the Montpelier Club "..and their ground was known as

Hall's and situated in Camberwell." William Powell referred to this book in his *Cricket Grounds of Surrey*. Read also stated that the club was "....believed to be an off shoot of Lord's..." If I had found Read's book at the start of my research I would have been even more confused, as to date I have found no evidence that Hall's was ever their home ground. It did host a variety of local club's home matches but not to my knowledge any of the Montpelier's.

I mentioned my study to Jeff Hancock the then Surrey C.C.C. librarian, who immediately put me in touch with George Smith, a fellow Surrey C.C.C. member who, by coincidence was also trying to establish the history of the club and its ground(s). Although we had researched along different tangents we were on common ground, in that neither of us had been able to locate the site of their home, and we had also discovered large gaps in their history.

I then used the Internet and was fortunate to find a map dated 1830 which clearly showed "Montpelier Gardens" and also "Beehive Tea Gardens". Also on the map was Montpelier Street and it was about the same length as when I later found it marked on an 1871 map. Nowadays the road is known as Pelier Street and is far shorter. During his studies George discovered that the name of the road had been truncated in 1938. The area around the site of the Montpelier Gardens ground has been built over twice since the club played there, and most of the roads have been renamed, thus making our job even harder.

But what of the Beehive ground and when, and why did they move there? When I began my research I was unaware that the club had used two grounds; this only came to light after I had dipped into *Scores and Biographies.* I have been able to gauge the rough date of their move to this ground, but there appears to be no reason shown anywhere for the move from Montpelier Gardens. However an article in Southwark reference library (also found by cricket historian and writer William Powell, who has also researched the club) does show that Montpelier Gardens went up for auction in July 1833, following the death of Mr. Ross, the landlord. It had also been put up for auction in January 1812 (see page 52).

What follows is a collection of information about the club and cricket in the locality that was found in various books, two national newspapers and a selection of scorecards covering some of these matches. The scorecards and match reports have been taken from two newspapers; *Bell's Life* which I trawled through from 1822 to 1858 and *The Era* between 1839 and 1858. I was about to take the book to the printers when I was directed to the latter newspaper, as I was told that it too covered sport. I checked original copies of the newspaper, which were in annual, heavy bound covers and found many more Montpelier match reports. There were many matches reported in both newspapers and many that featured in just one. The styles of reporting and lay-out were different in each and both were guilty of advertising matches, but not then reporting on them, or even reporting on matches that had not been advertised in their newspaper. The relevant match report is from

Bell's Life unless marked otherwise. There are many instances however when I have included two reports, in which case the second one is taken from *The Era* and this will be marked accordingly. If the lone report is from *The Era*, then this will be made clear prior to the start of the relevant report. Both newspapers were published on a Sunday.

I have also tried to highlight small errors in previous books on the subject and bring all of this into one book, which I hope will be of use to others who may be keen on researching this famous club. Cricket author and historian David Frith kindly passed on a copy of a poster advertising a match at the Beehive ground on August 28th 1843, although as he pointed out, *Scores and Biographies* shows the match to have been played on August 24th 1843. It is a shame that the Montpelier Club was not one of the teams contesting the match.

Throughout the book I will also guide the reader through the steps that George and I took to establish the locations of the grounds, and the pitfalls that we came up against. I am aware that although this book pulls various bits of information relating to the club, grounds and locality together, there are still huge chunks missing. Sadly much of the club's history appears not to have been put down on paper, scorebooks are missing and small mistakes were made, so I have included a lot of geographical information from my walks around the area. I hope these gaps will be filled in by someone in the future who manages to unearth more of the club's history.

Arthur Haygarth noted that he had been unable to obtain a copy of their scorebook, when a match of theirs against Mitcham played on June 28th 1837 at the Beehive ground was the first instance for twenty-four years of them being featured in his *Scores and Biographies*. However *Bell's Life* does record a few of their matches after 1831. Haygarth tells that the Montpelier Club sunk without trace about 1808, although he features one of their match reports in his book in 1813. As there is nothing recorded in his masterpieces between 1813-37, it is probable that the club dissolved sometime between these dates. This cannot therefore be a thorough club history - as surviving documents and recorded history do not appear to permit one.

It proved impossible to write a flowing historical and factual account of the club for these reasons. There were often conflicting match reports, inconsistent reports of matches; some were detailed, some very brief, and some were not reported on at all. Such a historical account was further hindered as despite much research, quite why the club was established and by whom does not appear to have been recorded. The style of journalism in *Bell's Life* is often very brief and plain, albeit factual, but little of the club's history ever made its way into their reports. Match reports for their embryonic years are covered in a variety of books and bring the reader from 1796 up to 1808 at least, after which they appear to vanish, until reports of their matches re-appear in *Bell's Life* after 1831. Research carried out by George Smith and I also had to be filtered into the compilation, and drawing from these widely different sources did initially give the draft copy three separate styles, one of which was much annotated. The Haygarth material, recent research and the *Bell's Life* and *The Era* material were all very useful, but very different in their styles. I was not happy with this lay-out as the book did not flow properly and the three sections were too different. Therefore I decided to filter all of the details and research from the many sources into the book, although this in turn gives it a diary style of approach to events. I hope that this style is agreeable; it would have been very hard to write it in any other way, as despite the club's matches featuring in *Bell's Life* post 1831, there is very little in the way of details or history to accompany them.

I have no doubt that lurking in other local newspapers will be other occasional reports, but time stopped me doing a thirty-year trawl through those newspapers. I did check *The Times* throughout its long history but found no match reports at all.

There is no consistency in the reporting of matches; different matches feature in *Bell's Life* and *The Era*, and also in the respective works of Britcher, Buckley, Denison, Haygarth and Waghorn on early matches, although there is plenty of overlap too. To feature all of the match reports would have been time and space consuming, and pointless, so I have been selective as to what is included.

If the match reports are dark, or hard to read, it is because that is the way they printed out from the microfilm I was checking, or the because copies of *Bell's Life* were scanned and saved onto microfilm, which I then took a copy of via a print-out facility, then re-photocopied to enlarge it. Then of course the printers of this book have scanned it again!

It appears that the main Montpelier Club drew players from other teams under their umbrella. There are reports for the Montpelier Monday, Tuesday, Thursday and Saturday teams in both Buckley and Haygarth's books. If we compare the Montpelier Saturday Club's fixture against Whitehall on July 22nd and 24th 1797 and the Montpelier Club's match against Woolwich on September 26th 1798, both played at Montpelier Gardens and both in *Fresh Light on 18th Century Cricket* by G.B. Buckley, we see that although only fourteen months separate the two matches, no player plays in both matches. In *Fresh Light on Pre-Victorian Cricket* by the same author, he covers a match between Montpelier Monday and Saturday Club and Montpelier Thursday Club on August 17th 1797, thus illustrating that there were at least three different teams to pool from. Perhaps like the Kennington Club (see fourth paragraph, page 18), one's job and class dictated which of the teams you played in. It is clear therefore that the club could call on a great numbers of players (plus "given" players) when they needed to put out a strong eleven.

Although little of their history appeared to have been recorded when I set out on this venture; a belief which was found to be true, I felt that what had been written down, along with details of their grounds and matches still needed placing between two covers for the first time. I hope that in the future others will become interested in the history of the club and can add to what I have detailed on the following pages.

This book has been sitting on my computer for three years, and I have travelled to Kennington and its libraries many times in that period in order to seek out more information. However I feel that there is much still unfound and I am frustrated that little is still known about many of the personalities associated with the club.

As this book progresses a worrying lack of written history concerning the club will unfold. Even Alcock struggled and wrote "Unfortunately few of the worthies who combined to form the Surrey County Cricket Club nearly 60 years ago are alive to tell the tale….. one thing seems to be beyond doubt: the club itself was indirectly the result of the removal of The Montpelier Cricket Club from The Beehive ground at Walworth. The Montpelier Cricket Club, was one of the, if not the strongest clubs of South London and had for several years been used to play at the Beehive".

In order to stop it reading like a till receipt I have broken up its diary-like style with maps, photographs and details of some of the players associated with the club. As they did not take part in a league, then the normal "ups and downs" of a cricket club will not feature, but the fact that they played in well organised matches and often travelled across the capital and even into different counties will be highlighted.

I am relieved though, to establish there was so much cricket being played in the Kennington area during this period. This fact brought me a problem; how to illustrate which club was playing at which ground at which time. Many of the clubs used other grounds for the odd match, which itself made the research harder.

It has been a hard but rewarding three years of research to bring this project to a conclusion, and I hope that its historical contents and associated findings and photographs will be a welcome addition to the historical side of the game. Overleaf I have listed those people who assisted in the compilation of this book and I would like to thank those unknown people who have added much helpful information to the Internet about local clubs and the area whom I have been unable to trace.

Meanwhile I must conclude by thanking George whose excellent level of research and knowledge which he willingly shared, and his good company and enthusiasm kept me going.

Philip Paine   February 2010

Acknowledgements

I would like to thank the following people for assisting me with this book:

Derek Carlaw
for sending information on the Rosemary Branch ground.

Derek Carr-Hill
for sending photographs and for his encouragement.

Cuming Museum, Southwark Council
for allowing publication of the photograph of the Montpelier Gardens plate.

Norman Epps
for sending details of matches from an unpublished manuscript by George Buckley.

David Frith
for sending a copy of the Beehive ground poster.

Roger Heavens
for sending information from Haygarth's *Scores and Biographies* volumes and details of matches from an unpublished manuscript by George Buckley.

Roy Hough
for sending details of the 1812 auction of Montpelier Tavern and the gardens.

Ian Maun and Roger Packham
for sending information from Britcher, Buckley and Haygarth's volumes.

Ordnance Survey
for allowing me to use the various maps.

George Smith
for passing on articles he wrote entitled *South London Cricket to 1845* and *Montpelier and Beehive Grounds*.

Gary Sutton
for sowing the seeds of this book.

Martin Wilson
for sending details of more Montpelier Club matches.

Books and Buildings

My research over these last three years has taken me to a wide variety of buildings and sent me scurrying into the pages of many different books and newspapers. I have decided to list below where I have been and which books and newspapers have aided my research, in order to save anybody who chooses to further study the club, from unnecessary journeys and research.

Books and Newspaper Referred to;

Surrey Cricket - Its History and Associations - Charles Alcock & Lord Alverstone
The History of Cricket - Harry Altham
The English Game of Cricket - Charles Box
A List of all the Principle Matches of Cricket - Samuel Britcher
Fresh Light on Pre-Victorian Cricket - George Buckley
Fresh Light on 18th Century Cricket - George Buckley
Cricketer's Companion - William Denison
Scores and Biographies - Arthur Haygarth
Surrey Cricket and Cricketers - Rev R. S. Holmes
The History of Surrey C.C.C. - David Lemmon
Off and On the Field - Henry Leveson-Gower
The History of Kennington and its Neighbourhood - Henry Montgomery
Cricket Grounds of Surrey - William Powell
The Annals of Cricket - Walter Read
History of County Cricket - Surrey - George Ross
Bell's Life
The Era
The Times

Places Visited:

Cuming Museum, Walworth
Lord's Library
Minet Library, Camberwell
Newspaper Library, Colindale
Surrey History Library, Woking
Southwark Reference Library
Southwark Local Studies Library, Walworth
Surrey C.C.C. library, Kennington Oval
Westminster City Reference Library, Leicester Square
The Internet

Chapters

1. Local History

2. The Hunt for the Ground(s)

3. The Montpelier Tea Gardens

4. The Early History of the Montpelier Club

i) *Scores and Biographies*
ii) John Tanner
iii) Harry Hampton
iv) Other Local Clubs

5. *Bell's Life* and *The Era* Match Reports 1831-47

i) Hampton and Hall's ground
ii) Beehive ground
iii) William Baker
iv) Charles Coltson
v) William Denison
vi) Edward Garland

6. Montpelier Quit Kennington Oval

7. *Bell's Life* and *The Era* Match Reports 1848-58

i) Thomas Lewis
ii) John Peto
iii) J. Spenceley
iv) Charles Whyting
v) Rosemary Branch ground
vi) The Oval

8. A Treasured Find

9. Conclusion

10. First, Lasts, Facts and Figures

i) First and last matches at four grounds
ii) Montpelier matches found in the works of Britcher, Buckley, Denison, Haygarth and Waghorn

Chapter One

Local History

Surrey County Cricket Club's home in the locality has put Kennington on the global map, and despite the ever-changing sponsorship deals in recent years; it is as the plain "Kennington Oval" or more often, "The Oval", that the ground is known to cricket lovers and those with a passing interest in the game.

The area has been chronicled well; the Saxons called the area Wealawyrd or Waleorde meaning "farm of the Britons", and in 1086 the Domesday Book recorded Walworth as having land for ploughing and growing corn, and eight acres of meadowland for cows. It was now a village in Surrey separated from Camberwell by a stream that ran by Walworth Common, which is now covered by the Aylesbury Estate. In 1337 the Manor of Kennington was given to the Black Prince.

The Vauxhall Pleasure Gardens were laid out in 1661, and the area around the club's grounds remained an area of leisure and recreation until the mid 19th century, when demand for housing saw the area carpeted with bricks and concrete. 1678 saw the first recorded execution on nearby Kennington Common when Sarah Elston was burnt for murdering her husband. The common was the South London equivalent of Tyburn (sited where Marble Arch now sits) and executions carried on for many years.

A 1681 map of the area shows Lattam-more (Lower Moor) now Lorrimore Square, which will feature later in the book. On June 16th 1724 the *St James Evening Post* advertised the Dartford v London cricket match on Kennington Common. The following year saw the first record of the *Green Man and Horns Tavern* "in" Kennington Common and the cricketers who played on the common used *The Horns* as a base. On August 7th 1729 the *London Evening Post* reported that "On Tuesday was played a great cricket match on Kennington Common between the Londoners and the Dartford men for a considerable sum of money, wager and bets, and the latter beat the former very much."

George Buckley's *Fresh Light on 18th Century Cricket (1697-1800)* refers to a notice in the *Whitehall Evening Post* of September 11th 1736 advertising a match between Mr Hesse's Club (Lambs Conduit Fields) and Borough of Southwark, on Kennington Common three days later. For the record this was 109 years before Surrey County Cricket Club, who would play just yards away, was formed.

On July 30th 1746 nine men of the Manchester Regiment who took part in the Jacobite Rising were hung, drawn and quartered on the common. The immediate locality saw a rich variety of entertainment and punishment, although 1799 witnessed the last hanging at the common; a fraudster from Camberwell called William Badger. In 1791 Michael Faraday, he of electrical fame was born in Newington Butts, very close to the Elephant and Castle roundabouts that today dispel and displace traffic around the area. In 1800 "the much respected Mr Briant" became landlord of *The Horns* tavern. He lived until 1852 and still has relatives living in the area.

George Buckley reports a game played on August 3rd 1752 on the same common, between Kennington Club and Fulham and another stating that Peckham beat Camberwell in two matches on Kennington Common and Peckham Rye.

F. S. Ashley-Cooper writes in Alcock and Alverstone's book *Surrey Cricket - Its History and Associations* that between 1700-20 the best known grounds in Kennington were the Walworth and Kennington Commons. He adds that in the 1720s Kennington Common became a famous cricketing centre, yet the Montpelier Club is not mentioned until page 61 of the book. For comparison Ashley Mote, author of *The Glory Days of Cricket* tells that Hambledon's first recorded match was on August 18th 1756 against Dartford, some forty years prior to the Montpelier C.C. coming to notice.

On the back of a re-produced 1871 map of Kennington published by Ordnance Survey is a brief history of the area written by Alan Godfrey. He wrote "Cricket was being played on Kennington and Walworth Commons by the mid 18th century, but the Oval took its name from the roads formed around it in the 1770s by William Clayton, as part of his scheme to grant building leases and thereby develop Kennington. The 'Oval' thus formed was intended to be left empty for Clayton's own use. However, little actual building development took place until Regent Bridge - started in 1811 by James Rennie as a stone bridge, but finally built in iron by James Walker - was opened in 1816 (and later became known as Vauxhall Bridge). This led to the development of Harleyford Road, and to houses replacing the market gardens in the streets around; but the 'Oval' remained a nursery ground for some years to come, with a few villas around it and something of the character of a park."

In 1824 St Mark's Church which still stands opposite The Oval underground station, was built on common land over the River Effra. The Surrey Zoological Gardens opened on Lorrimore Common in 1831 and was a mini Crystal Palace, displaying wild animals such as lions and tigers and offering the local folk the chance to walk amongst beautiful gardens. In 1832 hustings were set up on Kennington Common (outside *The Horns*) and April 10th 1848 witnessed the Chartist's "Monster Rally". On that day the first photograph of a crowd was taken by William Kilburn (probably from a position close to *The Horns* pub).

Alan Godfrey commented "But in 1840 the owners (of Vauxhall Gardens) went bankrupt and although there were various attempts to reopen the gardens, they finally closed for good in 1859. As Vauxhall Gardens declined, so the Surrey Zoological Gardens opened. This happened in 1831, just three years after the opening of the zoo in Regent's Park, and the Surrey rival soon had it own popularity - and the first giraffes of any English zoo. The Surrey Gardens also took over from Vauxhall the role of public entertainer, with music and historic tableaux. The zoo itself only survived until 1856, after which part of the site was used for a large concert hall; a few years later this was damaged by fire, but was rebuilt and restored - minus its corner pinnacles - as a temporary home for St. Thomas's Hospital, forced away from London Bridge by the railway. The old Manor House nearby was also used for the hospital, but the needs of housing soon reigned supreme, and in 1872 the Surrey Gardens were sold off, the concert hall and manor house demolished, and the gardens and lake made way for streets such as Sturgeon Road and Manor Place. The other significant open space on the map is Kennington Common, which had been transformed into a park in 1852."

Godfrey went on to say "In 1840 the Montpelier Club was formed, playing cricket at the grounds of the Bee Hive Tavern in Walworth. This land, however, was soon purchased for building use - the map shows clearly how little undeveloped land there would soon be - and in 1845 the club was able to lease the 'Oval' and convert the old market gardens into a cricket ground. Within months a Surrey Club had been formed." Clearly there is an error in the date of the club's formation, but Godfrey does add some worthwhile facts. The 1851 Great Exhibition proved formidable competition and the zoo had become run down, and by 1856 the animals had been auctioned to pay for the building of the Surrey Music Hall on the site.

This was a large three storey oblong building with corner octagonal staircase towers topped with ornamental turrets. The music hall held up to 12,000 people but sadly was destroyed by fire in 1861, and demolished in 1872. This is mentioned as it was next to where I eventually established the Beehive ground to have been located.

In 1852 Kennington Common was enclosed, the petition for its closure was led by the vicar of St Mark's church. In 1862 a railway was built through Walworth virtually going over the top of where the Montpelier Gardens cricket ground had been situated. A local small station called Walworth was in Fielding Street but it closed in 1906. In 1889 Charlie Chaplin was born above a shop in neighbouring East Street, famous now for its market, and located very close to where once was Walworth Common. The following year improvements in transport saw the City and South London railway linked to the Elephant and Castle - this later became part of the Northern Line on the underground system.

Electric trams arrived in the area in 1904, the Bakerloo underground line had come this far south by 1906, and 1940 saw Walworth suffer in the blitz. Come 1952 the trams had gone, the local Newington workhouse was demolished in 1969 and eight years after that, in the Queen's Jubilee year, the Aylesbury Estate was covering the site of Walworth Common.

A delve into the cricket archives will quickly reveal that the area was blessed with a number of cricket grounds prior to The Oval; the Beehive and Montpelier grounds in Walworth, Hampton's (later Hall's) ground in Camberwell, the Rosemary Branch ground, also in Camberwell, further south the Royal Veteran ground in Coldharbour Lane, Brixton and the two commons; Walworth and Kennington. All hosted their fair share of matches and it appears that it was easier in those days to find a cricket match to attend in the locality than today. The rapid expansion of the capital ensured that all bar the first and last venue disappeared under various developments. Kennington Common was split into two parts by the construction of the Camberwell New Road, and St. Mark's Church opposite Oval underground station now sits where the gallows were located. A total of 129 men and 12 women were known to have been executed at Kennington. The church itself was bombed in September 1940 and was listed for demolition, but partially re-opened in 1949 and fully re-opened on March 12th 1960.

Chapter Two

The Hunt for the Ground(s)

Whether I should have looked for the history of the Montpelier Cricket Club first, instead of trying to locate their home ground was a decision I turned over in my mind for many weeks. I had read a few Surrey County Cricket Club histories and they did not contain much information about their predecessors, so I decided to seek out their ground first. The only information that I had was that they left their ground about 1844 and moved into The Oval in time for the 1845 season.

I visited the area around *The Beehive* pub, in Walworth, southeast London to view the topography of the area, and to look for any flat pieces of ground. Friend and Surrey C.C.C. committee member Gary Sutton had stated that the club had been based very close to the pub. I found such a piece of land immediately behind the pub, and believed that if I could find an old map covering this small area the ground may be shown. Such maps for this area did not seem to exist for the 1840 era, although whilst in the local reference library I bought a map of the neighbourhood for 1871, which showed virtually the whole immediate area to have sunk beneath a large layer of concrete and bricks.

My quest took a "U" turn back to the club's history when, still at the library I was shown a copy of *The History of Kennington and its Neighbourhood.* It was published in 1889 and written by Henry Montgomery, the vicar of Kennington and later Bishop of Tasmania, but perhaps more famously, the father of Field Marshal Viscount Montgomery of El Alamein. Montgomery senior lived in a house next to The Oval, very close to Archbishop Tenison's Grammar School and it was here that his famous son was born too. In this interesting small book are some chapters about cricket and one about the Montpelier Club and the author writes "that some players adjourned to the Beehive grounds in Walworth. Here the Montpelier Club was formed about 1840". Although I was not certain at the time, this date for their formation is wrong, although in his defence the author may have been unaware of its earlier existence despite his accreditation as an eminent local historian.

On page 169 Montgomery tells that "In 1779 there was a landlord at "The Bee Hive" Tavern in Walworth named Keen …. (who) built a large mansion on his property called Walworth House: some years afterwards this house came into the possession of Mr Carter, a medical man with a large practice. Mr Carter cut off a portion of his grounds for building purposes, and the street erected there was called "Carter Street". On one side of it "The Bee Hive" Tavern was also erected;

and it had for a time the double meaning of "The Bee Hive and Cricketers," when the landlord of the tavern was a Mr Groom. The ground adjoining the Tavern was not built upon; it was called Wheeler's Fields and Lorrimore or Lothammoore. The gardens attached to the tavern were laid out by a Mr Bendal as a market garden, but afterwards as a place of resort, and extended over an area of five acres. The old tavern was a long low building with a railed gallery, covered with a verandah along its front."

Arthur Haygarth's detailed volumes of *Scores and Biographies* were to be my first dip into the cricket books of old, in the hope that some sort of address would be shown if he covered their home matches. I found reference to a match in 1796 played in Montpelier Gardens, Walworth, yet when I reached 1837 they were playing on the Beehive ground at Walworth. Surely this could not be the same ground? Were there two grounds? Or had one changed its name?

David Lemmon writes on page 14 of *The History of Surrey C.C.C.* that the Beehive Tavern stood where we now find Lorrimore Square. This appears to have been taken from Charles Alcock and Lord Alverstone's *Surrey Cricket: Its History and Associations* where, on page 345 it states "The Beehive Tavern, which stood where Lorrimore Square now is." *The Beehive* pub actually stands one block away, in Penrose Street on the corner of where Carter Street once began, before it was cut in half by a block of flats. The pub has stood there since at least 1799 (see previous page) so it is pivotal in the club's history, and I have found no evidence to suggest that it replaced another by the same name in Lorrimore Square. A John Heaps took the licence in 1827 and in 1832 William Starling took over.

H.H. Montgomery continues "Old inhabitants of Kennington can remember that cricket was played on the Common (now the Park) when the "Wednesday Club" and the "Thursday Club" were in existence. Players associated themselves partly according to position in society, and partly according to their degree of prowess, one set playing on a Wednesday and the other on a Thursday, as the names of the clubs denote. The landlord of the "Horns" lent them marquees, and doubtless provided the luncheons. I can get no more information about the matches on Kennington Common beyond the fact that they were played there and that good men were members of the clubs. But soon the Common was found to be too public for good matches, and the better players adjourned to "The Bee Hive" ground in Walworth." This is an interesting comment as it shows that the latter ground was associated with better players from its early days.

Referring back to Alcock and Alverstone's book; on page 345 it recounts "Mr. H.H. Quare, an old resident in Kennington, is of the opinion that the matches, if there were any prior to 1840 were mostly amongst the tradesmen of the neighbourhood. The Bishop of Tasmania (H.H. Montgomery) makes mention of a Wednesday Club and a Thursday Club as playing on the Common in the early days. A painstaking chronicler, no doubt he is right. But in a general way, it is safe to say the cricket on the Common was without form and void. Indeed, it was not until the "Beehive" cricket ground in Walworth came into existence that the cricketers who were in the habit of using Kennington Common had a chance of improving their condition."

Arthur Haygarth's *Scores and Biographies* first mentions the club when it shows that on June 24th and 25th 1796 the Thursday and Montpelier Cricket Club played Marylebone in Montpelier Gardens. In June the following year the Montpelier Wednesday Club played Marylebone at Montpelier, and I shall assume that this is the same ground. On July 12th and 13th 1797 England played Surrey and Middlesex on "Aram's New Ground, at Montpelier Gardens, Walworth" and this match is also recorded in Haygarth's book, and is the first time that Aram's name features in the title of the ground. Other venues in the book which I believe to be one and the same are: "New Ground at Montpelier Gardens", "Montpelier" and "Montpelier Gardens".

It is interesting to note that in 1796 it is referred to as the "New Ground", in 1802 as "Aram's New Ground" but just "Aram's Ground" by 1806. Documents show that the *Montpelier Tavern* and tea gardens passed from John Bendel to a Mr Aram "at least as far back as 1798" and Lord Beauclerk's highest score of 170 was for Homerton v Montpelier on Aram's ground in 1806, so we now have an idea when the club occupied this ground. Rather worryingly however the club is not included in the columns of page xvi of Volume One of Haygarth's book when he lists the well known cricket clubs of the era.

In *Scores and Biographies* an Aram played for Montpelier Saturday Club against Homerton on July 4th and 5th 1799 at Aram's New Ground, Walworth. He took no wickets, held no catches and, batting at number eleven was 0 not out in his only innings. His side won this match by nine wickets.

George Aram had an altar tomb in the original St Mary Church, Newington "In memory of Elizabeth Aram, daughter of George and Jane Aram who died in infancy, also George Aram, father of the above who died September 11th 1813 aged 47 years, born at Wells in Norfolk, Wm their son, who died May 29th 1808 aged 13 years".

In 1884 *The South London Chronicle* stated that John Bendel built the famous *Montpelier Tavern* and was the first licensee, a post which he held until 1810. The ground appears to have been used for about twelve years and matches are featured regularly in Haygarth's book until 1806. After the match against Homerton in 1806 reports dry up, except for one match at Lord's in July 1813 versus Marylebone, and we are left to wonder why.

On page 73 of *The Annals of Cricket* by W.W. Read published in 1896, it states that the club played a match at the New Ground at Montpelier Gardens on Monday July 25th 1796, but this match does not feature in *Scores and*

Biographies. Perhaps he errs with the month and is actually referring to the match that ended on June 25th which did feature in the said book? As mentioned in the introduction, on page 79 he adds that "the Montpelier Cricket Club was formed in 1796 and their ground was sited at Hall's in Camberwell. They had another ground at the "Beehive", Walworth and held their meetings at "The Horn's", Kennington". This gives more detail than other writers regarding the embryonic years of the club and suggests that they had yet another ground in Hall's. However despite much research I cannot find any evidence of them playing at Hall's ground, although it was reasonably close to the Beehive ground and hosted a variety of team's matches.

The suburb of Camberwell is only half a mile south of Walworth, and I was interested to know where Hall's ground was located. Most likely it fell under a mass of city expansion as the city grew southwards. *The Horns* is of note as this tavern was where Surrey C.C.C. was formed in 1845; although it was bombed in the Second World War and is no more. It can be seen on the right-hand side of the print on page 72.

We get a different slant from the pages of H.S. Altham's *History of Cricket* when he states "with 1810 this great chapter in Surrey history ends. From then to 1844 only eleven county games are recorded……Surrey cricket was now disintegrated amongst a host of prosperous and powerful clubs such as Montpelier…. The present Surrey Club is really the creation of the Montpelier Cricket Club." This clearly suggests that the Surrey Club shrunk in its magnitude whilst the Montpelier Club continued to grow. We know that their matches were no longer being reported in *Scores and Biographies*, except for the one at Lord's in 1813 against Marylebone, so where did they go? It was at this stage that I realized that I had a major project on my hands, as I had no idea of how many grounds I was looking for, and who held the power in these early days. Further, much of the information in books that I was using appeared contradictory.

A local map dated 1824 (see page 57) shows "cricket ground" adjoining Montpelier Gardens to the south and perhaps this is indicative of cricket still being played there in the 1820s. On the wall of the local reference library is a map of the area dated 1851, which unlike the 1871 map shows little extra building in the immediate area, although there are no signs of any cricket grounds.

George Smith found a copy of *Sketches of Southwark Old and New* by Robert Woodger Bowers published in 1905, which states that "the "Beehive" which, together with Montpelier Gardens, were in old times pleasant and popular resorts of the lovers of the national game of cricket." This assisted greatly as it confirmed my belief that there were possibly two grounds, albeit both in close proximity.

If we return to Montgomery's local history book again, he adds that "The Beehive tavern was erected on one side of Carter Street" and this is where it is found today as Penrose Street junctions with the truncated Carter Street. He also mentions that the pub was known as *The Beehive and Cricketers* and that the landlord was Mr Groom. However further research has been unable to prove that the pub went by this name, or was ever officially registered as such.

In William Powell's recent *Cricket Grounds of Surrey* about the various grounds used by Surrey C.C.C., he allocates two pages to the Montpelier Club, and draws from similar sources to those mentioned above. He was unable to ascertain when Aram's New Ground gave way to the Beehive ground as the club's main ground, but his conclusion that the former was "near, if not or contiguous to the Beehive and Cricketer's Ground", proved accurate. William also suggests that there were two grounds having referred to *The English Game of Cricket* by Charles Box published in 1877. On page 198 Box writes "the Beehive and Montpelier Clubs, Walworth served as such independently of Hall's ground near the Canal Church at Camberwell" when explaining where the Surrey cricketers came from. This is most helpful as it locates Hall's ground and gives further evidence that there were two grounds in Walworth and at least two clubs.

If we return to W.W. Read's *Annals of Cricket* it states on page 118 that the Montpelier Club's "headquarters were at this time at the "Beehive and Cricketers" in Walworth near Lorrimore Square. Here is a match played upon the ground on June 29th 1841 not long before it was required by the builder." This gives us an indication when and for what reason the club vacated the Beehive ground. The match referred to was Montpelier Club v Islington Albion C.C. and it occurred five years before the last match on the ground. It is also interesting to note that Read states that the pub was near Lorrimore Square, as six years later, Charles Alcock wrongly stated that it was actually <u>in</u> Lorrimore Square. Just after page 252 in Read's book there is a map showing the grounds of eighteen of the capital's prominent cricket clubs. The Oval is shown along with Kennington Common, however the Beehive ground is shown being located on the other side of Walworth Road and about 400 yards further north, virtually on the site of the current Town Hall. Was Read's book wrong or was he about to solve the problem once and for all? I desperately needed to find other documents to finally locate this ground. I was also still trying to find when the club first played at the Beehive ground.

It should be noted that Read's book was also the only one that I have found to state that the club was 1) possibly an off-shoot from Lord's, 2) that they played at Hall's and 3) that their main ground was located where Southwark Town Hall now stands. However after my research the last two of these "facts" turned out to be incorrect and the first one remains unfounded.

The Illustrated London News proved fruitless as a source, as it did not begin until 1842, nor did I find any mention of matches played at any of the other grounds. An article on the Internet mentions that "the club was formed in 1795 and became one of the strongest teams in southeast London. In 1845 their ground was given up for development and they moved to The Oval, becoming one of the founders of the Surrey County Cricket Club. The gardens must have gone by 1850." This gives another date of formation for the club plus a date of leaving, and added that the "gardens area was big enough to accommodate a cricket ground." Also found on the Internet under *New Picture of London*, are details of street names for the capital in 1819. It appears that this was printed for Samuel Leigh of 18 Strand, London (close to Trafalgar Square) and we find Montpelier Gardens, Walworth listed. If it is the cricket ground and associated buildings that made up the tea garden attached to the Montpelier Tavern, and not another street this indicates that the street was still in existence eleven years after it last featured in Haygarth's volumes.

Neither George Smith nor I could ascertain when the Montpelier Gardens ground gave way to the Beehive ground. But he had located its rough position, with the help of a poorly detailed map dated 1813 which showed the Gardens. The ground appeared to have been sited roughly where the cricket ground sized Sutherland Square is found today, and with the benefit of better maps that I discovered after this, he was very close in his supposition.

There is no trace of Montpelier Street on the above mentioned map of 1813, nor is it apparent on the 1824 map. The 1827 map shows the street but it is not named. However the 1830 map shows the street and names it. I had presumed that the club was named after the gardens in which they played which was verified by cricket historian and writer John Goulstone.

Stephen Humphrey, the archivist for the Southwark Local Studies Library, informed me that Montpelier is taken from the French town of Montpellier (note the 2 l's). He then helpfully added "In the 18th and 19th centuries, good health was considered to depend especially on fresh air, and the town of Montpellier was ranked as a particularly healthy place. And so Georgian streets all over England were often named after it, in the hope that they would be better regarded. Montpelier Street in Walworth was named after the Montpelier Gardens, which were pleasure gardens that first operated in the late 18th century.

The change from Montpelier to Pelier took place at the insistence of the London County Council, which was the authority responsible for street-naming in London down to 1965. The council had a policy of removing instances of multiple uses of a name. In some cases, a new name would be totally different, but in changing Walworth's Montpelier, the name was simply shortened to leave a completely meaningless word."

The Internet provided me with my largest piece of assistance to date and helped pinpoint both grounds - when I found an 1830 map of the area that clearly showed West Lane (renamed on July 24th 1868 as Penrose Street) separating Montpelier Gardens and the smaller triangular shaped Beehive Tea Gardens (see page 71). The latter are sited opposite where *The Beehive* is found today. The two grounds mentioned in *Scores and Biographies* are therefore correctly titled, as there were two different venues in close proximity.

An 1827 map that I found (see page 58) showed Montpelier Gardens in the same place that other maps have placed it, yet the Beehive ground opposite is not shown. This apparent oversight can be easily explained; the Beehive ground first appears in *Scores and Biographies* with the Dartford and Beehive Club fixture on September 15th-16th 1831, so possibly it would not have been built in 1827, the year that *The Beehive* pub was first licensed. Perhaps John Heap the licensee then decided to make the gardens a suitable venue to host cricket matches?

Bit by bit my quest was falling into shape, and various matches at the two venues combined with the potted histories that different sources provided, allowed me to estimate dates of formation and occupation of grounds.

The final piece of the jigsaw came when I was able to enlarge the 1830 map found on the Internet, to the same size as the 1871 map that I had bought in the library. By laying one on top of the other the Montpelier Gardens ground is seen to be the same shape as the outline on the map and to have been located where Olney Street (now Fielding Street) is found today (see map on page 207). Just south of this there is a small area of grass, and on the right is Pelier Street which George and I by separate routes had established had been called Montpelier Street prior to 1938. Other documentation states that "Montpelier Gardens is to be found at the end of Montpelier Street". I did not link the present day Pelier Street with the ground that I was looking for until the very latter part of my research.

We have very limited records of matches played over twelve years at the Montpelier Gardens ground until 1808; an indication as to when they moved into the Beehive ground where they enhanced their reputation as a top club, and details of their matches there from 1831 until they left in 1844. Despite having located both grounds and Hall's ground too, like George I am still wondering what happened to the club between 1808-1831 if one ignores their lone appearance at Lord's in July 1813? This would surely have been answered if Haygarth had secured access to that scorebook for 1837.

Sketch of the Kennington Area Locating Eight Grounds.

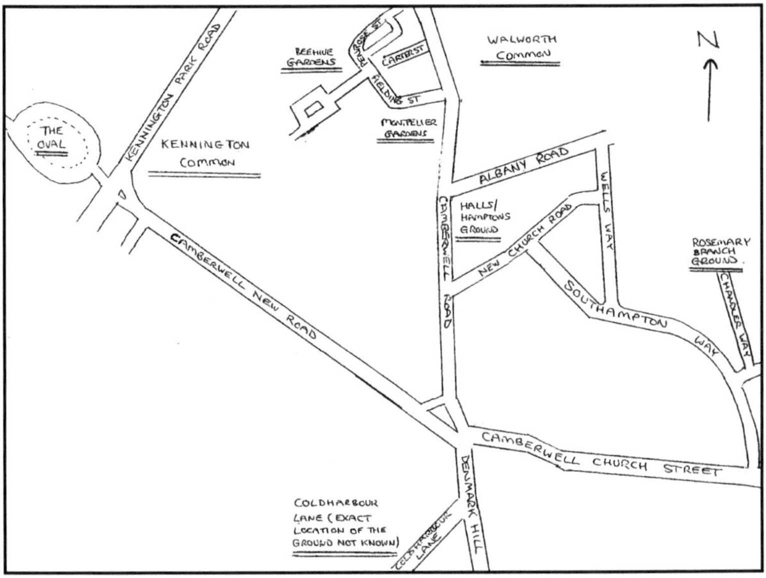

This rough sketch map shows eight grounds in the locality; all of which are mentioned in this book. The proximity to each other is easily noted and some clubs moved between and shared them. Some grounds were mentioned more in *Bell's Life*, whilst others were covered more in other publications such as; Britcher's, Buckley's, Denison's and Haygarth's.

Map of Kennington Manor 1785.

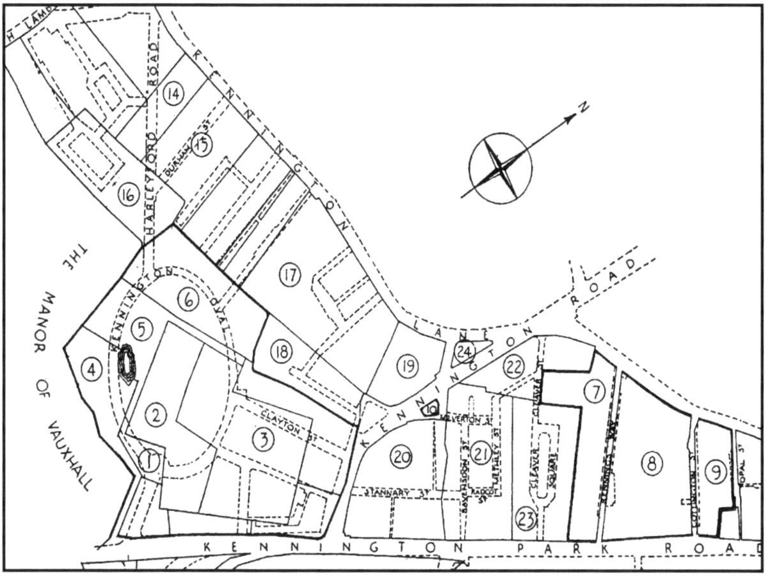

This detailed map shows the layout and owners of land around Kennington Manor in 1785, following Hodgkinson and Middleton's survey. The location of the future Kennington Oval cricket ground is marked and easy to see and Kennington Common is located below Kennington Park Road. The Beehive and Montpelier grounds would in time be located off of this map, but to its southeast. William Clayton, owner of plots 1-9 is commemorated with the modern day Clayton Street, close to Kennington Oval cricket ground.

Kennington Wednesday v Thursday Club
July 25th 1794.

On Kennington Common, in Surrey, July 25, 1794.

Thursday Club.	1st Inn.		2nd Inn.
— Briden, Esq., b Rubegall	0	— run out	2
— Ray, c Farrance	28	— st Warren	12
J. Beeston, b J. Miller	5	— b J. Miller	1
J. Goldham, b Rubegall	4	— run out	18
W. Barton, st Warren	3	— run out	2
— Dale, c J. Miller	3	— c J. Miller	0
T. Lord, c H. Miller	11	— b Rubegall	31
W. Beeston, b J. Miller	0	— c Farrance	5
— Shepherd, not out	3	— b Rubegall	4
— Wall, run out	3	— st Warren	3
— Earnshaw, c Duplock	0	— not out	1
Byes	5	Byes	0
	65		79

170 CRICKET SCORES AND BIOGRAPHIES.

Kennington Wednesday Club.	1st Inn.		2nd Inn.
— Clark, b Lord	10	— c Briden	3
J. Miller, st J. Beeston	14	— b J. Beeston	5
— Rubegall, b Lord	20	— c J. Beeston	3
— Farrance, b Lord	0	— b J. Beeston	6
— Johnson, st J. Beeston	6	— run out	0
— Watts, c Wall	2	— b Shepherd	10
H. Miller, b Lord	0	— b Lord	10
— Warren, b Lord	8	— b J. Beeston	1
— Duplock, b Lord	7	— b Lord	6
John Tanner, Esq., c Dale	10	— not out	4
— Newman, not out	2	— b Goldham	1
Byes	8	Byes	0
	87		49

The Thursday Club winning by 8 runs.

The "Marylebone Thursday Club" playing above, must not be mistaken for the Marylebone. The Thursday was, it is believed, a Tradespeople's Club, meeting at Lord's on Thursdays, as the Kennington did on Wednesdays.

This is the earliest scorecard of a match in the Kennington area to feature in Haygarth's *Scores and Biographies*. John Tanner who features later in the book bats at number ten for the Wednesday club. It is interesting to note the comment below the scores, about the Thursday Club being "a Tradespeople's Club". The Thursday Club was based at Lord's and came to notice again in June 1796 when they combined with the Montpelier Club to form an eleven.

Chapter Three

The Montpelier Tea Gardens

History tells us that the Montpelier Club played from at least 1796 in Montpelier Gardens, but we are informed little more about these gardens. However on the Internet I found a web-site dedicated to all things Montpelier, which detailed various areas so named. I e-mailed the writers three times asking for permission to use the material, but never received a reply. I have therefore edited it to include only references to the Walworth Montpelier material, and hope that the compilers are not upset by my using it.

"After Montpellier Row in Twickenham (a handsome terrace of about 1720, overlooking the Thames), the next Montpel(l)ier in the London area was in Walworth. Here the name was attached to a pleasure garden set up by one John Bendall. It was one of several such attractions on the southern fringes of the then built-up area, where Londoners could take the air and enjoy a number of amusements. Established in the mid-to-late 18th century, and in business for nigh on a century, the Montpelier Tea Gardens (and tavern) had wide and favourable renown in their day, doubtless doing much to spread awareness of the name in London and beyond.

Other 19th-century south London appearances of Montpel(l)ier - the nearest is in Peckham - seem very likely to derive from it. In the absence of specific indications, in Walworth the Montpelier name can be assumed to have been chosen to suggest general salubriousness: although the site was originally quite large and open - thus meeting the "airy" criterion usually associated with Montpel(l)ier elsewhere - unlike several others the Walworth example is on relatively level ground not noticeably higher than its surroundings.

The Montpelier Tea Garden at Walworth is of intrinsic interest, and it is worth detailing some of its features as they must have helped form the early 19th-century view of what "Montpelier" meant in an English setting. Its exact origins are uncertain, but lie in the second half of the 18th century - perhaps about 1780.

The first proprietor was John Bendal or Bendall, who at first ran the 5 acres on which it stood, to the west of the Walworth Road, as a market garden. At that time it was largely surrounded by open ground - Wheeler's Fields and the broad expanse known as Lorrimore or Lattermore. The Poor Rate records for Newington show that John Bendall had a property with a rateable value of £34 in Walworth by 1782; before that the records are patchy, but the preceding surviving rate-books, for 1760-64, show no sign of him.

So, while the Montpelier establishment could possibly be as early as 1765, more conservatively we can assume a date of about 1780. According to Cuming, having built the Montpelier Tavern, Bendall then "laid out the lands in a tasteful manner with a spacious greensward and gravel-walks flanked with choice shrubs and trees, the whole area being belted with fine lofty elm trees". William Hazlitt, the essayist, born in 1778, used to be taken there by his father, and recalled with pleasure his "infant wanderings" there.

The above description of the grounds is taken from the *South London Chronicle*, which in 1884 published an article on the tavern and tea gardens written by a keen local antiquarian, H Syer Cuming. The detail he gives of the tavern is full enough to suggest an eye-witness account: "The old tavern was a very picturesque structure, and retained its primal aspect until its removal to give place to the present palace. It was a long and rather low building in which lath and plaster and weather boarding played a principal part. (In fact, the earliest maps depict a square building, which became elongated to the north by 1841.) The white front faced the south and had a railed gallery covered by a verandah running the whole length of the building, which was reached by a flight of steps at its eastern end, and from this gallery access was gained to the great room where many a stately banquet was served.... The floor of the gallery formed the roof of the bar where refreshments were furnished to the frequenters of the gardens, and between the windows of the house backing this department were suspended several huge turtle shells, mementoes of the soup which had been at divers times consumed within the walls of the tavern. The public bar was at the end of the house next Princes Street (later Carter Street), which led up to the gardens from the Walworth Road....

The tea gardens in front of the tavern were a large, irregular space, neither square, round, nor oval, but a sort of compound of all three forms in one. A good part of its borders were filled up with gaily painted boxes, each with benches fixed to the back and sides, and with a table in the middle, and here persons were wont to be served with tea at 6d per head. Dotted about were turfy banks or low knolls, crowned by ponderous examples of the gigantic clam-shell (Tridaena gigas), and in the centre was the broad level grass plot upon which the volunteers of old used to assemble for drill, and where, on Monday September 2nd 1799, they were presented with their colours, which, when peace was restored, were hung above the communion table in St Mary's Church, Newington.

One of the features of the Montpelier Gardens was a cold bath enclosed in a wooden shed near the entrance to the grounds. Each person desirous of its benefit had to pay one shilling for its use. Bendall laid out the southwest portion of his domain as a small labyrinth or maze, which, though inferior in extent to the one at Hampton Court was considered to display much ingenuity in design. The northwestern part of the estate was a flower garden, where might be purchased plants and shrubs, and seeds, and where choice tulips were exhibited under canvas awnings, and Bendall's tulip show was at one time a thing to talk about.... Attached to the maze, and just outside the southwestern entrance to the tea gardens, was Bendall's dwelling, known in later times as "The Maze Cottage".

It was a square, rough-cast, one-storeyed building, with sloping, slated roof. In the front were two Gothic windows and a Gothic four-panelled door, reached by two stone steps, the erection looking much like a mansion in a toy city. Standing with your back to the Montpelier so as to face the cottage, there was on the left a little stream, crossed by a rustic wooden bridge, which led to Wheeler's Fields, and on the right was the entrance to the maze, for admission to which 2d was demanded. This wonderful contrivance fell into a sad state of ruin in its later days.

The Maze Cottage is the subject of the only known illustration of any feature on the Montpelier site. It has been suggested that the cottage gave Dickens a model for Mr Wemmick's residence - a toy house and a bridge - in *Great Expectations*. (Although the Montpelier Tea Garden may never have been in quite the same league as the often-illustrated Vauxhall or Surrey Gardens, it seems impossible that it went completely undepicted over its long life: discovery of an illustration is awaited with interest.)

The garden area was big enough to accommodate a cricket ground, and in July 1796 the newly-formed Montpelier Club played their first match there. On August 10th and 11th that year "the same ground was the scene of a match of a rather painful, if curious, character. The game, like all cricket of the period, was played for high stakes - in this case 1,000 guineas - and the players were selected (by two noble lords) from the pensioners of Greenwich Hospital: eleven men with one leg against eleven with one arm. The match began at ten, but about three a riotous crowd broke in, demolished the gates and fences, and stopped the proceedings till six o'clock, when play was resumed. On the second day the elevens reappeared, being brought to the scene of the action in three Greenwich stage-coaches, not without flags and music. The match was played out, and the one-legged men beat the poor one-arms by 103"."

This detailed article is of much interest as it tells us that the club was "newly formed in 1796" and played their first match in the gardens, thus removing any lingering doubts that they existed before 1796, or played at other grounds. It is also interesting to read two paragraphs above, about the scarcity of an illustration of the gardens. This is another example of part of the club's history being so hard to find, although the etching on the next page may go some way to rectifying this.

The Montpelier Gardens ground.

This marvellous representation of the ground was by Henry Alken (1785-1851), a prolific painter of sporting works that included hunting, racing and steeple chasing scenes and was featured in *Cricket*, a book published by *Country Life* in 1903. I found a copy of it in a different book and below it was "A match played at the Montpelier Gardens, Walworth, in 1796 between Greenwich pensioners with one arm and one leg for a purse of £1,000. The match generated such excitement that there was nearly a riot". On the following page there is a report of the match taken from *The Times*.

One Arm v One Leg Match Report

"Yesterday a curious match was played at Montpelier Gardens," reported *The Times* on August 10th 1796, "between 11 of the Greenwich (sailor) pensioners, wanting an arm each, against the same number of their fellow-sufferers with each a wooden leg. Thousands of spectators showed up at nine o'clock August 9th to cheer on the two teams of seadogs - one with hooked arms, the other with peg legs. The game was a hotly contested one; the crowd was "highly entertained with the exertions of the old veterans of the ocean, who never acted upon their most inveterate enemy with more energy." The crowd grew quickly and soon an unruly mob of 5,000 was pressing at the fence, wanting to enter. Also wanting to gain entry were a lot of pickpockets, who descended upon the spectators in pairs, each holding the end of a long rope. They ran through the crowd, sweeping their legs from under them, and sending men and powdered wigs flying, and in the confusion, the thieves dived in and relieved spectators of their watches and wallets. Fights broke out, the gates gave way, and the riotous crowd poured over the grounds.

Constables swarmed in and caught one or two thieves, but three hours passed before enough sanity was restored for the game to restart. The match, having stretched through an entire day, had to be called off due to darkness."

On the New Ground, Montpelier Gardens, at Walworth,
August 9 and 10, 1796.

One Leg (Greenwich Pensioners).	1st Inn.		2nd Inn.
— Farrell, b Terry	5	— c Hearn	1
— Cade, b Mudd	4	— b Hearn	0
— Johnson, b Mudd	0	— b Terry	0
— Boswell, b Terry	6	— b Terry	3
— Pullen, b Terry	13	— b Terry	27
— Brice, b Terry	4	— b Hearn	19
— Fearn, not out	30	— run out	5
— Cooper, b Terry	4	— b Terry	13
— Clark, b Mudd	9	— b Terry	4
— Glasscock, b Mudd	0	— b Terry	20
— Walker, b Mudd	0	— not out	4
Byes	18	Byes	8
	93		104

One Arm (Greenwich Pensioners).	1st Inn.		2nd Inn.
— Peat, b Brice	1	— not out	5
— Lower, b Fearn	0	— b Fearn	0
— Allen, b Fearn	6	— b Fearn	1
— Norris, b Fearn	0	— b Fearn	1
— Hearn, b Fearn	3	— run out	3
— Craddick, b Fearn	9	— b Fearn	0
— Terry, hit w	0	— run out	1
— Mudd, b Brice	5	— b Fearn	8
— Shearry, c Cooper	10	— b Fearn	5
— Robinson, b Fearn	0	— b Brice	0
— Leighton, not out	1	— b Fearn	7
Byes	6	Byes	22
	41		53

The One Leg winning by 103 runs.

Map of the area in 1795.

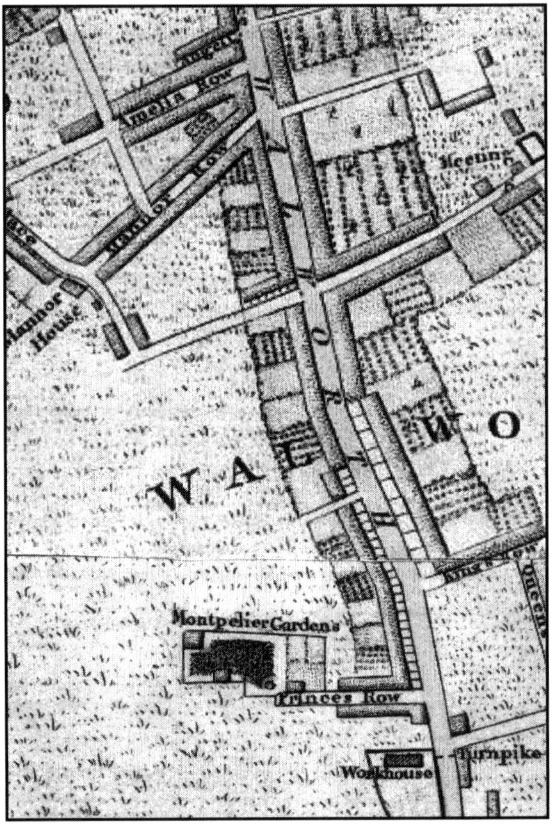

This map by Carey clearly shows the rural nature of the area, yet Walworth Road is still prominent on the right-hand side. It is interesting to see a Manor House, Turnpike and Workhouse marked on the map and none are hemmed in by other buildings. Princes Row, re-named Princes Street in 1868 (see map on page 205), has since been demolished and built over.

Montpelier + Thursday v Marylebone, June 24th and 25th 1796.

CRICKET SCORES AND BIOGRAPHIES.

On the New Ground, at Montpelier Gardens, Walworth, London, June 24 and 25, 1796.

Marylebone.	1st Inn.	2nd Inn.	
Earl of Winchilsea, c Warren	6	b Lord	0
Lord F. Beauclerk, st Warren	37	run out	3
Hon. E. Bligh, st Warren	1	run out	2
Hon. H. Tufton, c Jones	17	st Warren	1
Hon. J. Tufton, b Tanner	0	not out	32
Hon. A. Upton, c Tanner	8	c Turner	7
J. L. Kaye, Esq., st Warren	6	c Tanner	0
— Mellish, Esq., run out	8	c Butler	8
G. Louch, Esq., b Turner	22	st Warren	2
T. Boxall, c Jones	13	c Butler	6
— Sylvester, not out	10	b Turner	5
Bye	1	Byes	0
	129		67

Thursday and Montpelier Clubs.	1st Inn.	2nd Inn.	
— Smith, b Boxall	1	b Boxall	5
— Butler, st H. Tufton	12	b Boxall	16
— Jones, b Beauclerk	7	c Upton	0
— Warren, c Beauclerk	1	c Tufton	7
T. Lord, c Louch	4	c Boxall	19
J. Beeston, c H. Tufton	0	c Beauclerk	6
G. Boult, Esq., b Boxall	1	run out	3
W. Barton, st H. Tufton	15	b Beauclerk	4
J. Goldham, run out	4	c H. Tufton	27
J. Tanner, Esq., run out	0	not out	1
— Turner, not out	0	c Upton	0
Byes	0	Byes	0
	45		88

The M. C. C. winning by 63 runs.
The second innings of the M. C. C. adds up 66.
Warren stumped five and caught one.

This is the first Montpelier Club match to feature in Haygarth's *Scores and Biographies*. The Thursday Club played at Lord's and combined with the Montpelier Club for this fixture against Marylebone at Montpelier Gardens. If the club were not as W.W. Read says "….believed to be an off shoot of Lord's" then they certainly had a good relationship with them as this combined eleven shows. In mid-July the two teams played again, but this time at Lord's.

Montpelier Wednesday v Marylebone June 12th and 13th 1797.

At Montpelier, June 12 and 13, 1797.

Marylebone.	1st Inn.	2nd Inn.	
Hon. J. Tufton, l b w	6	b Rubegall	0
Hon. E. Bligh, run out	1	c Tanner	2
Hon. H. Tufton, b Tanner	0	st Wells	21
Lord F. Beauclerk, b Tanner	62	st Wells	3
Hon. Colonel Lennox, c Wells	10	b Tanner	0
Earl of Winchilsea, c Wells	2	b Tanner	0
Hon. A. Upton, b Tanner	2	hit w	1
Hon. C. Douglas, c Pontifex	3	b Rubegall	9
G. Louch, Esq., c Wells	28	c Dale	22
Captain Lambert, st Wells	0	b Rubegall	1
T. Mellish, Esq., not out	3	not out	0
Byes	0	Byes	2
	117		61

Montpelier Wednesday Club.	1st Inn.	2nd Inn.	
— Pontifex, Esq., c J. Tufton	5	run out	2
— Butler, st — Tufton	19	c Beauclerk	1
J. Tanner, Esq., b Beauclerk	3	c J. Tufton	16
J. Aylward, c J. Tufton	13	b H. Tufton	1
J. Goldham, c Lambert	9	b H. Tufton	22
— Wells, c H. Tufton	7	b Beauclerk	2
G. Boult, Esq., sen., b Beauclerk	2	not out	9
— Rubegall, b Beauclerk	3	c J. Tufton	7
— Dale, not out	4	c Beauclerk	5
— Boult, Esq., jun., c J. Tufton	2	c J. Tufton	1
— Turner, run out	1	c J. Tufton	1
Bye	1	Byes	0
	69		67

The M. C. C. winning by 42 runs.

Wells (who must not be mistaken for the Surrey player) stumped two and caught three. J. Tufton caught 7.

Thanks to a large score by Lord Beauclerk, Marylebone took a healthy first innings lead of 48 runs. Although dismissed cheaply in their second innings, good bowling by H. Tufton and Beauclerk saw them home by 42 runs as only two Montpelier batsmen reached double-figures. J. Tufton took seven catches for Marylebone too. Dale and Goldham played for Thursday on July 25th 1794, but for Montpelier this time, thus showing another link between the two clubs.

Pelier Street, Walworth.

This photograph was taken looking north and shows the now truncated road. The bridge on the right carries trains from Blackfriars to the southern suburbs of the capital and into Kent. It was here on the corner with Fielding Street that Walworth station was located until it closed in 1906. Further up on the right are car repair yards and on the left are small blocks of flats. At the end, just visible is a children's playground, part of which covers the site of Montpelier Gardens although not where the cricket ground was located inside the gardens.

Fielding Street, Walworth.

This appropriately named road which curves southeast from Penrose Street and follows the northeast limit of the Montpelier Gardens ground, covers what was Olney Street in 1871 and then junctions with the busy Walworth Road. Olney Street has been truncated and just the western section (out of view) now remains. Small blocks of flats now sit on what was once the middle section of Olney Street and cover what was the centre of the playing surface.

Langdale Close, Walworth.

Langdale Close runs due south from Fielding Street then curves sharply to the east and covers a small part of the western side of the playing area. This photograph shows the opening of the road and is taken looking south. The block of flats on the left in the photograph is the same one as the one on the right in the photograph on the previous page, so the two can be joined together to give a panoramic view of the area.

Fielding Street, Walworth.

The original street sign high up above a shop clearly shows Olney Street, but below it is affixed a sign denoting Fielding Street; its new name. The street runs due west off the busy Walworth Road and contains terraced houses which I feel certain would have been there when the 1871 map was compiled. Most of the streets in the immediate vicinity have had name changes; Hill Street was lengthened to Hillingdon Street, Montpelier Street became Pelier Street, Beresford Street became John Ruskin Street, and Henry Street, still the same design and length, became Draco Street. My research would have been a lot easier if they had been left alone and the area would have kept better ties with its past.

Pelier Park, Walworth.

Pelier Park now covers part of the site of Montpelier Gardens. The grey metal, box-style railway bridge, where Pelier Street begins, is visible at the rear on the right-hand side and close by was the now demolished Walworth railway station.

Map of the area today.

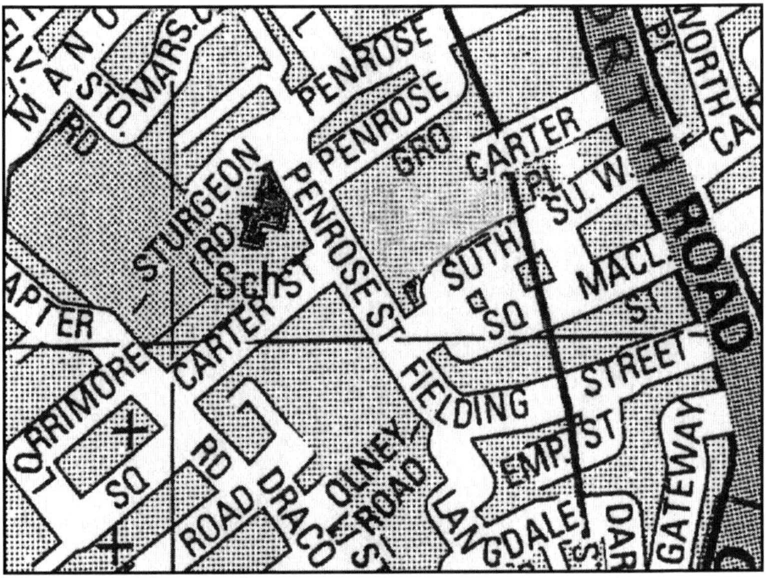

This modern day map shows how Carter Street was cut in half by modern redevelopment. The aptly named Fielding Street covers the northern tip of where the Montpelier Gardens ground was once located and Langdale Close sits on top of the playing surface. The site of the Beehive ground is where "Sch" is marked on the northern side of Carter Street. The two grounds were but a minute's walk apart.

Chapter Four

The Early History of the Montpelier Club

Any records about the beginning of the club appear to have been lost in the passage of time. Unlike Surrey C.C.C. who emerged half a century later, there appears to be no records concerning who formed the club, or why they were set-up. However if we look more laterally, there are mentions about the club which are valid and worthy of closer examination.

As stated already, the writers about Surrey C.C.C. found very little about their predecessor club. However from different sources there is no doubt that by 1796 the club was established. The *Wikipedia* site on the Internet tells that the club "was prominent in English cricket about 1796 when it began to compete against M.C.C. and other leading "town clubs"." Details of their early matches appear in the records of the early chroniclers such as Britcher, Buckley and Haygarth.

Why the club was so called was solved by John Goulstone who said that they were named after the gardens in which they played, which in turn were named after the street that led to the gardens. The *Wikipedia* entry imparts a piece of information that I have found nowhere else "Montpelier was a victim of the Napoleonic War and the strength of the team waned after 1800 as the war progressed. It became a minor club in playing terms but remained influential in membership terms and was still a leading club in Surrey when the formation of a county club was first proposed in the 1840s."

On page six of *Surrey Cricket and Cricketers* by Rev R. S. Holmes (1896) which I found at the Surrey History Centre in Woking is "between 1779 and 1788 - i.e for eight years - Surrey played no matches at all; why I cannot learn. Perhaps for the same reason that the club practically disappeared in 1810" and in 1810 "Surrey practically dropped out of cricket for 35 years…" Cricket in the county must have waned during this period.

H.S. Altham's *A History of Cricket* (1926) re-iterates this as on pages 103 and 104 he writes "With 1810, this chapter in Surrey history ends, and for the next 34 years the county as such is practically non-existent, in that in the whole of that time only 11 county games are recorded …. Surrey cricket was now disintegrated amongst a host of prosperous and powerful clubs such as Montpelier …" and "The present Surrey Club is really the creation of the Montpelier Cricket Club."

In William Powell's *Cricket Grounds of Surrey* he notes the comments by W.W. Read in *Annals of Cricket* who, on page 79 says "The Montpelier Club was formed in 1796 and their ground was known as Hall's and situated in Camberwell.

They had another ground at the "Beehive" Walworth …" I am glad to find another source telling that the club was formed in 1796 and wondered whether the club did play at Hall's as a smaller club, prior to moving the short distance to Montpelier Gardens in time for the 1796 season. Research that comes to light later in the book however suggests that this is not correct, as one newspaper reported on June 8th 1834 that Harry Hampton sold his ground to a Mr Hall. Unless the ground was owned by a different Mr Hall forty years prior to this sale. Read carries on "It was an important club, and believed to be an off shoot of Lord's and was soon sufficiently strong enough to play the Marylebone Club." The comment that the club could be an off shoot from Lord's is interesting, and has not been mentioned by anyone else, but it must not be discounted. One interesting point to note is that seven of the first nine Montpelier C.C. fixtures to feature in *Scores and Biographies* are against M.C.C. and three of these were played at Lord's. Two were combined with Thursday Club, about whom John Bryant and Keith Warsop wrote in the *Cricket Statistician* (Spring 2009) and confirmed that they were a club based at Lord's. They wrote "The Thursday Club played at Lord's and included many Middlesex players so is often confused with Middlesex. However it is possible to distinguish true Middlesex teams from the Thursday Club. Apart from the team composition, it is relevant to look at the opposition; a match against another county is likely to have been Middlesex rather than Thursday."

The first important match was against M.C.C. "for three hundred guineas a side" at Montpelier Gardens on June 24th and 25th 1796 (see page 33), a match which they lost by 63 runs. On July 13th, 14th and 15th they played a return match at Lord's as "Thursday and Montpelier Clubs with T.A. Smith and Stephens" and lost by six wickets. Bryant and Warsop also note "…it should be pointed out that the two between MCC and a combined Montpelier/Thursday side (24 Jun and 13 Jul) are of a relatively high standard and include some professionals. It was possible that these games were arranged in place of the usual MCC v Middlesex fixtures, which did not come off in 1796."

In Britcher's works is a report for a match against Middlesex at Montpelier Gardens on July 25th (Middlesex won by an innings and 19 runs). In the Montpelier team was G. Boult who had been a member of the Hambledon team and who hailed from Berkshire. Britcher also reported the match against Highgate at Montpelier Gardens on August 15th (Montpelier won by 6 runs). On August 12th they linked with Kennington to play Thursday Club at the same venue and lost by three wickets despite having the assistance of the famous James Aylward who scored 16 and 34 in their totals of 120 and 112. John Goldham who played four first-class matches in all and often for England, London and Middlesex, played for the club for the third time and John Pontifex, a merchant and coppersmith, who played thirteen first-class matches for Middlesex amongst others scored 5 and 0. On August 26th a combined Montpelier and Kennington team played the Thursday

Club at Montpelier Gardens and lost by three wickets, and against the same opposition a fortnight later at Montpelier Gardens the match is shown in Haygarth as "postponed", although the Thursday Club scored 205 and 101 and Montpelier and Kennington 179 and 78-8. Pontifex scored 0 and 2, Goldham 23 and 32 and James Aylward, aged 55 scored 98 and 28.

Perhaps the absence of the M.C.C. v Middlesex fixture opened the door and allowed them to gain a more important footing on the cricket ladder? On June 12th 1797 Montpelier Wednesday played M.C.C. at Montpelier Gardens and won by 42 runs. Pontifex scored 5 and 2, James Aylward 13 and 1 and Goldham 9 and 22. Two weeks later they played at Lord's against M.C.C. (Britcher says Mary-Le-Bone) "for five hundred guineas a side" and the home team won by 5 wickets. Although overlooked by Haygarth, Britcher includes the Montpelier v Whitehall match on July 22nd + 24th at Montpelier Gardens (Whitehall won by 5 runs). Again in Britcher's but not in Haygarth's works are the Montpelier Wednesday Club's matches against Fulham on August 1st + 2nd at Parson's Green and Parson's Green on August 9th at Montpelier Gardens. (Fulham won the former by an innings and 13 runs and Parson's Green won the latter by 8 wickets). Britcher also reported the Montpelier Saturday's match on August 2nd against Whitehall which they won by 23 runs. Good proof here then of the size of the club, as they put two elevens out on August 2nd. On page 30 of Buckley's other book; *Fresh Light on Pre-Victorian Cricket*, the Montpelier Monday and Saturday against Montpelier Thursday match at Montpelier Gardens on August 1st 1797 is featured. The Monday and Saturday eleven scored 49 and 114 and the Thursday eleven managed 53 and 57. The match was originally reported in the *Morning Post* on August 17th. The match against M.C.C. on September 4th at Montpelier Gardens is featured in Haygarth's *Scores and Biographies* and Montpelier won by 6 wickets. Aylward scored 11 and 12, J. Hammond 41 and 31 and Goldham 0.

In 1798 Haygarth reports on just two matches; May 28th against M.C.C. at Lord's (Montpelier won by 55 runs with T. Boxall scoring 10 and 11 but Pontifex bagging a pair) and June 13th against M.C.C. at Montpelier Gardens (M.C.C. won by 176 runs with Boxall scoring 4 and 7, W. Fennex 4 and 4 and T. Burgoyne 7 and 1). Perhaps there were fewer matches this season as Britcher includes only three, albeit different ones; June 25th + 26th against Whitehall at Montpelier Gardens (Montpelier won by 10 wickets), September 26th against Woolwich at Montpelier Gardens (Montpelier won by 138 runs and Woolwich were dismissed for just 24) and October 8th + 9th against Woolwich at Woolwich (match shown as "postponed with Woolwich needing 13 runs to win" Montpelier 50 and 69 and Woolwich 67 and 40-7).

1799 saw just five of their matches reported; Haygarth reported three; against Richmond and Brentford on June 17th at Montpelier Gardens (Montpelier won by 91 runs with Hampton scoring 24 and 4, Wells 20 and 5 and Rubegall 22 and 1), the Saturday club against Homerton on July 4th (Montpelier won by 9 wickets although the names of the eleven are all unfamiliar) at Montpelier Gardens and against Homerton on July 19th (Homerton won by 5 wickets) played at Homerton. Britcher reported on the return match against Richmond and Brentford at Richmond Green on June 27th + 28th match (Montpelier won by 48 runs) and the above two matches against Homerton match on July 4th and July 19th.

1800 saw five matches reported; Haygarth took care of the two against Homerton; the first on June 25th at an unknown venue (Montpelier won by an innings and 5 runs and again none of the eleven are familiar names) and the return on July 3rd at Homerton as Montpelier Thursday which they lost by 4 wickets (which saw ten of the same team appear again). Britcher meanwhile reported the match against Richmond at Montpelier Gardens on June 26th (which Montpelier won by 52 runs and which saw none of the players from the 1799 match feature), the return match on July 2nd + 3rd at Richmond (Richmond won by 69 runs) and the match against Woolwich on July 24th + 25th at Woolwich (Woolwich won by 8 wickets), along with the June 25th and July 3rd matches against Homerton.

The first year of the new century saw a vast difference of matches reported. Haygarth included only the match against Homerton on June 30th at Homerton (Montpelier won by 18 runs, yet only the names of C. Mortimer 0 and 3, Peppercorn 13 and 19, John Nyren 36 and 10 and Barton 3 and 1 are familiar), whereas Britcher reported six; against Homerton at Homerton on June 11th (Montpelier won by 3 wickets), Homerton on June 3rd at Montpelier Gardens (Montpelier won by 18 runs), Deptford at Montpelier Gardens on August 6th (Montpelier Thursday won by 25 runs), Deptford at Blackheath on August 22nd (Montpelier won by 7 wickets), Kennington on Kennington Common on September 3rd (Kennington won by 5 wickets) and against Woolwich on September 21st at Woolwich (Drawn). George Buckley, another compiler of early matches included the June 11th and September 21st matches in his works, but was unique in finding an August 14th match against Deptford played at Blackheath (Montpelier Thursday won by 7 wickets after scores of 30, 38, 33 and 36-3), although maybe this is the match which Britcher says occurred on August 22nd.

In 1802 Haygarth included only the Homerton match played on July 6th at Montpelier Gardens which was shown as "postponed" although Montpelier scored 123 and 33 and the visitors 68 and 44-2. John Nyren scored 66 and 4, Peppercorn 6 and 8 but C. Mortimer bagged a pair. Britcher however again excelled with six: versus Homerton on July 12th at Montpelier Gardens (Homerton won by 5 wickets), Woolwich on July 13th at Montpelier Gardens (Woolwich won by 7 wickets), Woolwich on July 19th at Woolwich (no result shown), Richmond on August 2nd at Montpelier Gardens (Montpelier won by 13 runs), Homerton on August 12th at Montpelier Gardens (Montpelier won by an innings and 22 runs) and Richmond on September 3rd at Richmond Green which ended in a tie.

Buckley chipped in with six too; versus Homerton on June 24th at Homerton (Montpelier won by 3 wickets), Woolwich on July 13th as above, Woolwich on July 26th for which he gives the result as a win for Montpelier by 40 runs, but which could be the July 19th match in the above paragraph, Homerton on August 12th as above, Homerton and Richmond on August 18th (Montpelier won by 13 runs) and the tied match against Richmond on September 13th.

In 1803 Haygarth's only reference to the club was their match against M.C.C. at Lord's on June 29th (M.C.C. scored 165 and 258 and the visitors 36 and the result is shown as "Montpelier gave up the match". W. Barton scored 14, J. Tanner 8 and Hampton 2. Haygarth next features them (with Beldham) in their match against Homerton on June 12th 1806 at Montpelier Gardens. The home eleven scored 112 and 74-7 and Homerton (with Lord Beauclerk who scored 2 and 170) 58 and 265. Their last appearance in his works for many a year came with their match against Marylebone at Lord's on July 21st 1813; which is shown as "unfinished" although Montpelier scored 158 and 114 and Marylebone 123 and 103-4. Hampton, Tanner and Noah Mann junior played and in the opposition eleven were J. Hammond, Hon. E. Bligh and G. Osbaldeston.

Britcher and Buckley both covered the August 31st 1803 match against Homerton (Homerton won by 30 runs and Pontifex scored 33 and 15) and their interest then ceases too. On page 51 of Buckley's *Fresh Light on Pre-Victorian Cricket* there are details of the Montpelier Tuesday versus Montpelier Friday match played at Montpelier Gardens on July 7th 1808. Tuesday scored 66 and 171 and Friday 60 and 87 and the match was originally covered in the *Morning Post* on July 9th. With this match the gap in *Scores and Biographies* between 1806-13 is interrupted, although it was an "in-house" match.

On page 163 of Buckley's book under a title of "JOHN NYREN's scores which are unrecorded in *Scores and Biographies* are listed eight more Montpelier matches (see page 227). It is noted that "These matches were recorded in the *Courier*". These eight matches were played between June 11th 1801 and August 31st 1803 and three show Montpelier and five Montpelier Saturday as the relevant team. It is interesting to note though that only two of the eight matches were home fixtures; Montpelier Saturday v Homerton on August 12th 1802 and Homerton and Richmond (located many miles apart) a week later.

On page 179 there is mention of the Homerton v Montpelier match played on July 6th and 10th 1802 at Montpelier Gardens. Underneath is "It was Montpelier Saturday Club playing (*Scores and Biographies* says Montpelier Club). They won the first match on June 24th by three wickets; and won the third at Woolwich on August 12th by an innings and 22."

With no disrespect to either Buckley or Haygarth, there is no consistency in the reporting of the matches of the various elevens that the club put out. Between 1796-1803 Haygarth's *Scores and Biographies* features eighteen matches,

Buckley adds another six and then we must add John Nyren's matches that are not recorded in *Scores and Biographies* which add eight more to the total. So we are now aware of thirty-two matches played by the club in this period.

I went to Lord's library in May 2008 and although there appeared to be no books about the club or any with specific mention of it, I was guided to the records compiled by Samuel Britcher, one time scorer for M.C.C., who collated reports on cricket matches between 1790-1805. The first mention of the club in his books is the match against M.C.C. on June 24th and 25th 1796 at Montpelier Gardens which Haygarth also covered. He says "The Montpelier Club was formed at a ground that had recently opened tea gardens, in Walworth, South London. By 1797, two years after this match, the gardens were home to at least three clubs - the Montpelier Monday, Wednesday, Saturdays - to which were added at least a Thursday club by 1800, and a Tuesday club by 1808 - what could be termed as a working week." He errors that there is two years between 1796 and 1797, but tells that other elevens played under the Montpelier name.

On examination of his books many more Montpelier C.C. matches come to light along with other matches played at Montpelier Gardens between 1796-1803, which often included brief comments about the matches. In all he mentions six matches played in each of 1796, 1797 and 1798, four in 1799, five in 1800, six in both 1801 and 1802 and one in 1803. Along with the familiar oppositions of Homerton, Richmond and Woolwich, he unearths matches against Deptford, Fulham, Highgate, Kennington, Parson's Green and Richmond and Brentford.

If we compare the thirty-two matches covered in Buckley and Haygarth's respective works with those found by Britcher, and deduct the duplicates, the total of known Montpelier C.C. matches rises from thirty-two to fifty-eight - an impressive increase. It is also interesting to see that Britcher too was unable to unearth more than one match after 1802.

It would be 1813 before Montpelier would grace Haygarth's *Scores and Biographies* again and then nearly another twenty-four years before they would again be considered worthy of inclusion. Between July 1799 and July 1813 just nine of their matches appeared in *Scores and Biographies*, and their opposition each time was Homerton or M.C.C.. Despite these valid inclusions it is clear to see that reported matches ebbed off after the 1803 season.

Perhaps the club were still going, despite few their matches after 1803 being recorded anywhere but playing at a lower-level? It was Arthur Haygarth, who many years later, noted in his *Scores and Biographies* when he featured a Montpelier match played on June 28th 1837 "It is a great pity that neither the Montpelier nor Mitcham score books could be obtained by the compiler, as they played many good matches about this time."

Scores and Biographies - Arthur Haygarth

As you will notice throughout this book, there is no consistency in which reports feature in compilations and newspapers. Cricket historian Roger Packham told me that it was often the club secretary's job to send off a match report with a fee to the local sporting newspaper to ensure its inclusion. As you will see in *Bell's Life* some seasons witness a multitude of reports for local teams and in other seasons not many are included.

There is some overlap but also much difference in the reports to be found in Haygarth's *Scores and Biographies* and the respective works of Bentley, Britcher, Buckley and Denison.

I contacted *Scores and Biographies* expert Roger Heavens to try to establish how Haygarth determined which matches to include in his tomes and which to omit. His reply was very informative so is included in full below:

"Arthur was very much his own man and whether he would have approved of my research into his life is doubtful. One thing he did not abide was outsiders with no real knowledge of the game pontificating about it!

We must remember that he knew ALL the players and the teams he was writing about. He knew their strengths and weaknesses and what teams and what players were important at the time. There was no first-class cricket in the early days so Haygarth inserted all games that he considered important both with regard to players and teams. For example most M.C.C., touring teams, England in its various guises, counties regarded as better than the others (Sussex, Kent, Notts, Yorks, Lancs, Surrey, Gloucs) games are there but not all I Zingari. If you look at the names playing you can see what I mean. In addition if a side made under 20 or more that 500 - or had a batsman scoring 100 runs over two innings (in the early days) and centuries - they were included. The selection was certainly not random so you can safely say that games he did not record were, in his opinion, not worthy of saving. However he did want the books to be bigger - but costs prevented that - so there are games of value that he has not used. I imagine he cut out minor county matches and games between insignificant sides even when they played good teams - but the names would become important then.

Not an easy question to answer but I hope that gives you a flavour of his mindset."

Montpelier C.C. Players

Throughout the book at timely intervals I have included some pen-pictures of some of those cricketers who played for the Montpelier Club. The www.cricketarchive.co.uk website lists fifty-five players who played for them in either first-class or miscellaneous matches. There were of course many more who played in lesser matches between 1796-1806 who are not listed on this excellent cricket statistical website.

The web-site lists fifteen matches during this period, a mixture of first-class and miscellaneous matches. Like Haygarth and comments by other writers, they list their first Montpelier Club match in 1796 (with Thursday Club against Marylebone at Montpelier Gardens). Matches are listed annually until 1800, after which only the match against Homerton in 1806 is featured.

Some of those who played for the club were regulars for many years, such as Baker, Coltson, Lewis and Spenceley. Others were well-known names who played just occasionally; such as Aylward, Beldham, Fennex, Goldman, Hammond and Pontifex, and of course there were many who played just a handful of matches and who have been all but forgotten.

I have ignored most of those about whom much has been written and are well known, and chosen some of the players who are not so well known, or who loyally served the club for many years. I have weaved what can be found about them on the Internet with some statistical details and reports found in newspapers and I hope that this helps bring the lives of these respective players a little more to the fore.

John Tanner

(1772-1858)

Although he is the earliest player to feature in these pen pictures we do have a year of birth for him and an accurate date and place of death (Sutton March 23rd 1858). He first came to notice in 1794 when he played for Kennington Wednesday against Marylebone Thursday Club on Kennington Common, a match that Haygarth recorded in his *Scores and Biographies*. He scored 10 and 4 as his side lost by eight runs. He also he played for the Montpelier and Thursday Club against M.C.C. at Lord's on May 9th-11th 1796 and took two wickets as his side won by three wickets. He batted at number ten in the first innings but failed to score and at number eight second time round and scored 4 runs and also held one catch. He played again for the same team against the same opposition and at the same ground at the end of the month. He features in *Scores and Biographies* again for Montpelier and Thursday against M.C.C. at Aram's New Ground, Montpelier Gardens, Walworth on June 24th and 25th 1796 in which he scored 0 and 1 not out, held two catches and took a wicket. Despite this, Montpelier lost by 63 runs.

His fourth match was for the Montpelier and Kennington clubs against the Thursday Club at Lord's on August 12th and 13th 1796. So we can see that he started playing for a team based at Lord's and then opposed them. The following year on June 12th and 13th 1797 he played for the full Montpelier team against M.C.C. at Montpelier Gardens, the first of three matches against them, so his colours were by now nailed to the south of the Thames. On July 12th and 13th he played for England against Surrey and Middlesex at Montpelier Gardens and scored 3 not out and 8. During the first innings he bowled John Walker for no score, although Surrey and Middlesex won the match by four wickets.

In 1798 he played for Montpelier against M.C.C. at Lord's and the following year for the Thursday Club against M.C.C. at Lord's. He opened the batting for Montpelier against Brentford and Richmond in 1799 and scored 14 and 0 in their match on Richmond Green, but most of the bowling analyses for this match have been lost. In 1800 he played for Surrey v England at Lord's, for Woolwich v M.C.C. at Woolwich and then for Montpelier against Woolwich at the same ground. There is no record of him in 1801, but in 1802 and 1803 he played for Surrey against England at Lord's and in 1804 for England against M.C.C. at Lord's. In 1806 he played his last match for Montpelier; against Homerton at Montpelier Gardens and scored 0 and 24 and held a catch. Homerton scored 58 and 265 and Montpelier replied with 112 and 74-7.

He did not appear to surface in 1807 in any reported match, but the next year played for M.C.C. against Middlesex at Lord's and twice for Surrey against

England at Lord's. For Surrey in the latter two matches he scored 0 and 9 not out and held two catches as Surrey won by 60 runs, and then 30 and 0 and held one catch as they won again by three wickets. He played for Surrey twice against England at Lord's in 1809 and once in 1810, and between 1810-18 for a myriad of minor teams; Lord F. Beauclerk's XI, Colonel Byng's XI, Under 38's, B. Aislabie's XI, D.J.W. Kinnaird's XI, St John's Wood, Epsom, W. Ward's XI and G. Osbaldeston's XI, mainly at Lord's before making an appearance for Hampshire against Epsom at Epsom Downs in August 1819. In July 1821 he opened the batting for M.C.C. against Godalming at Godalming and scored 4 and 6 and took three wickets in the first innings, as M.C.C. won by 64 runs. From 1819 until his last match in 1826 for M.C.C. against Middlesex at Lord's when he scored 13 not out and 0 and took a wicket in both innings, he played for the Gentlemen and M.C.C..

In a long career that included 40 first-class matches (and no doubt many other lesser matches) he scored 385 runs at 6.31 in 72 innings with a top score of 34 and took 41 wickets although his bowling averages have been lost. He also held 27 catches and made one stumping.

Montpelier v Homerton
June 12th 1806.

On Aram's Ground, at Montpelier, June 12, 1806.

Homerton, with Lord F. Beauclerk.	1st Inn.		2nd Inn.
— Peppercorn, Esq., b Pontifex	1	— b Pontifex	4
Sir H. Martin, run out	5	— run out	12
— Warren, Esq., b Pontifex	8	— b Beldham	19
Lord F. Beauclerk, b Beldham	2	— st Beldham	170
J. Nyren, b Pontifex	15	— c Tanner	18
F. Ladbroke, Esq., c Lambourn	7	— c Roffy	3
— Madden, Esq., b Pontifex	7	— b Hampton	6
— Holland, Esq., b Pontifex	0	— not out	20
T. Vigne, Esq., b Pontifex	4	— b Pontifex	7
R. Walpole, Esq., b Pontifex	8	— c Beldham	5
B. Aislabie, Esq., not out	0	— b Pontifex	0
Bye	1	Bye	1
	58		265

Montpelier, with Beldham.	1st Inn.		2nd Inn.
Harry Hampton, st Vigne	64	— b Beauclerk	0
— Eldridge, Esq., b Beauclerk	2	— c Beauclerk	0
— Hart, Esq., b Beauclerk	2	— b Beauclerk	16
W. Beldham, run out	4	— c Beauclerk	16
— Roffy, Esq., b Beauclerk	0		
— Pontifex, Esq., b Beauclerk	0	— c Nyren	0
J. Tanner, Esq., b Warren	0	— b Beauclerk	24
— Blake, Esq., b Holland	20	— st Vigne	5
— Vane, Esq., st Vigne	9	— not out	13
— Lambourn, Esq., b Beauclerk	4		
— Turner, Esq., not out	4		
Byes	3	Byes	0
	112		74

Montpelier gave up the match.

It must be observed (in justice to other cricketers) that Lord F. Beauclerk's runs were made against inferior bowling and fielding, except Beldham's.

After this match at Montpelier Gardens there were hardly any other Montpelier ones that came to light. The visitors scored 58; John Nyren being the only player to record a score of double-figures. The home team then took a healthy lead after Harry Hampton's 64 and Blake's 20. Lord Beauclerk replied with 170 in Homerton's 265 and, set 212 to win, Montpelier "gave up the match" with the score on 74-7. Beauclerk had a hand in five of the dismissals in both innings.

Sale of Montpelier Gardens in 1812.

The Montpelier Tavern, Tea-gardens, and Cricket-ground, Walworth.—By Messrs. HOGGART and PHILLIPS, at the Mart, opposite the Bank of England, THIS DAY, at 12 o'clock, in two Lots, unless an acceptable offer is previously made by private contract.

Lot 1. THE LEASE and beneficial TRADE of the established and respectable TAVERN and TEA-GARDENS, known as the MONTPELIER, eligibly situated at Walworth. The house contains an assembly-room, 73 feet by 23 feet; dining-rooms for large and small parties, commodious bar, excellent kitchen, and suitable accommodations for conducting an extensive business; the annual returns of which, for the last 3 years, have been upwards of 5000l. with tea-gardens, fish-pond, and skittle-grounds. Lot 2. The Lease of an enclosure of rich Land, used as a cricket-ground, and two excellent gardens, containing altogether about 18 acres, immediately adjoining the premises. To be viewed; and particulars had of Mr. Wood, solicitor, No. 12, Richmond-buildings, Dean street, Soho; on the premises; at the Mart; and of Messrs. Hoggart and Phillips, 62, Old Broad-street.

This advert was placed in *The Times* on Friday January 17th 1812. Dimensions of the assembly room are given along with mentions of other rooms and the expected annual turn-over. It adds "The lease of an enclosure of rich land, used as a cricket ground, and two excellent gardens, containing all together 18 acres, immediately adjoining the premises." All considered this was a large piece of land with buildings that were up for sale. Mr Wood, a solicitor of Dean Street, Soho was the man to see, to get details along with Messrs Hoggart and Phillips of Old Broad Street.

Harry Hampton

(17??-18??)

It is unfortunate that his dates of birth and death have been lost. He will be probably best known as being the owner of the ground in Camberwell near the church, which hosted so many important matches. If the cricketer mentioned in the next paragraph is indeed him, than I will guess that he was born about 1778 which would have seen his cricket career start when he was about nineteen and continue until thirty-five, and he would have sold his cricket ground when aged about fifty-six.

Noting the comments on page 66 about there being a J. and H. Hampton who were indistinguishable, it is impossible to say for certain that he is the man listed just as "Hampton" who played for Montpelier against Marylebone at Montpelier on September 4th, 5th and 6th 1797, who batted at number five and scored 6 and 3 and held a catch as his team won by six wickets. The same surname appeared for the same club and batting at the same number, in their match against the same opposition at Lord's on May 28th and 29th 1798 and scored 33 and 11, and again on June 13th and 14th against Marylebone at Walworth when the player scored 3 and 1 and took one wicket. A Hampton played against Richmond and Brentford on June 17th and 18th 1799 at Walworth, and batted at number three and scored 24 and 4, took three wickets and held three catches. In the return match the following week, he scored 27 and 7, took two wickets and held two catches.

Hampton's next appearance in *Scores and Biographies* came for a match against Marylebone on June 29th and 30th 1803 and he scored 2 at number ten and took one wicket as Montpelier were thrashed. Marylebone scored 165 and 258 (Lord Beauclerk 73 and 110 not out) and Montpelier 36 and Haygarth comments that Beauclerk's scores "were against very inferior bowling and fielding" and "Montpelier gave up the match" and that "This is one of the most one-sided matches that ever was played."

Haygarth notes that H. Hampton played for the Twelve first chosen in 1805, and his full name is finally given in *Scores and Biographies* for the match against Homerton on June 12th 1806 at Montpelier Gardens, when as opening bat he scored 64 and 0 and took one wicket.

Harry Hampton played five first-class matches between 1802-11; the first three came for England against Surrey at Lord's in 1802, 1803 and 1805. His fourth first-class match was for Kent against England at Bowman's Lodge ground in Dartford in August 1806. His fifth and last first-class appearance came for B. Aislabie's X1 against G. Osbaldeston's X1 at Lord's in July 1811 and in most of these matches he batted in the lower-order.

Scores and Biographies shows a Hampton playing for the club against Marylebone at Lord's in July 1813 (see below) and he batted at number ten and scored 10 and 2. Harry Hampton's ground was sold to Mr Hall in mid-1834 but it continued to host a variety of local cricket matches. His name also comes to light when research is carried out on Nicholas Felix (Wanostrocht), who it is said on the www.Cricinfo.com website "learnt his cricket with the East Surrey Club under the coaching of Harry Hampton whose ground was at Camberwell."

He enjoyed a long career in the game and put much back into it after retirement and his five-match first-class career realised 36 runs in nine innings at 5.14. He also held one catch.

At Lord's, July 21, 22, and 23, 1813.

Montpelier, with Sherman.	1st Inn.		2nd Inn.
— Harris, b Budd	2	c Hammond	10
— Hardy, b Budd	0	b Hammond	26
— Sherman, b Hammond	12	c Hammond	0
— Mann, b Osbaldeston	58	c Warren	0
— Smith, c Budd	0	b Rice	32
— Roffey, c Schabner	17	b Hammond	0
— Clayton, hit w	5	l b w	21
— Davies, b Hammond	17	b Budd	2
— Tijon, not out	25	run out	15
— Hampton, b Hammond	10	hit w	2
J. Tanner, Esq., b Budd	10	not out	3
Byes	2	Byes	3
	158		114

CRICKET SCORES AND BIOGRAPHIES.

Marylebone, with Hammond.	1st Inn.		2nd Inn.
H. Repton, Esq., c Sherman	13	not out	6
Captain Hawkins, b Tanner	1		
J. Poulet, Esq., b Hardy	1		
A. Schabner, Esq., b Tanner	2	b Tanner	4
E. H. Budd, Esq., b Roffey	39		
J. Hammond, c Tanner	29	b Hardy	14
Hon. E. Bligh, c Clayton	17	b Tanner	10
T. Burgoyne, Esq., c Smith	0		
C. Warren, Esq., run out	5		23
James Rice, Esq., not out	1		
G. Osbaldeston, Esq., b Tanner	8	run out	46
Byes	7	Byes	0
	123		103

Unfinished.

The Horn's Tavern, Kennington
1820.

This print was taken from *Old and New London - a Narrative of its History, its People and its Places* (Volume six) by Edward Walford M.A.. This series of volumes was published in 1897. Opposite the pub was Kennington Common (later enclosed and now known as Kennington Park) where many matches that attracted thousands to watch, were played in the eighteenth and nineteenth centuries.

The Horn's Tavern, Kennington c1910.

Although this photograph of the pub and assembly rooms, which are iconic in the history of Surrey C.C.C., is out of sequence in the book, it allows one to compare it with the sketch on the previous page, which depicts the building about ninety years earlier. The building was re-built in 1887, but badly damaged by a flying bomb which fell on August 16th 1944. It was then demolished and the current office block that sits upon this site was erected about 1965.

Map of the area in 1824.

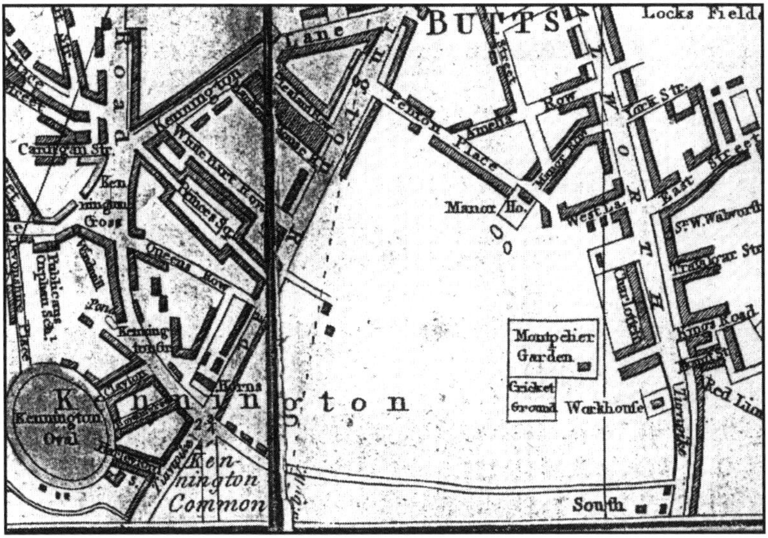

This map is not as detailed as others that feature in the book, but it is interesting to note that the cartographer has shown the cricket ground to be separate from Montpelier Gardens. To the west are Kennington Oval and Kennington Common and both venues hosted a large amount of matches in the nineteenth century. Walworth Common which itself hosted plenty of cricket matches in the mid and latter parts of the eighteenth century, but which is now covered by a large council estate was located just off the map by Lock's Fields in the top-right corner.

Map of the area in 1827.

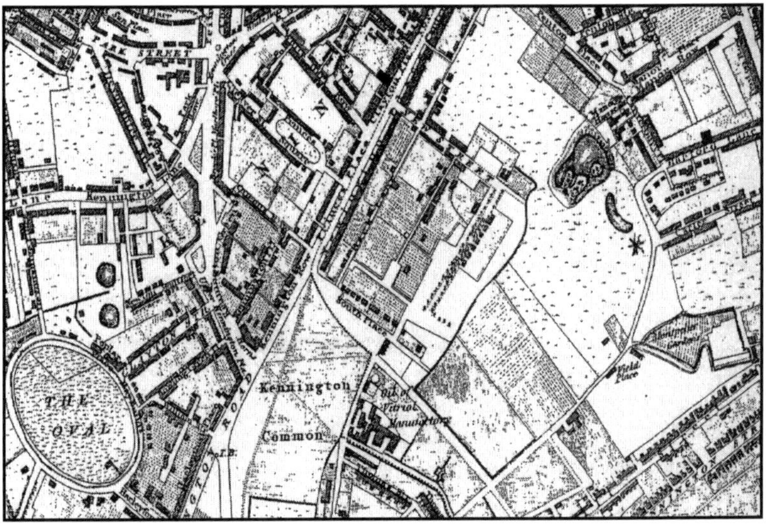

The clarity of this map and the fact that it features The Oval, Montpelier Gardens and Kennington Common makes it my favourite one in the book. *The Beehive* pub was first licensed in 1827 but the Beehive ground is missing, however this is probably accounted for by the fact that it did not host its first match until 1831.

Other Local Clubs

After a slow start cricket coverage in *Bell's Life* grew quickly and it reported on a good cross-section of local cricket, although Montpelier C.C. only played a few of their neighbours. I wanted to highlight the amount of other cricket being played in the locality, but this would have created huge problems. Some teams quite clearly were little more than pub elevens, others ground-shared and the history of most would be impossible to establish, as their matches never made it into *Scores and Biographies*. I was also fortunate to find reports detailing the name changes of teams too; Kennington Saturday became Camberwell Clarence and New East Surrey became Camberwell St George.

Between 1825-55 I found reference to at least thirty-nine other teams in the immediate vicinity of Kennington. I have included some of their match reports, just to highlight them, or if they are educational, informative, quirky or relevant and I hope that what I have include meets with approval.

I have drawn up a list of these other local clubs (see below and next page) and in another column have given the first date that I found one of their match reports in *Bell's Life*. This can only be a rough guide as to the year of their emergence, as they may have played earlier matches which were not reported, or I may have missed an earlier mention in the newspaper. Some of the clubs, of which Kennington and the Montpelier were two, went on to play at another, or other grounds in the locality. This may be because they grew in size, or their normal ground was unavailable; it could have also have been because the opposition was a decent team and a large or better ground was required to host them.

I am reliant on the newspaper actually naming the ground in the report, and this was not always forthcoming. Where a ground is not shown it is because the club played an away match, or it was not mentioned in any reports.

It is interesting to note the longevity of Kennington C.C.'s residence on the local common, the number of teams that played at Hall's Ground in Southampton Street, Camberwell and the number of grounds that the Montpelier Club played at. Although the latter were based at four grounds in all, they were not averse to leaving whichever was their base for that season, in order to play at one of the other three. I will assume then, that some grounds were more suitable for bigger matches than others.

	Team	First to Note	Home Ground
1	Kennington Saturday	17-7-1825	Kennington Common
2	Kennington Junior	17-7-1825	Kennington Common
3	Camberwell Thursday	27-8-1826	Kennington Common
4	Kennington Wednesday	06-8-1826	Kennington Common

5	Kennington	15-7-1827	Kennington Common
6	Kennington Albion	15-7-1827	Kennington Common
7	Camberwell	26-8-1827	
8	Camberwell Star	22-6-1828	Hampton's
9	Surrey Vauxhall	27-7-1828	
10	Camberwell Union	11-10-1829	
11	East Surrey	01-8-1830	Hampton's
12	Beehive	08-5-1831	Beehive
13	Montpelier	28-8-1831	Beehive
14	Kennington Tuesday	04-9-1831	Beehive
15	Camberwell Clarence	08-6-1834	Hall's
16	Surrey Clarence	19-7-1835	Hall's
17	St George's Camberwell	26-7-1835	Hall's
18	Vauxhall	16-8-1835	Ford's Field, Vauxhall
19	Beehive Victoria	02-7-1836	Beehive
20	New East Surrey	09-6-1837	Staton's (Hall's)
21	Upper Camberwell	28-7-1837	Royal Veteran
22	Walworth Amateurs	06-10-1837	
23	South London	23-6-1839	Beehive
24	Union, Kennington	17-5-1840	
25	Beehive Union	19-7-1840	
26	Camberwell Vauxhall	09-5-1840	Hall's
27	Vauxhall Clarence	03-10-1841	Kennington Common
28	Kennington Albion	02-10-1842	
29	Kennington Royal Standard	30-7-1843	
30	West Surrey	20-8-1843	Wandsworth Road
31	Harleyford	11-8-1844	Beehive
32	Walworth Union	07-9-1845	Beehive
33	Surrey Paragon	13-8-1848	Oval
34	Surrey Phoenix	09-9-1849	
35	West Surrey (re-formed)	01-12-1850	Wandsworth Road
36	St George's (Surrey)	27-4-1851	Old Kent Road
37	Surrey Union	08-6-1851	Oval
38	Kennington Oval	04-7-1852	Oval
39	Camberwell Amateurs	23-7-1854	Rosemary Branch
40	Kennington Park	22-4-1855	

Chapter Five

Bell's Life and *The Era* Match Reports

(1831-47)

The Newspaper Library at Colindale in North London posted me a long list of newspapers from the area and era that could provide cricket reports. I was able to whittle this list down to just four newspapers which included *Bell's Life*, which proved to be by far the best source. It was available from 1822 on microfilm, and gave the current politics and news on a national scale. Within its few pages, normally on page four, a variety of sports were usually well-covered. In the summer months, boxing got most coverage, but angling, coursing, pigeon shooting and wrestling also got a few paragraphs, along with cricket.

I made a few trips up the Northern Line to the library but was relieved to find that Westminster Library near Leicester Square in the heart of the capital also had copies of the newspaper on microfilm. Thus the vast majority of my research was conducted in the premises of the latter. The library also had copies of *The Era*.

Bell's Life usually featured two or three matches in full, and by that I mean that it detailed the scores in both innings of each team, which was often accompanied underneath by a reasonable or very short report of the match. Very occasionally there was a lengthy report of the match. It is important to note that I will refer to these irrespective of the length of the accompanying reports (if indeed there were any) as "full match reports". Below these came more columns highlighting a lot of lesser matches, normally just a couple of lines, but on a national scale. It was within these columns of "round-ups" that I found what I was after, although many such entries were of just two lines. I was unsure how to feature my notes in my book, so I have often left them in an annotated style. Some reports have been selected to give a flavour of the matches occurring during this era, because they relate to the geographical area, or, because they place teams at particular grounds. It was hard to decide which reports to include and which to omit, so I have chosen to include all of the mentions of Montpelier C.C. matches, however brief. I have also included other local reports to give an idea of the other teams based in the area. The newspaper featured many such matches in the 1830s and 1840s, but, come the next decade few local matches were covered. There is also often no overlap of match reports that feature in the works of Britcher, Buckley, Denison or Haygarth. Clearly these different authors decided for themselves what to cover in their respective books, and also what not to. It should be noted that the first

Montpelier C.C. who played at Montpelier Gardens had faded away prior to the first edition of *Bell's Life*.

Some reports are included to show just how far afield (and often abroad) the newspaper featured cricket and others as previously mentioned if they were educational, informative, quirky or relevant. Many reports were often little more than a couple of lines in length, most begin with "a match will be played at…." or "a match was played between …". Despite their brevity, credit must be given to the editors for including details of these early matches and from so many different areas.

Bell's Life was published on a Sunday and was initially less helpful about the Montpelier Club than Haygarth's volumes. Cricket is featured in the newspaper from its outset in 1822, albeit very infrequently. In 1823 coverage improved and we read of matches involving All-England, Mary-le-bonne, Epsom, Nottingham and Sheffield. Sadly cricket coverage went backwards in 1824 and 1825, but, come 1826 it was being reported in much more depth and on August 6th Kennington's match against Ripley on Kennington Common was featured which saw Kennington win by nine runs, and "no less than 4,000 persons were present". The same season saw reports on matches involving Brighton, Camberwell Thursday, Dorking, Hackney Albion, Kennington Wednesday, Leeds, Midhurst, Northampton, Stowmarket and Wakefield amongst others. Decent coverage carried on until 1830 and from the newspaper's beginning the following teams local to Kennington had been covered in some respect; Kennington Saturday, Kennington Junior, Camberwell Thursday, Kennington Wednesday, Kennington, Kennington Albion, Camberwell, Camberwell Star, Surrey Vauxhall, Camberwell Union and East Surrey. Until 1831 the Montpelier Club was not mentioned and this adds to the belief that the club folded after the Napoleonic War.

Instead of trying to pen a history of the club from its re-appearance or, perhaps it should be termed, second phase, I will use the match reports to portray the re-emergence, exploits and success of the club. Exact details are very rare so what will emerge is a potted history, although being told in the fashion of the era which will hopefully give it a contemporary flavour.

So, in date order is a selection of the often very brief match reports in an annotated style, to give a flavour of what cricket matches were reported in the newspaper. The early years give a wide flavour of match reports and they gradually tighten-up to concentrate on clubs in the Kennington area.

1831

This year sees the first mention (on July 17th) of the Montpelier Club, although there is no comment on its re-formation, or why they played at Lord's and then in a report on July 31st, at the Beehive Club. If we refer back to W.W. Read's comments, there is also the lingering doubt that this may be evidence of their connection with Lord's. Did they cross the Thames to find a new home midway through the season?

May 8th - An advert in the newspaper invites "A challenge to the counties of Hertford and Essex. The gentlemen of the Tuesday's Bee-hive Walworth club (their first mention), are open to play the Gentlemen of the above County clubs, a friendly match at cricket - for any sum from 20 guineas to 100 guineas within a month, upon application to J. Heaps at the Beehive, Carter Street, Walworth." Heaps as mentioned earlier had become licensee of the pub in 1827, so was clearly a direct link with the club, and perhaps an organiser of matches at the ground.

May 22nd - "East Surrey at Hampton's ground are in the field and now meet on Wednesday's during the season. From Chislehurst, Hornchurch, Old Westminster, Canonbury, Hackney, Regency, Hampstead, The Paddington, Montpelier, Woolwich and many others in town and county, much is expected..." We are teased with the word Montpelier but this time there is no prefix, surely it must be the first mention of the one we are interested in? If so, we have the Beehive and Montpelier Clubs coming to press attention early in the same year.

Jun 5th - "A match will be played on Friday next in the Roebuck ground, Lewisham, Kent between the Dartford and Lewisham clubs."

In Rennel Street, close to the Lewisham indoor shopping centre and railway station, is a pub called *The Roebuck*. It is behind the site of the now demolished Lewisham Odeon, where many of the country's top pop groups once performed.

Jun 19th - At the bottom of a one-column report on cricket is "a match will take place at the Bee-hive New Cricket Ground, Carter Street, Walworth between eleven gentlemen of the Blackheath Union Club and eleven well-known players of the Bee-hive Club for 100 sovereigns." This is the first mention of both the Beehive club and their ground and shows that they had their own ground. *The Beehive* pub is still to be found close by.

Jun 26th - There are no reports on the above match, but there is a mention that "a match will be played on Thursday next at Camberwell between eleven gentlemen of the East Surrey Club and eleven gentlemen of the Hornchurch Club, therefore East Surrey were still at Camberwell and had not made the Beehive ground their new home.

Jul 3rd - There is a report on the return match between Blackheath and the Beehive Walworth Club at Blackheath which the Beehive team won by an innings. There is also mention of the new cricket ground at Bromley, Kent although this was not the famous White Hart Cricket Field, as that operated between 1751-1892. Incidentally, there is a large plaque commemorating this ground which is located in Queen's Gardens at the rear of *The Glades* shopping centre. On July 4th Kennington Wednesday Club were due to play the Lewisham Club on Kennington Common. The Bee-hive Walworth Club were also to play Chelsea Union on Thursday July 7th at the Wellington Club in Chelsea.

Jul 17th - "On Saturday week eleven gentlemen of The Charterhouse School (sited in London at this time) and a similar number of The Montpelier Club played a match at Lord's ground in the presence of a respectable muster of the admirers of the game." There had been earlier reports of a Lord's Montpelier Club and a Blackheath Montpelier Club, but can we conclude that it is our Montpelier Club that they are referring to? The match is not reported in *Scores and Biographies*.

The newspaper adds "on Monday the 25th instant, a match will be played at Camberwell between The Walworth Bee-hive club and Camberwell." This would have been a local derby as the two teams played their home matches within a mile of each other.

Jul 31st - The newspaper reported on the above mentioned match, but states that "a match was played at the Montpelier Club on Tuesday last between Hampton's Club and The Beehive Walworth Club which was decided in favour of the little Bees in one innings and 15 runs to spare." Camberwell are referred to as Hampton's Club (he owned the ground) but it initially stated that the match was to be played at Camberwell, yet the match report states that it was played at Montpelier Club. Perhaps the date and venue were changed at the last minute? The newspaper goes on to say that "a grand Match will be played at The Bee-hive cricket ground, Carter Street, Walworth on Tuesday week between Dartford and 2 county players and eleven of the Bee-hive club."

Aug 7th - The newspaper's main headline highlights the opening of the new London Bridge by His Majesty, "Amongst joyous peals of bells from the 100 neighbouring churches." In the sports section is a short report telling "on Thursday next Charterhouse School will contend with The Montpelier Club at Mary-la-Bonne. The following players were listed to play for The Montpelier eleven: Ballantyne, Maddock, Walker, Clarkson, Cooper, Morrice, Dutton, Lindselle, Yewens, Yeats and Mackinnon. This is the first team-list that we have for the club.

Aug 28th - Under a full match report for Mary-la-Bonne v Hornchurch it mentions "an excellent match was played at Dartford Brent on Monday last between nine of Dartford (plus Wenman and Mills) and the "little Bees of Walworth." Underneath it continues "a match was played at the Bee Hive Ground Carter-street, Walworth on Wednesday last, between Brompton and the Montpelier Club which was won by the latter with eight wickets to spare." From this article we can now deduce the Beehive Club and the Montpelier Club both used the Beehive ground.

Sep 4th - The newspaper mentions Kennington Tuesday playing on Kennington Common. It is their first mention in the newspaper.

Sep 18th - "The third match between Dartford plus Wenman and Mills and Little Bees of Walworth was played on Thursday and Friday at Heap's ground, Carter Street, Walworth which terminated as follows. Dartford 25 and 46 Little Bees 93 thus wining the match single handed with 22 runs to spare." The match was "honoured by the presence of the Queen, Duchess of Saxe Welmar, Prince George of Cambridge and several of the Nobility who were visiting the Zoological Gardens and appeared highly delighted at the activity displayed by the Little Bears." Surely they mean the Little Bees? It should be added that the Zoological Gardens bordered the Beehive ground.

Sep 25th - The newspaper reports on the fourth match between Dartford and The Little Bees which was played at Dartford Brent. Dartford scored 247 and 142-8, Little Bees 24, and needing 364 runs (should be 366) "the Little Bees resigned the contest."

So, at the end of the season, we have read of the Montpelier Club playing at Lord's and the Beehive ground, the Beehive Club playing at Heap's (the Beehive ground) and the Montpelier Gardens ground hosting the Hampton's and Beehive clubs. But there is no report that tells of the Montpelier Club playing at Montpelier Gardens.

Although our club have played at Lord's and W.W. Read commented that they "were believed to be an offshoot of Lord's (see page 4), there is also no evidence so far of them actually being based at the ground.

Continued on page 77.

Hampton's and Hall's Ground

This ground was clearly an impressive set-up and hosted a variety of teams, from local minor matches up to East Surrey's matches. *Bell's Life* reported on June 8th 1834 that Harry Hampton had sold it to a Mr Hall and on July 20th 1834 the opening of the new pavilion. Match reports featured in *Bell's Life*, show that Camberwell, Camberwell Star, Kennington, Licensed Victuallers, St George's Camberwell and East Surrey all played as the home team at the ground. Cottage Green, Camberwell where Harry Hampton's ground stood still exists and borders Burgess Industrial Park.

Hampton played for Montpelier at Aram's Ground, Walworth on June 12th 1806 and opened the batting against Homerton. He top-scored in the first innings with 64 but failed to score in his second innings. On page 152 of volume one of *Scores and Biographies* Haygarth writes "the name Hampton first appears in this match (Marylebone v Kent at Dartford Brent June 29th and 30th 1793). There were two who played occasionally in matches of note - J. and H.; but owing to the initials being generally omitted in the old score, performances of each cannot be separated. Not the slightest account of either could be obtained by the compiler of this work; where and when they died, ages, occupations, & c., therefore they remain unknown. It is believed, however, that they came out of Surrey, but it is by no means certain. Harry Hampton at one time kept a cricket ground at Camberwell, much patronised by suburban clubs. J. Hampton's name is found on the Twelve first chosen v. next Twenty-three in 1805; he must therefore, have been a pretty good man in some capacity or other, perhaps as a field."

On November 4th 2007 I went to look for any signs of this ground. The canal church as previously stated was mentioned on page 198 of *The English Game of Cricket* by Charles Box published in 1877, is still in situ (at 55 Wells Way, Camberwell and featured on pages 188 and 189 of this book), although it has been converted into flats. Next door is a large building with "Public Wash-house" carved into the stonework, now home to the Lynn A.C. Boxing Club. There is a plaque on the right side of the front elevation that states that it was the foundation stone for the baths. It was laid on Thursday July 25th 1901 on land given by the Right Honourable Llangattock. Another plaque, on the same elevation was the foundation stone for a public library, again laid on July 25th 1901. Thus the building had two roles from its opening day.

The canal has been filled in and its route is now part of Burgess Park. On one side of the church is a new housing estate, but on the other side is a large park. I could not find any trace of the pavilion, whose opening was reported in *Bell's Life* on July 20th 1834, but there were a sprinkling of old buildings in the vicinity.

The Beehive Ground

Exactly when or why the Montpelier Club moved to the Beehive ground is yet to be established; although 1831 would appear to be a good bet as in *Bell's Life* on June 19th 1831 the ground is referred to as Beehive New Ground. No precise dates are evident in any documents that I have studied, or in any books that I used in my research, and the ground is noticeably smaller than the Montpelier Gardens ground. The local map of 1830 shows the area to be largely rural and with just five main roads. However come 1871, the map shows the entire area covered with terraced houses and both grounds are lost under such development.

The first reported match at the new ground was in August 1831, between the Montpelier Club and Brompton, although as it is late in the season perhaps there were earlier ones that went unreported in *Bell's Life*. The club is mentioned briefly in the newspaper on May 22nd 1831, although it did not regularly feature any of their match reports until a few years later. Where the Beehive Club, who played at this ground went to after their first appearance in the newspaper in May 1831 is a mystery, and sadly there appear to be no clues. They also vanish from press reports in the newspaper after 1833.

The Montpelier Club were based at the Montpelier Gardens ground from at least June 1796 until July 1808 (or 1835 if we accept the comments made by W.W. Read in his *Annals of Cricket* book). They arrived at the Beehive ground at the latest by August 1831 and played there until at least July 1844 when *Bell's Life* reported their match against Clapton.

It is reported that they left the Beehive ground in 1844 after pressure from developers, which in turn probably led to some soul-searching by ex-players and the two famous meetings at *The Horns* pub in 1845, that witnessed the formation of the county club that we know today.

A page on the Internet dedicated to running tracks has a page on the ground and states that "some sort of track was in use here from 9th April 1844". The track must have had a very short life, perhaps for just one summer. Sadly whoever put this onto the Internet was unable to locate the ground giving their address solely as "Walworth", and were unable to give details as to what sort of track was in place too.

So to conclude; it appears to be twelve years residence at the Montpelier Gardens ground, and at least thirteen at the Beehive ground. Had the club's scorebook been obtained by Haygarth then this part of the club's history would have been a lot clearer and this era not so vague. It is even more frustrating as at this time they were re-emerging after more than twenty years out of view.

A Match Advert.

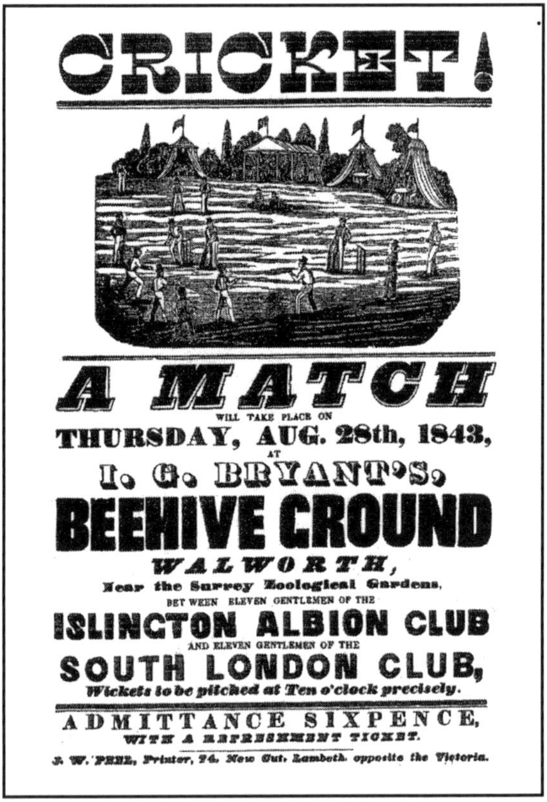

This impressive poster was passed to me by erudite cricket historian and writer David Frith from his own collection and I am very grateful as it adds a contemporary flavour. It is very informative, giving the location of the ground, the owner and an admission price, but in just over three years the ground was no more. *Scores and Biographies* gives a slightly different date for the match however and it is a shame that the match does not feature the Montpelier Club.

Site of the Beehive Ground.

This photo was taken a few yards south of the *Beehive* pub, and shows the site of the ground opposite the pub. The Beehive Tea Gardens were smaller than Montpelier Gardens, and the site is now covered by a school, a small block of flats and a road that contains large Victorian style houses.

Site of the Beehive Ground.

On the opposite side of Carter Street to the school shown on the previous photograph are a small block of flats. Behind them is this large and flat area of grass which, judging from old maps was also within the boundary of the triangular-shaped Beehive ground.

Map of the area in 1830.

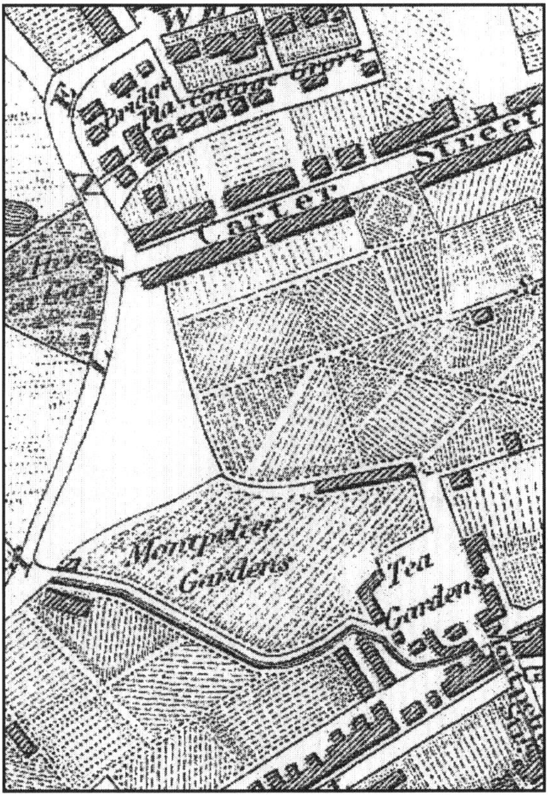

Both grounds can be seen on this map and Montpelier Street (now Pelier Street). *The Beehive* pub was located on the north side of Carter Street at the junction with West Lane (now Penrose Street). If one compares the shape of Montpelier Gardens with the boundary line highlighted on the 1871 map (page 207) they are almost identical. The recently vacated Carter Street police station sat for over 130 years on the southern side of the street just in from Walworth Road and joins a number of other stations closed in South London in the last few years.

Kennington Common in 1830.

KENNINGTON COMMON AND CHURCH IN 1830.

I bought this old print for ten pounds in 1997, when I discovered it in a box stacked with other prints of the capital, in a shop in Cecil Court in central London. The shop owner agreed to frame the "over one hundred years old" print for another fiver so that made it even more of a bargain. *The Horn's* on the right is where Surrey C.C.C. was formed in 1845 and it overlooked cricket matches played on the common. St Mark's Church is on the left and the small octagonal building just to its right is still there. The view is southwards along what is now Kennington Park, which in turn is really an enclosed Kennington Common.

Kennington Common in 2008.

This photograph gives a contemporary view of the scene on the previous page. Behind the trees on the left is St Mark's Church which is clearly visible on the older print of the same area. The layout of the roads is also virtually the same although the traffic is many times heavier now. *The Horn's* sited on the right of the print was bombed in World War Two and an ugly office block now sits in its place. I tried to take the photograph very close to where the artist who compiled the featured print would have sat, but tall hedges and a large fence made it impossible to align this and the print absolutely.

The Beehive pub, Penrose Street, Walworth.

The pub sits in front of a large block of flats which I initially believed to be the site of the Montpelier Ground. A good menu is advertised outside and customers can partake of the food and drink on a small west-facing terrace. Three doors on the south side lead into the pub, which is clean and tidy both inside and out. Outside a range of plants and some umbrellas add to the ambience of the building which I feel will not have changed much at all since the first licensee was registered back in 1827. I am also glad to see that it has not taken on a glitzy appearance, changed its name or become a theme pub and that it still displays original brickwork.

Map of the area in 1832.

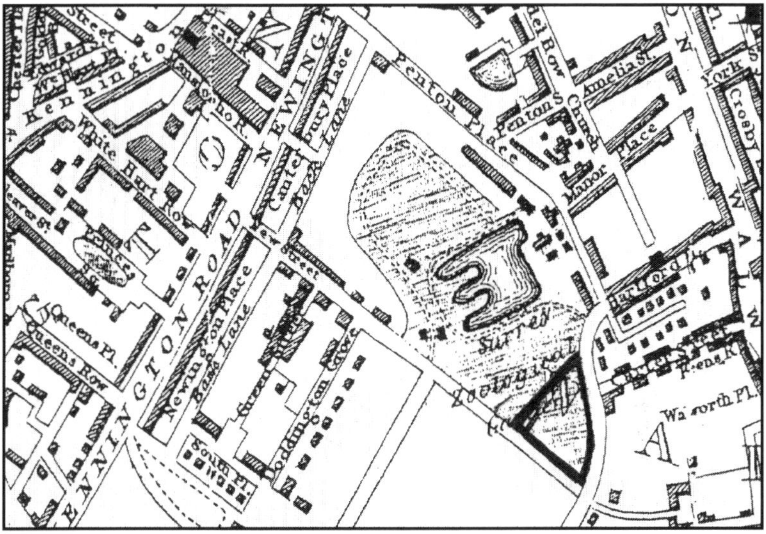

This map is one of my favourites due to its clarity and detailed structure. I have highlighted the triangular boundary of Beehive Gardens which is adjacent to the Surrey Zoological Gardens.

Map of the area c1837.

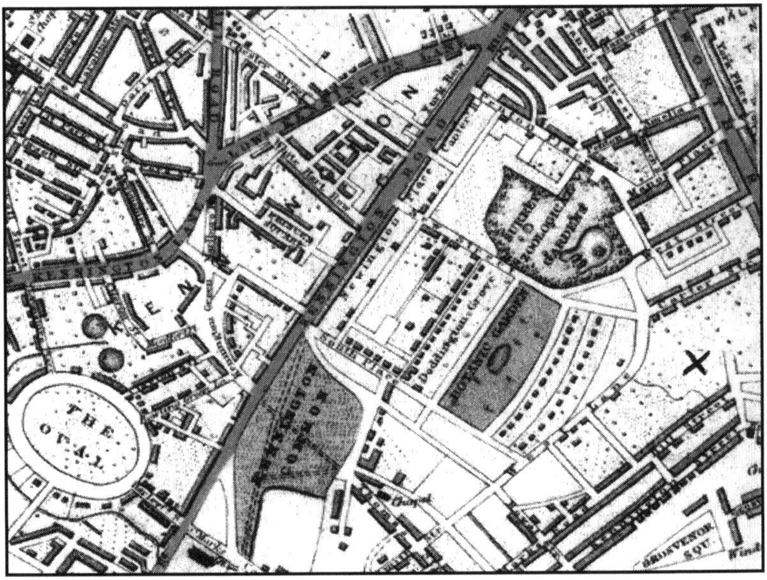

I have been unable to date this map which was found on a web-site dedicated to music halls and those who entertained in them. This map was found on the page given over to the Surrey Music Hall which was built on the site of the Surrey Zoological Gardens after the closure of the latter. The triangular site below the gardens is the unmarked location of Beehive Gardens, although it is located in a slightly different place to its position on the map on the previous page. The neighbouring cricket venues of Kennington Common and The Oval are clearly visible too. An "X" marks the spot where Montpelier Gardens was located and it is strange that they have been omitted, as they are evident on earlier ones, such as the 1795 map on page 32 and the 1824 map on page 57.

1832

Jun 10th - Tucked away at the base of the round-up is "a match will be played at Heap's Cricket Ground, the Beehive, carter-street, Walworth tomorrow (Monday) June 11th between the Mile End Club and the Montpelier Club."

Jun 24th - There are two mentions for the Montpelier Club this week. Firstly an advert for their match against "Eleven Gentlemen of the Richmond Club" at Heap's ground (the Beehive) on the twenty-ninth and then the result of their match on the eleventh against Mile End. Mile End scored 47 and 25, and Montpelier 46 and 30 to win by four runs (see below).

24/6/32

...mmon, betw... ...f Hounslow,

A match will be played at Heap's Cricket-ground, the "Beehive," Carter-street, Walworth, on Friday, June 29th, between eleven gentlemen of the Richmond Club and eleven gentlemen of the Montpelier Club. Wickets to be pitched at ten o'clock precisely, and the game played out.

A Match was played at Heap's Cricket-ground, the Beehive, Carter-street, Walworth, on Tuesday, the 11th instant, between eleven Gentlemen of the Mile-end Club, and eleven Gentlemen of the Montpelier Club, which terminated as follows:—Mile-end; 1st innings, 47; 2d ditto, 25; total, 72.—Montpelier; 1st innings, 46; 2d ditto, 30; total, 76. Thus winning the match by four runs, which was well contested by both parties.

Jul 8th - Again at the bottom of the cricket round-up is "return match between Richmond Union Club and Montpelier Club for 50 sovs will be played at Heap's cricket ground, the Beehive, Carter-street, Walworth on Thursday week."

Jul 15th - Reports on the Kennington Wednesday club's match against Mitcham. Mitcham scored 59 and 52 to beat Kennington who managed 59 and 37. There would be "a return match on Kennington Common on the 25th."

Jul 22nd - After a full match report on Lord Strathavon's side v Sir St. V. Cotton's side at Lord's (Sir St. V. Cotton's side won by an innings and 24 runs), the newspaper reports that "Kennington Wednesday club will play their return match with the Mitcham club on Wednesday next on Kennington Common, after which they will be open to play any eleven within 20 miles of London."

Aug 5th - Following a full match report on Winchester v Eton match the newspaper reports that Kennington Wednesday v Mitcham was played on the 25th and 28th (yes, a three-day gap) and that Kennington with 60 and 64, beat Mitcham

40 and 81 by three runs. The newspaper then comments that Mr Bucket kept wicket for Kennington, and "was the admiration of some thousand spectators, amongst whom we were gratified to see a number of very elegantly dressed females." After the match both teams dined at *The Cock* in Kennington.

Aug 12th - Under a full match report for the Eton v Harrow match at Lord's is reported "The East Surrey and West Kent club's played a match on Tuesday last, when the East Surrey proved victorious, with 7 wickets to spare. The match took place at Hampton's ground, Camberwell."

Aug 26th - "The return match of the Kennington club and the County of Surrey will be played on Kennington Common on Wednesday Sept 5th."

Sep 9th - The newspaper gives full match reports on the Everton club's win over Rochdale, the recent match between the Dundee Cricket and Dundee Athletic Club and Bury v Woodbridge. Closer to home is a report on a single wicket match on Clapham Common between Mr William Sewell of Mitcham and Mr Guinn of Clapham for 5 sovs. Mr Sewell scored 0 and 9 and lost to Mr Guinn's 7 and 3 not out.

Cricket reports then quickly ebb off and there are few of any interest in the Sept 16th edition and none at all in the Sept 23rd and 30th editions. Oct 7th has but a very small round-up, and Oct 14th marks the final cricket report of the season with a small advert for the forthcoming Sheffield v Nottingham match to be played in Hyde Park, Sheffield for 100 sovereigns.

This season has seen no mention of the Beehive Club, affectionately nick-named "Little Bees" by the newspaper last year. However there have been two reports about Montpelier matches and an advert for one too.

1833

May 19th - "The season at Lord's will be opened with a match between Mary-la-bonne and East Surrey." The East Surrey team was Reed, Plank, Everett, Rich, Rich, Wildman, Howkins, Craven, Denison, Jackson and Routh. Mary-le-bonne scored 130 (Cobbett 30 not out) to easily beat East Surrey who scored 70 and 13 (only three players scored). The newspaper also advertised that "a match will be played on Thursday next between the East Surrey club and the Mile End club at the cricket ground, Cottage-green, Camberwell." I shall be brave and assume that this is Hampton's ground, called by a different name and thus we have now pin-pointed its position.

Jun 30th - There is a full match report on the recent East Surrey v West Kent match. West Kent scored 62 and 29 to lose by an innings to East Surrey's 114. Felix played for East Surrey and Buller, Jenner, Kynaston and Lord Clanbrock for the opposition. Also reported is a match between Peckham C.C. and Clapton C.C. on Wednesday 26th on Peckham Rye Common, which "after 7 hours spirited play terminated in the success of the former by a majority of 37 runs." Peckham scored 163 and Clapton 126.

The Morning Advertiser dated July 5th 1833 contains an advert for a "Sale by Auction....Montpelier Tea Garden and Tea Gardens ... in consequence of the death of Mr Ross." David Ross had been licensee since 1817. Although the club seemed to disappear after their match against Marylebone at Lord's in July 1813 I did wonder if they still played lesser and unreported matches at their ground. But as no other teams are recorded as playing there, I feel that this is unlikely so perhaps David Ross decided not to allow cricket within the boundaries of his Gardens when he took over? Or am I being harsh on him? Checking the Newington Justices Records further we find that prior to him, John Hutchin(s) was landlord between 1812-16 and John Price in 1810 (there is nobody shown for 1811) so perhaps one of these terminated the Montpelier Club's tenure at the Gardens?

Jul 21st - The newspaper gives a full match report to Mary-la-Bonne v Left-Handed hitters at Lord's which resulted in "majority in favour of left-hitters 149." The home side had scored 52 and 77 and the left-handed players 199 and 79.

Under this report is another of a match last Monday on Kennington Common between eleven of Kennington and eleven of Paddington. Kennington won by 64 runs as they scored 72 and 91 and Paddington 51 and 48. At Hampton's ground in Camberwell, eleven of Camberwell beat eleven of Burstow by 28 runs. The Camberwell club scored 87 and 71 and the visitors 53 and 77.

Jul 28th - The cricket section opens with a long and detailed report about the single wicket contest between Fuller Pilch and Marsden at Norwich. Below this is a short report on the Montpelier Club's match against Mile End New Globe at Montpelier Gardens. At the close of the first day's play the Montpelier had been dismissed for 165 and the visitors for 182. This is an interesting report as it tells that the club played at Montpelier Gardens. It is unlikely to be a typing error and although the newspaper occasionally refers to them playing at the Montpelier

Ground, this is more specific with the venue. Perhaps Montpelier Gardens was still in existence at this time and the club used both it and the Beehive ground?

Sparrow shooting is the next sport to be covered. The featured event took place at The Red House Inclosure at Battersea for 50 pounds. The winner killed all bar one of his birds and the loser 28 out of 30.

Aug 4th - The cricket section opens with full match reports on Eton v Winchester and Eton v Harrow; both played at Lord's. Below these is mention of Mr Bradbury's forthcoming single wicket contest against Mr Brock to be played at Finch's new ground, Putney. Also mentioned is next Friday's match at Hampton's ground between St George's Camberwell and Guy's Hospital.

Aug 18th - Full match report on Kent v England match played on Monday at Chislehurst. Kent scored 117 and 17-2 and England 84 and 48. Mention is also made of the Barham v Dover played at Broome Park, next Thursday's East Surrey v Chislehurst at Hampton's ground and tomorrow's match at Burton-on-Trent between Leicestershire and Burton.

Aug 25th - A match in northern France makes the newspaper so adds to the diversity; St. Omer v Boulogne, played on August 1st at St. Omer. The home team scored 171 and the visitors 64 and 59. In the return match played at Boulogne on August 15th, Boulogne scored 109 and 58 and St. Omer 61 and 43. The newspaper stated "The ground at St Omer is an open plain, a fine sward, on a freestone bottom, which makes it particularly elastic. The ground in Boulogne is a meadow, which was cropped last year."

Tuesday last saw Kennington Wednesday Club v Epsom on Kennington Common which the home side won by 191 runs. Kennington scored 146 and 131 and Epsom 42 and 44. Mr Tew and Mr Kennedy played a one wicket match at Hampton's ground. Mr Tew scored 13 and 31 and Mr Kennedy 4 and 7. "Mr T winning both matches."

Sep 1st - The main report concerns the recent Richmond v Reigate match at Richmond, which was interrupted when a "mob then rushed upon the Reigate players, with most abusive language and seized them, three or four upon one, striking them in the most cowardly manner … the police rescued the umpire." The Reigate players quickly left in their coach at which "stones were thrown, two of which hit the players Killick and Lanaway." Below this is a report which begins with the customary "A match was played" on Monday at the Greyhound ground, Dulwich between Camberwell and Dulwich Junior Club which Camberwell won.

The following invitation also appeared: "The gentlemen of Kennington Wednesday club are open to play any club within 20 miles of London."

Sep 8th - A long letter opens the cricket section regarding the fracas at the recent Richmond v Reigate match written by "an inhabitant and eye-witness". Meanwhile Students of Guy's Hospital beat eleven of St George's Club, Camberwell at Hampton's ground. The newspaper also mentioned that "a match will be played tomorrow" between Union Club, Camberwell and Clapton at Hampton's ground.

Sep 22nd - In the smaller reports section "a match will be played" on Tuesday at Hampton's ground between Guy's Hospital and St George's Club.

Sep 29th - Full match report on Kennington v Seven Parishes; the latter team made up of players from "Mitcham, Esher, Wandsworth, Richmond, Kingston, Wimbledon, &c". It was played on a Monday and Tuesday on Wimbledon Green and saw Kennington score 139 and the home team 33 and 75.

There is also a long report on a match between the Watchmaker's Arms and Red Horse Union clubs of Coventry, which the former won. Boston beat Tadcaster and Kennington Wednesday club would play "Eleven players collected by Mr Finch from Putney and the surrounding parishes. The members of the Kennington club hope to have the pleasure of meeting some of their late opponents to assist Mr Finch in his endeavours to find a victorious party over the invincibles."

For the second season, there is no mention of the Beehive Club a.k.a. "The Little Bees" in the newspaper and hardly any mentions of our club either.

1834

This season sees some detailed reports, along with the customary short ones which usually cover the local clubs. Matches from across the country are again reported, and there is a welcome addition this year with the column of "Matches to Come" which highlights forthcoming fixtures. This season sees Hampton's ground in Camberwell change hands, the re-naming of one local club and two detailed and very welcome reports on the opening of the pavilion, at what was previously Hampton's ground. The reports this season seem more focused and there are still many teams in the Kennington area being reported on, which allows us to note which club was playing at which ground.

Jun 8th - Full match report on Epsom v Clarence played on Epsom Downs and short report on the Camberwell Clarence's win against Charlton at Hall's ground in Camberwell. Charlton's defeat the newspaper suggests, could be "attributed to their playing without spiked shoes, a circumstance almost unpardonable." This is an important short report as it is the first mention of Harry Hampton's ground now being under the ownership of a Mr Hall. In William Denison's *Sketches of the Players* published in 1846 he writes about James Dean, "In due time, Dean came up to London and was quickly brought into action by Hall, who succeeded Harry Hampton as the proprietor of the then Cricket Ground at Camberwell."

In the match round-up "a match will be played on Wednesday next week at Hall's Ground, Camberwell between Gravesend and Camberwell Clarence Club (late Kennington Wednesday Club)." This short report is also important as it highlights a name change for one of the local teams, and a radical one at that. Sadly though, there is no reason given for this change.

Jun 15th - Under "Other Matches to Come" is listed Mary-la-Bonne v East Surrey at Hall's ground Camberwell on July 25th.

Jun 22nd - The column opens with a full match report on Eton v Harrow, won by Harrow by four wickets and Mary-la-Bonne v Oxford, a one-day two innings match which ended as a draw. There are shorter reports on Clapham Albion v Camberwell Clarence on Clapham Common for fifty sovereigns a side. The newspaper very commendably also reports "On Friday next the opening of the new pavilion at Mr Hall's cricket ground Camberwell will take place in commemoration of which the gentlemen of the East Surrey and Union clubs with their friends intend having a day's play and the opening dinner, the President's of both clubs will preside at the table. The room, which is a very handsome building, commands an excellent view of the whole of the ground, and is capable of dining nearly 100 guests and which must now be considered as a second only to the Pavilion at Marylebone for beauty and convenience. For play, also the Camberwell Clubs can boast of some as good a players as any clubs of the day, and with the assistance of some of the county players, some first rate matches may be expected this season. The exertions and perseverance of the proprietor have not been spared to give convenience and accommodation to the different clubs that frequent his ground, and who in return seem determined to give him that encouragement that may ultimately repay him for what he has done."

I visited the site of Hall's ground in November 2007 but could find no sign of any building that could have been a pavilion. The area was bombed during the last war and there has been substantial re-building in the area, so its site may now well be covered.

Jun 29th - "The Walworth Montpelier Club intend playing a match with the Windsor and Eton Junior Club, at Windsor on Monday next."

Jul 6th - Under "Matches to Come" Clapham were to play Camberwell at Hall's ground and "On Thursday the 26th a match came off at the Montpelier, Walworth, between eleven gentlemen of the Merchants Taylor's School Club and eleven of St Paul's School. St Paul's scored 22 and 85 and Merchant Taylor's 98 and 10-0 to win by ten wickets".

Jul 13th - There is a full match report covering Kent v England at Lord's which England won by eight wickets. They chased 33 in their second innings for victory. Under "Matches to Come" we read that on Tuesday next the Camberwell Club will play Clapham at Hall's ground and on July 23rd "a match will take place between eleven of the Reigate Club and eleven gentlemen of the St George's Club at Hall's Ground in Camberwell" and "On Friday July 25th the grand match between Mary-la-Bonne and East Surrey will take place at Hall's Ground."

Jul 20th - Full match reports on Royal Clarence v Epsom at Moulsey Heath and Reigate v Brighton at Reigate and underneath, two welcome and detailed reports. The first report tells that "On Monday last week a match was played at the Beehive Club Ground, Carter-street, Walworth between eleven gentlemen of the Hampton Crown Club and eleven gentlemen of the Montpelier, Walworth. The field was numerously and respectfully attended and many ladies of the neighbourhood honoured the game by their presence, the gallantry of the Club having provided special accommodation for them. The game at the conclusion of the play stood as follows: Montpelier 128 and 13 and Hampton 98 and 16 with two wickets to go down thus rendering it most probable that had the game have been played out, the Montpelier would have beaten them apparently in one innings."

The second report is under the heading "Opening of the Pavilion at Hall's Ground, Camberwell" and continues "This event was celebrated on Thursday by a grand dinner, to which many admirers of cricket, and friends of the landlord sat down - John Pinham Esq in the Chair. The entertainment was more than usually sumptuous, and the wines first rate. On the cloth being removed, the usual loyal and patriotic toasts were given from the chair, the national anthem, and the appropriate songs succeeded the respective toasts, the whole of which were given in excellent style by several gentleman forming part of a company. On a gentleman proposing the health of the landlord, a high and deserved eulogy was passed upon Mr Hall for the spirited manner in which he supported the noble game of cricket, and his manly exertions to provide the interest and comforts of those gentleman who frequented his ground. The toast was received with a loud and long-continued applause. Mr Hall in retiring thanks, observed, that he had been a cricketer for many years, and had always had the interests of the game at heart. He felt exceedingly proud at the kind feeling evince towards him, his wife, and family; and he assured those gentlemen who had honoured him with their presence, that he should continues to exhort himself until he hoped not only to rival the Mary-la-Bonne club, but all others within 300 miles of London, in bringing famous matches on his own ground replete with first-class players of the present day, and all the scientific displays which have hitherto characterised some of the first Clubs in the Kingdom (cheers) ….."

I wish that there were far more of these detailed types of reports, in order to illuminate players, clubs and grounds much better. These facts aside, the newspaper has to date been happy to mention teams with scant regard to any other accompanying facts.

Jul 27th - Full match report on Yorkshire v Norfolk played at Hyde Park, Sheffield and in the round-up Surrey and Sussex Union beat St George's at Hall's by ten wickets, and Mary-la-Bonne v East Surrey at Hall's ended in a tie although "the score forwarded to us is in such an imperfect state, as to render it impossible to make it out."

Aug 3rd - Under "Matches to Come" Montpelier, Walworth would play Windsor and Eton Junior Club again on the Montpelier ground tomorrow, and Montpelier would play Kingsland Star at the same ground on Thursday next. It is not clear whether they mean the Beehive ground or Montpelier Gardens ground here. At Hall's, Mitcham would be the Camberwell Clarence Club's opposition, and on Friday next Camberwell Union would entertain Wanstead. In the results section, Lynn beat Spalding and on Hampton Common, Minchinhampton beat Gloucester by 5 runs over two innings.

Aug 10th - A report on Montpelier v Windsor and Eton "Montpelier with Messrs Lambert, Bocket, Trimmel, Colston, Baker, Foulds, Hodgkins, Lewis, Twigg, Williams and Berman, scored 50. The visitors then scored 100 and Montpelier replied with 82. The visitors then scored the required 33 for the loss of three wickets."

If we go back three years earlier to the report on August 7th 1831 there are no players with the same name.

Aug 17th - In the shorter reports there is a second one that informs the reader "On Monday last some of the finest play was witnessed at Walworth between the Montpelier who of late years have beaten everything brought against them and the Windsor and Eton Juniors Club..... although it was excellent play the match throughout was a one-sided affair: indeed from beginning to end it was St James's Palace to a sentry box."

This is also an interesting report as it is the first albeit in an unusual style to show how dominating the Montpelier Club was during this period. It is odd therefore that to date there have been no full match reports concerning any of their matches featured in the newspaper.

Aug 24th - There is a report about a match played on Wednesday on Kennington Common between Kennington Saturdays Club and Mitcham Albion. It reports "Afterwards the clubs dined together at the *Cock Tavern*, Walworth, Kennington Green where a most excellent dinner was provided by Mr Merry, the landlord." The newspaper also reported that "The East Surrey and Montpelier Walworth Clubs met on Tuesday for a day's play at Hall's Ground, Camberwell." East Surrey scored 73 and 77 and Montpelier 101. Montpelier "won on first innings, there not being light to play any longer." Another fairly local ground is mentioned when the newspaper reports "a match will be played at the Greyhound, Dulwich on Wednesday next between Blackheath and Dulwich for 22 sovereigns."

Aug 31st - In amongst some short reports are Camberwell Clarence v Brighton at Hall's, Camberwell, which began on Thursday "Clarence went in first and scored 56 .... Brighton marked 25 ..... Clarence then resumed the bat, and made their score altogether 105, thus leaving Brighton 81 to get to win. On Friday Brighton had four wickets lowered for seven runs ... when rain put an end to the game."

Sep 14th - Under "Matches to Come, Kennington Saturday Club "will have a day's play on the Common, on Wednesday next, after which they will dine together at Mr Merry's, the Cock Tavern, Kennington Green as a "wind-up" for the present season."

Sep 21st - Full match reports on Sheffield v Nottingham and Chislehurst v Norfolk and underneath in the briefer reports mention is made that the Kennington Saturday Club's match on the Common was between two teams calling themselves "County of Surrey" and "All England". The Surrey team, who scored

84 and 23-6 contained Denison, Gentle, Hillyer, Le Neve and Witham and the "England" team who scored 88 and 70 contained Bocket, Groom, Hatch and Steven. Bad light brought play to an early finish after a collapse by Surrey. At the meal Mr Emmens, Club President took the chair and Mr Lyons officiated as Deputy.

"The Montpelier Club will meet at their ground, Carter-street, Walworth, on Thursday next for a day's play as a finale of a most successful season, they having played matches with the East Surrey, the Hampton, the Windsor and Eton, and the Kingsland clubs, losing only the return match with the Windsor and Eton." This report is of note as it refers to the ground at Carter-street being "their ground".

Sep 28th - The cricket column opens with a list of new and altered "Laws of Cricket" and there are full match reports on Goodwood v Midhurst and Guards v Postmen (played in Vincent Square, Westminster, London). The Postmen scored 53 and 152 and the Guards 35 and 48. There were no reports of any local interest in this week's newspaper.

There is no mention of the Beehive Club in the newspaper this season, although their Beehive Gardens ground is still being used by the Montpelier Club who also appear to still be using the Montpelier Gardens ground.

1835

I will limit this season's and future ones, to reports relating to the teams local to Kennington, unless there is anything of interest. It is worth noting that this season's reports are better laid out, more detailed and more teams are mentioned.

May 17th - The Marylebone Club (note how it is now spelt) "celebrated their anniversary by a dinner at Ellis's Hotel, St James's Street." Their forthcoming matches are listed, plus the changes and alterations to the "Laws of Cricket" which ran to a whole column. The newspaper reports that "Several clubs meet at Hall's ground, Camberwell, the Clarence on Mondays, the East Surrey's on Wednesdays, the Union on Thursdays and the St. George's on Saturday. Another club is forming, and it is supposed the members of it will meet on Fridays."

May 24th - The newspaper reports "The Walworth Montpelier Club meet very strong this season, and are commencing operations with spirit. Their first match is appointed for Thursday next, when they will meet the East Surrey Club on the Walworth ground."

From this vague reference we are again unable to deduce which ground the newspaper is referring to.

May 31st - Full match report on Montpelier v East Surrey, which is the first instance in the newspaper of their getting such thorough coverage. "The match between these two clubs was played on Thursday last at the Walworth ground in the presence of a numerous assemblage of spectators, among whom were several gentlemen from Lord's who came to see the crack bowler Mynn, do dreadful execution upon those who had never before stood against." This one-day match saw Montpelier score 97 and 124 and East Surrey total 85. The Montpelier eleven was: Bocquet, Lambert, Foulds, Coltson, Baker, Hogarth, Elt, Peto, Dension, Collis and Clark. Mynn took four wickets in the first innings and three in the second.

If we compare this eleven to the one listed less than a year ago, on August 10th 1834, even allowing for spelling errors there are only four who played in both matches, so it is appears to be good evidence that the club had a large playing membership.

Jun 7th - "On Thursday next, a match will be played at Hall's ground, Camberwell between eleven of Blackheath and eleven of the Camberwell Clarence Club."

Jun 14th - "A single wicket match for £20 will be played at Hall's ground, Camberwell on Tuesday next at twelve o'clock between Mr A Rich, - Lucas esq and Mr John Grinham, against Messrs Hall, Bennett and Heath. The match .... has caused a considerable deal of betting, the odds at present are five and six to four in favour of Mr Hall's side."

Jun 28th - "The Kennington Saturday Club will play their first match of the present season with the gentlemen of the Mitcham Albion Club, on Thursday next, at Mitcham Green."

Jul 5th - "The match between the Reigate and the Camberwell Clarence Clubs took place on Monday on the Reigate ground, Lillywhite being given to the Reigate and A. Mynn esq. to the Camberwell. Reigate won by 48 runs. The Camberwell eleven was: A. Mynn, Hadland, Bennett, Grinham, Hall, Heath, Finch, Day, Harding, Messenger and Ashby. There is no sharing of players with the Montpelier Club, whose eleven is listed on May 31st." This last comment is a clear indication that players inter-changed between clubs.

The newspaper continues "On Wednesday and Thursday the 18th and 19th a return match will be played at Hall's ground, Camberwell between Reigate with Lillywhite given against the Camberwell Clarence Club." and "A match is made between the Camberwell Clarence Club against seven colts of Sussex with J. and W. Broadbridge, Taylor of North Chapel and Millyard of which timely notice will be given when played at Hall's ground."

Jul 12th - "On Friday the return match between eleven gentlemen of the East Surrey Club against eleven gentlemen of the Bee Hive, will be played at Hall's Ground, Camberwell."

Jul 19th - Full match report on Windsor and Eton v Walworth Montpelier which was played at The Brocas, Eton. The home team scored 145 and 62 and Montpelier whose team was: Croucher, Lambert, Lewis, Colston, Baker, Peto, Denison, Elt, Williams, Bernon and Goodchild, managed 77 and 16-2. Also reported is "The return match is fixed to take place at the Bee Hive ground, Walworth on the 17th August."

"A match between the Leeds, Kent Club and the Surrey Clarence Club (their first mention in *Bell's Life*), with Cobbett given, came off at Hall's ground, Camberwell on Thursday and Friday the 9th and 10th inst. The Leeds club was victorious after a most interesting game by five wickets."

"The return match between Mitcham Albion Club and Kennington Saturday will be played on Kennington Common next Wednesday. The Kennington eleven would be: T. Emmons, H. Powell, C. Powell, J. Pinham, H. Stilling, J. Wheat, F. Withern, D. Withern, Esqrs, Messrs Heath, Alder and Coomber."

"A single wicket match will be played at Hall's ground, Camberwell on Wednesday next between Redgate and Goode and A. Mynn Esq and Marsden for 20 sovereigns. Wickets to be pitched at nine o'clock precisely."

Jul 26th - Full match reports on Gentlemen v Players, Harrow v Eton, Carlisle v 34th Regiment, Wanstead v Clapton and Manchester v Liverpool, and the brief reports which follow these are noticeably more detailed than those from the season before:

East Surrey v Walworth Montpelier was played at Camberwell on Friday the 17th. East Surrey scored 137 and Montpelier 84 and 37-5 as the match ended as a draw. The East Surrey eleven was: Marsh, Plank, Felix, Mynn, A. Rich, Coe,

Reed, Craven, Spencer, Dyer and Wildman. The Montpelier eleven was: Bocquet, Foules, Hogarth, Peto, Lewis, Coltson, Baker, Trinnell, Dennison, Elt and Williams.

The newspaper continued "The Walworth Montpelier Club and the Windsor and Eton Junior play a match at the Beehive Ground, Walworth on the 17th of August."

Aug 2nd - "On Tuesday next there will be a general meeting of the members of the Montpelier (Walworth) Club, for election of a president and the transaction of the business. The return match between Montpelier and Ripley clubs will be played on the Walworth ground on the 6th inst. A match will be played on the same ground on the 12th inst., between the Putney and Montpelier Clubs, and on the 17th inst. On the Walworth Ground, the return match between the Windsor and Eton Junior and Montpelier will take place."

From this interesting report we can see that the club were now playing regularly and not on the same day every week.

Aug 16th - This week's reports sees the first mention of another local ground, albeit in a different direction from The Oval. The newspaper starts off with its familiar "A match was played" and continues "on Tuesday at Ford's Fields near Vauxhall between Vauxhall Club (their first mention in the newspaper) and Camberwell Clarence Club which the former won by six runs. The ground was numerously attended and after the match the company adjourned to Mr. Keasley's Three Compasses, Vauxhall."

Below this came a short report of interest; "On Friday next a match will be played at Hall's Ground, Southampton Street, Camberwell between Camberwell Clarence and the Clapton Club. On Tuesday August 25th the return match between the Vauxhall Club and the Camberwell Club, will be played at Hall's Ground, Camberwell."

This is the first time that the road in which Hall's famous ground is located has been mentioned.

Aug 23rd - The club's second full match report comes with Windsor and Eton Juniors v Montpelier, perhaps due to the club growing in stature? "On Monday last the return match between the Windsor and Eton Junior and the Montpelier (Walworth) Club was played at the Beehive Ground, Walworth." The Montpelier team scored 97 and 106 and the visitors 80.

The newspaper continues "Eleven of the Montpelier played a return match with the Ripley at Walworth on the 6th ultimo which ended with daylight as follows: Montpelier 77 and 78-5, Ripley 121. On the 13th inst the Montpelier Club played a match at Walworth against the Putney Victoria Club which was decided as follows: Montpelier 111 and 81, Victoria 61 and 56. Montpelier won by 81 runs."

Sep 6th - "On Friday the 29th ultimo the return match between the Victoria and the Montpelier (Walworth) Clubs took place at Finch's Ground, Putney which was decided in favour of the former by 26 runs." Also "A match was played at the Beehive, Walworth last week for £10 and a dinner between eleven tradesmen of Walworth and eleven tradesmen of Newington, which after a severe contest was won by Walworth by 5 runs."

Sep 20th - "On Wednesday next a single wicket match will be played at the Beehive Ground, between two gentlemen whose names are not at present much known to the cricketing worlds, but who bid fair to take the lead in that manly game - viz - Messrs Hammond and Kiddle."

Oct 4th - "The St George Club met last week at Hall's Ground for a day's play being the last time of their meeting this season." The weather was "very unfavourable", but the club succeeded in playing two innings per side. The dinner was served by Mr Hall "in his usually excellent manner and embraced some of the best fare of the season." The Club's President was Charles Ebsworth.

1836

May 22nd - "Any club within 30 miles of London wishing for an early match, can, no doubt, have their wishes complied with by application to Mr Hall at the Camberwell Ground, as various clubs play there, and he can accommodate them with either a strong or younger club." This advert confirms that Hall's ground was home to many clubs based in the area.

Jun 5th - There is an interesting report which states "The East Surrey club had an excellent day's play, eleven a side on Wednesday, at Hall's Ground, Camberwell. We hear that this club is about to be dissolved and that the gentlemen belonging to it intend to join the other Club's on Hall's ground."

Although helpful, the newspaper fails to illustrate which team the club played against and worse, why the club, perhaps with ability on a par with the Montpelier

Club, was being dissolved. It is another example of a lack of quality journalism in the newspaper.

The newspaper continued, "The Montpelier Walworth Club with some of them barred, play the Victoria Putney club on Finch's ground, at the latter place on Thursday week".

So far this season there has been no mention of any of the Montpelier midweek teams e.g. the Wednesday and Friday elevens.

Jun 12th - The newspaper sadly had to report "Mr. Benjamin Dark, who was long known as the celebrated cricket-bat maker at Lord's Ground died suddenly last week, leaving a widow and numerous family to deplore his loss."

Jun 19th - Full match report on - Montpelier v Putney Victoria Club match at the Bee Hive ground, Walworth (see two pages on), which saw the Montpelier Club win by five wickets.

Jun 26th - The weekly round-up mentions "return match between Camberwell Clarence and the Gravesend Orange Clubs will be played tomorrow (Monday) at Gravesend" and "a match will be played tomorrow (Monday) at Hall's Ground, Camberwell between the Vellum Makers and the Bookbinders in the employ of Mr Smith of Lock-fields and Long acre." Below this is another brief report.

"The Montpelier Walworth and the Putney Victoria clubs play their return match at the Beehive Ground, Walworth on Thursday next."

Jul 3rd - A full match report for the Montpelier Walworth v Putney Victoria match at the Beehive ground. The hosts amassed 262 and the visitors 68 and 52, so romped to victory by an innings (see three pages on).

The newspaper carried a short report on the Vellum v Bookbinders match the week before - "The game was decided in favour of the parchment and velum makers. Nearly a hundred persons engaged in Mr Smith's extensive establishments, dined in the evening in the Pavilion, at the cricket ground on which occasion Mr Smith took the chair. The dinner was in Hall's usual excellent style, and after a pleasant evening the company separated, Mr Smith being loudly cheered on leaving the room."

Jul 17th - Full match report on Mitcham v Camberwell Clarence Club which saw Mitcham record scores of 64 and 53-8 and the visitors 107. The newspaper reports

"Had the Mitcham sent in their men in proper time there would have been time, not only for the Mitcham to have concluded their second innings but for the Clarence to have resumed to bat."

The newspaper goes on and perhaps balances the argument by reporting "Clarence not arriving on the ground at the usual time" and that "A party of nearly 40 sat down to dinner at The White Hart - Mr Oakes in the chair."

Another interesting match was reported on; "A single wicket match for £20 a side was played on the Beehive Ground, Carter-street, Walworth on Wednesday between Messrs Trimmel and Lewis of Montpelier Cricket Club and Messrs Wright and Lovell of Waltham Abbey." The Montpelier duo scored 10 and 11 and the duo from north of The Thames scored 0 and 21 and the match ended as a tie.

This week's healthy cricket reporting continued, "On Saturday week a match came off at the Beehive Ground, Walworth between eleven gents of St Paul's and eleven of the Merchant Taylor's Club, in which the latter came off victorious, with eleven wickets to go down."

Jul 24th - Full match report on Windsor and Eton Junior Club v Walworth Montpelier Club played last Monday in the Brocas, Eton. The home team scored 93 and 37 and Montpelier 57 and 74-2. The newspaper reported "The fielding of the Montpelier was wretchedly bad in the first innings, but altogether as good in the second. The return match will take place at the Beehive Ground, Walworth on the 15th of August."

The weekly round-up mentioned Kilburn (55 and 44) v Montpelier (50 and 107) which was played last Thursday.

Jul 31st - The newspaper reported "A match will be played on Monday week on Kennington Common between eleven master-waggoners on the road between London and Portsmouth and eleven of the County of Surrey for £50 a side; wickets to be pitched at eleven o'clock."

Aug 7th - Despite a healthy two columns given over to cricket reports, the only one of local interest is "A single wicket match for £10 a side was played at Hall's Ground on Tuesday last between Lambert and W. H. and C. Corbett against Morrison, Macpherson, Kibble and Knowles (all members of the Camberwell St George's Club) which terminated in favour of the afore mentioned gentlemen in their second innings, without the loss of a wicket."

MONTPELIER AND PUTNEY VICTORIA CLUBS.

The match between the Putney Victoria and the Walworth Montpelier (with three members barred, came off on Thursday at Finch's Ground, Putney, as follows —

VICTORIA.	1st inn.		2d do.
King, bowled by Lewis	0	bowled by Lewis	2
E. Mackeson, bowled by ditto	0	caught by Challis	0
G. Whyting, bowled by ditto	2	bowled by Lewis	5
Byron, bowled by ditto	7	bowled by Denison	3
Cooper, stumped by Coltson	3	thrown out by Coltson	7
L. Mackeson, bowled by Lewis	5	bowled by Lewis	12
C. Whyting, bowled by Denison	10	bowled by ditto	17
Wells, stumped by Coltson	0	bowled by ditto	5
James Lee, bowled by Denison	21	bowled by ditto	3
John Lee, bowled by Lewis	3	not out	3
Roper, not out	0	bowled by Denison	0
Byes	4	Byes 6, wide ball 1	7
Total	—52	Total	—64

MONTPELIER.	1st inn.		2d do.
Beman, caught by E. Mackeson	0		
Coltson, run out	0	bowled by C. Whyting	1
Dawson, caught by E. Mackeson	4		
Elt, caught by ditto	8	caught by James Lee	0
Trimnell, bowled by G. Whyting	7	bowled by C. Whyting	1
Lewis, caught by E. Mackeson	1	not out	17
Denison, before wicket	3	bowled by King	10
Challis, bowled by G. Whyting	0	not out	2
Blundell, caught by E. Mackeson	2		
Kiddle, not out	6	caught by G. Whyting	0
Ayrey, bowled by C. Whyting	7		
Byes 22, wide balls 11	33	Byes 3, wide balls	21
Total	—63	Total	—54

The Montpelier winning by five wickets.—The bowling of Lewis and Denison, on the Montpelier side, who were not changed during the whole day, was the admiration of a numerous concourse of spectators. The return match is fixed to come off at the Bee Hive, Walworth, on the 30th inst. The Montpelier have a match on hand with the Windsor and Eton Junior, which they expect will very shortly come off

June 17th 1836

MONTPELIER AND PUTNEY VICTORIA CLUBS.

The return match between these Clubs was played on Thursday at the Bee Hive Ground, Walworth, the Montpelier winning in one innings by 142 runs, as will be seen by the following score :—

VICTORIA.	1st inn.		2d do.
G. Whyting, caught by Trimnell	24	bowled by Elt	2
Cooper, thrown out—Lewis	0	bowled by Lewis	8
Demay, caught by Hastings	14	bowled by Elt	6
Byron, caught by Peto	0	bowled by ditto	15
C. Whyting, run out	6	caught by Peto	4
L. Mackeson, caught by Denison	0	caught by Trimnell	2
James Lee, caught by Trimnell	12	bowled by Lewis	0
Wells, caught by Elt	1	cau. by Foulds (Denison)	2
E. Mackeson, caught by Lewis	5	bowled by Lewis	0
John Lee, caught by Trimnell	1	not out	0
W. Mackeson, not out	0	bowled by Elt	4
Bye 1, no balls 4	5	Byes 8, wide ball 1	9
Total	—68	Total	—52

MONTPELIER.	1st inn.
Blunden, caught by C. Whyting	3
Challis, bowled by G. Whyting	44
Peto, run out	47
Denison, hit wicket	1
Coltson, bowled by C. Whyting	84
Lewis, bowled by ditto	1
Trimnell, bowled by G. Whyting	14
Elt, bowled by ditto	0
Beman, bowled by E. Mackeson	17
Kiddle, caught by Byron	5
Hastings, not out	0
Byes 32, wide balls 34	66
Total	—262

The following matches were also advertised:
Montpelier v Copenhagen on Wednesday at Walworth Ground and
Montpelier v Kilburn at Beehive Ground on Monday (the 22nd).

Initially I assumed that "the Walworth Ground" was definitely the Beehive ground by a different name, but in the above fixtures, both grounds are mentioned. I will be brave enough to suggest that this is a printer error.

Aug 14th - Full match report on Montpelier v Copenhagen which saw Montpelier score 77 and 167 and the visitors 59 and 38-2. The newspaper reported "This match was made by barring nine members of the Montpelier and eight members of the Copenhagen, and afforded a very excellent specimen of what may be expected of these two clubs at a future time."

Aug 21st - The return match between Copenhagen and Montpelier was played "At Islington on Thursday. We do not have room for the whole of the score". The newspaper did however inform that Copenhagen scored 84 and 88 and the visitors 109 and added "After scoring 15, night put an end to the game, leaving them 48 runs to get with eight wickets standing."

Aug 28th - Full match report on Montpelier (223) v Kilburn (65 and 29) played at Walworth last Monday. The newspaper reported "The Montpelier winning, in one innings, by 129 runs - being the eighth successful match that they have played this season." The newspaper further reported that The Epsom v Camberwell Clarence Club was "not played out" due to rain.

There is also an advert for the Licensed Victualler's match of Middlesex and Surrey to be played at Lord's tomorrow. The return match will be played on Monday September 5th at Hall's ground, Camberwell.

Sep 4th - With regard to the above Victualler's match; it was "not finished, Middlesex leaving Surrey about 60 to get in the second innings … the whole of the money received for admission in the Ground was appropriated …. to the fund for building the new Licensed Victualler's School in Kennington Lane."

Sep 11th - The newspaper reports "On Monday the return match between the Licensed Victuallers of Surrey and Middlesex came off at Hall's Ground, Camberwell. The company was not so numerous as expected. The game was not finished Middlesex getting in their first innings 129, Surrey 74. Middlesex then got about 60 runs with six wickets down."

The following intriguing match was also advertised:

Eleven Druids of the Camberwell Green Lodge v Eleven Druids of the Hammersmith Lodge at Hall's ground on Wednesday.

The newspaper continued "The Montpelier Club which has been successful in every match played this season, intend meeting on Thursday, the 15th', for a day's play between their first eleven and the next eighteen members of the their clubs." At least six of these matches have been reported in *Bell's Life* although they were not playing matches very frequently.

The above report is further evidence of how large and powerful a club the Montpelier were, and we are left to wonder why if they played any matches between 1813-31 they were not featured in the sports media.

Sep 18th - "The day's play of the Walworth Montpelier - viz: the first eleven and the next eighteen of the members, came off on Thursday, in favour of the former, who played in their usual excellent manner, to the admiration of the spectators."

1837

This is the first season for many years that sees the Montpelier Club in *Scores and Biographies,* so it will be interesting to note if their opposition was of a better quality, as Haygarth was selective about what he included in his tomes.

May 14th - "On Wednesday next, a new club under the name of the Surrey Union Club, will be formed at Hall's Ground, Camberwell which bids fair to become not only a strong club in numbers, but likewise a fair Club in play. Mr Dawson of the Clarence club, held at the same ground, has been called upon to become Secretary under whose management it cannot fail, with the assistance expected from several other gents, to become a formidable club."

The newspaper reported on a visit to the Montpelier Club at their Beehive Club base - see below.

The Montpelier Club, who meet at the Bee-hive ground, Walworth, assembled numerously on Tuesday. The ground was in admirable order, and after several hours' play the members and their friends adjourned to the Club-house, for the transaction of business. It having been agreed upon that a new tent should be purchased by the Club, several makers entered the lists of competition. Five or six tents were erected on the ground for inspection, and after some discussion it was at length decided, by a majority of two, that the one made by Edgington should be purchased, and the Treasurer received orders to pay for it instanter, which was accordingly done. The Club days are Tuesdays and Fridays, and the members appear to be only waiting for an invitation, to "come out" more prominently. We were much pleased to see "the Starlings" at the Bee-hive in full feather and delightful plumage.

The Kennington Saturday Club opened their season on the Common yesterday week. They met numerously, and appear anxious for a trial with some other Club. Yesterday they were to meet again, and afterwards to partake of a dinner handsomely given them by Mr. Merry, the late landlord of the Cock Tavern (the Club-house), and the present one, Mr. Davy, as a farewell to the old, and an introduction to the new proprietor. The Club, it is expected, will go on merrily this season, several new members having been already added to the list.

This is an interesting report as it is the only one that I have found which refers to the club as "the starlings", which may have been their nick-name. The surname of licensee of *The Beehive* pub from 1832 until his death in 1835 was Starling, and although this report comes two years after his death, perhaps the club were still known by this title?

Jun 11th - Under "Cricketting" (note the two "t"'s) on the front page of the newspaper this week. The Kennington v Beehive Victoria match is reported on (see next page), although there is no clue given as to where the match took place. It would also be interesting to know more details about Beehive Victoria (their first mention) - were they a re-appearance of the Beehive Club, under a slightly different name?

Jun 18th - There are no reports of local interest but we read "On Wednesday next a match will be played at Hall's Ground, Camberwell between 11 gentlemen of the St George's Club, Camberwell and 11 gentlemen of Camberwell Waterloo Club." Further down is "The return match between the Kennington Saturday Club and the Beehive Victoria Club will take place tomorrow at the Bee-Hive Ground, Walworth. Wickets to be pitched at ten o'clock."

June 11 1837

KENNINGTON AND BEE HIVE VICTORIA CLUBS.

This match came off on Tuesday, and attracted a large assemblage of spectators. The Kennington won by a single run only, and certainly very unexpectedly, for after the first innings of both parties 20 to 1 against Kennington went begging; but, as the Kenningtonians were awake to the "glorious uncertainty" of cricket, they went steadily to work in their second hands, and by the exertions and superior batting of Messrs. Withern and Garrett succeeded in scoring 121, which left their opponents 41 to get; but, through the excellent bowling of Brooks, added to the careful fielding of the rest of the Club, they only obtained 40, losing the match, as before stated, by one run. Nine of the Victoria wickets, in the second hands, were lowered for 16 runs; and of the style of hittng on the part of Kennington, some idea may be formed when we state that Mr. Withern scored an eight, a six, two fives, two fours, and four threes; and Mr. Garratt, two fives, two fours, &c. On the other side, Mr. Hersee scored a six, a five, and two threes; Mills, two fours, and six threes; Henton, several threes; Davies, a six and a four; and Alder several threes.—The following is the score:—

KENNINGTON.	1st inn.		2d do.
Howard, caught by Davies	8	bowled by Coomber	0
Russell, bowled by Coomber	0	bowled by Alder	1
Brooks, bowled by ditto	2	caught by Mills	10
Powell, bowled by Alder	10	bowled by Alder	8
Pinhorn, bowled by ditto	0	bowled by ditto	5
Wheat, bowled by Coomber	1	bowled by Coomber	0
Withern, caught by Lambert	13	bowled by Alder	54
Roffey, bowled by Alder	8	caught by Mills	0
Herbert, run out	1	caught by Green	0
Emmens, bowled by Coomber	0	caught by Jones	7
Garratt, not out	0	not out	29
Byes, &c.	4	Byes, &c.	7
Total	—47	Total	—121

BEE HIVE VICTORIA.	1st inn.		2d do.
Brott, bowled by Withern	5	bowled by Brooks	1
Townley, bowled by ditto	2	bowled by ditto	1
Green, caught by Emmens	10	caught by Howard	0
Jones, bowled by Brooks	3	bowled by Brooks	0
Alder, leg before wicket	14	bowled by ditto	4
Hersee, run out	0	stumped by ditto	22
Mills, caught by Powell	39	not out	0
Lambert, caught by Wheat	4	bowled by Powell	2
Henton, bowled by Brooks	20	bowled by Brooks	2
Davies, bowled by ditto	17	leg before wicket	2
Coomber, not out	7	bowled by Brooks	3
Byes, &c.	6	Byes, &c.	3
Total	—127	Total	—40

Jun 25th - The death of King William is the headline this week and it tells that "Our sailor King, William the Fourth died on Tuesday morning last at Windsor Castle". He was in his 72nd year and a detailed account of his post-mortem was also printed for readers to feast on.

In the round-up is "On Wednesday next the Montpelier (Walworth) Club play a match with the Mitcham Union, at the Bee-Hive Ground, Walworth. It will be seen from the following list of players that the Montpelier gentlemen have a phalanx of science to contend against and it is imagined that it is the strongest eleven that they will have to play against this season. Montpelier: Foulds, Lewis, Baker, Coltson, Hogarth, Trimnell, Denison, Peto, Elt, C. Whything and G. Whything. Mitcham: C.H. Oakes Esq, H.J. Hoare Esq, J. Barnard Esq and Messrs Bayley, Bowyer, Good, T. Sewell, W. Sewell, Shepherd, Lilley and Lunt."

Jul 2nd - "At the BeeHive Ground, Walworth Montpelier scored 117 and 87-8 and Mitcham 146. The newspaper reported that "the hitting on the Montpelier side was excellent." and "W. Sewell also hit away in a most effective manner, and left his wicket standing." (He scored 13 not out).

The Beehive ground next appears in *Scores and Biographies* regarding a match on June 28th 1837, when the Montpelier Club plays Mitcham. It is their first mention in the book for twenty-four years. Underneath the match details is "It is a great pity that neither the Montpelier nor Mitcham score books could be obtained by the compiler, as they played many good matches about this time." Haygarth must have been very frustrated to have been unable to view these scorebooks, and how I echo this over a hundred and seventy years later! With their aid perhaps a deeper history could have been written and we would have had conclusive evidence of when and where the club played its matches in this period? It would also have shortened the gap in their apparent absence from the cricket field between 1813-31. Perhaps they kept playing matches, but of a lower standard and against less renowned opposition? On page 100 of W.W. Read's book he looks back briefly at seasons past, and notes that in 1831 at Scholar's ground, Westminster there was a match between Old Westminster Club and Eleven of Lord's Montpelier Club. Is this our club under a slightly different name? This was not the first time that a connection between the words Lord's and Montpelier had been mentioned by W.W. Read in his book.

On page 106 he notes that in 1835 at the Montpelier Ground, Walworth there was a match between Montpelier Club and Mile End New Globe Clubs. This appears to show that matches were being played, but that they were of a lesser standard or importance to be included in Haygarth's book.

Bell's Life makes no comment about the club's return to better level matches (such were needed to be considered by Haygarth as worthy for inclusion in his works) although they are now referred to as Walworth Montpelier.

To date there have been no reports on the newly formed Surrey Union Club nor have any of their fixtures been advertised. The return Kennington v Beehive Victoria match played at the Beehive ground, resulted in Beehive scoring 123 and 115 and Kennington 123. The newspaper reports "Unfortunately the muster was not completed until a late hour which prevented the match being played out …. After a most excellent day's play, the members retired to the Beehive, where dinner was served up in the usual splendid manner." This last line adds to my belief that the Beehive Victoria was in some way connected to the Beehive Club.

Jul 16th - "A match will be played on Kennington Common on Tuesday the 25th inst. between eleven of the Vauxhall Union Club and eleven gentlemen picked from the County of Surrey for £50 a side. Wickets to be pitched at nine o'clock." Note that only one eleven is referred to as "gentlemen".

Jul 23rd - "Cricketting" again makes the front page and it reports "The return match was played on Wednesday at Mitcham. The Mitcham went in first and scored 69. The Montpelier upon whom the genius of ill-luck appeared to have sat, then went in, and came out with a score of 29 only, their opponents leading them 40. Mitcham in their second innings fetched 68. At this time we left the ground, and as neither party had forwarded to us the particulars, we are unable to give the result of the match."

Jul 30th - The newspaper reported that it has last week's Mitcham v Montpelier scores: "In the second innings of Montpelier, Foulds scored 7 not-out, Baker 0, Lewis 0, there were three byes, making it 10-2 with two wickets down, when night put an end to the game." The newspaper went on "On Wednesday next a match will be played at Bee-hive Ground, Walworth between two elevens of the Montpelier Club whose names commence with the letters A-K and L-Z."

Aug 20th - The newspaper contains a good article about a visit to the Montpelier Club at their Beehive ground (see next page). A few of the players are named and the newspaper found the players to be "hard at it" and the grounds to be "well worth visiting."

MONTPELIER CLUB.—We visited the Walworth ground on Tuesday, and found the members "hard at it," playing a match among themselves, in which Messrs. Baker, Twigg, Barton, and two or three other gentlemen played admirably. Mr. Baker, after scoring upwards of 30 runs, brought out his bat, and Mr. Twigg showed as a second Box, by the manner in which he kept wicket. His batting was also excellent. Several others also played in good style. The Bee-hive grounds are well worth visiting; they are delightfully situated, and a number of persons of both sexes frequently congregate, and become spectators of the sports of the field, which are not confined to cricket, inasmuch as some excellent matches at bowls, and other out-door amusements are daily carried on.

Sep 10th - "On Tuesday last a match was played at Hall's Ground, Camberwell between eleven of Bromley and eleven of Camberwell Clarence, the Bromley scoring in their first innings 67, and the Camberwell 80, when darkness put an end to the game."

So far this season there have been no full match reports on any Montpelier matches and just two of their matches have been reported on. There have been no reports on any Surrey Union matches either and very little reported on the many teams who played their matches on Kennington Common.

Sep 17th - "A match will be played tomorrow on Kennington Common between eleven gents of the Kennington Saturday Club and eleven of the County of Surrey. The parties meet at nine o'clock at Mr Davey's the Cock Tavern, and commence the match at ten, in order that it may be played out."

Sep 24th - The newspaper's date is erroneously shown as September 23rd and it contains little of cheer. "On Tuesday next a match will be played on the Beehive Ground, Walworth by the members of the Montpelier Club, as the finishing day's play of the season."

Map of the area in 1837.

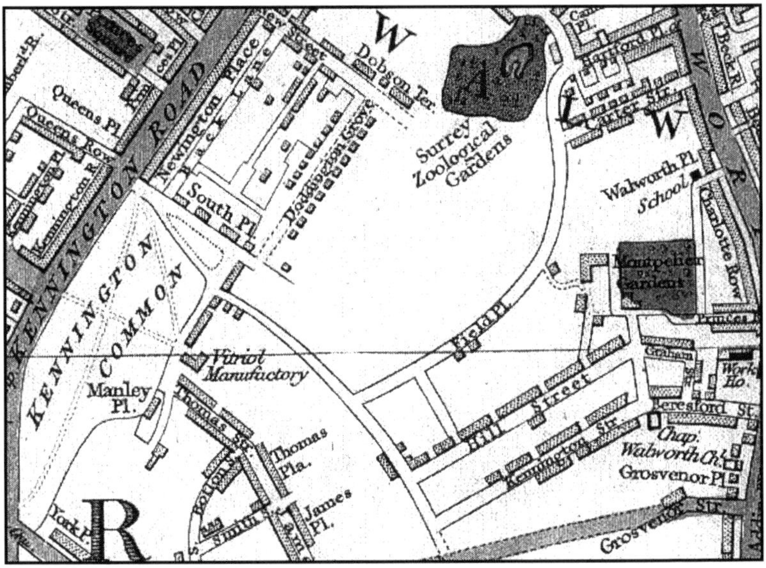

This map is part of one entitled "Cary's New Plan of London and its Vicinity 1837" and its clarity is to be commended. It clearly shows Carter Street, Field Place, which was later to be covered by the modern day Penrose Street, and two prominent sites of local cricket; Montpelier Gardens and Kennington Common. Strangely despite it featuring on the 1830 map, there is no sign of Beehive Gardens although the famous Surrey Zoological Gardens which were next door, are shown.

1838

Jun 17th - No reports of a local interest just a mention that "The members of the Montpelier Club have been in active practice in order to meet the gents of the Lingfield Club tomorrow (Monday). From the equality of the clubs, the match excites considerable interest. The return match is expected to come off on Monday fortnight at the BeeHive, Walworth."

Jun 24th - The Lingfield v Montpelier match report is featured (see below) which saw the Surrey team lose by 40 runs. Lingfield would become a regular opposition for the next few years. The only other report of local interest is "The Camberwell Clarence Club are open to play and Club within 20 miles of London. Applications to be made to Mr Hall of the Camberwell Ground."

MONTPELIER AND LINGFIELD.

The match between the above clubs came off on Monday, at Lingfield, as follows, viz.:—

LINGFIELD.	1st inn.		2d do.
Mr. Chapman, bowl by C. Whyting	3	run out	8
Saunders, caught by Peto	24	bowled by Peto	3
Hooker, caught by Lewis	1	bowled by Lewis	19
Cheal, caught by C. Whyting	16	caught by Williams	2
Longley, caught by Trimnell	8	leg before wicket	7
Scott, leg before wicket	0	not out	5
Holmden, caught by Williams	2	bowled by Lewis	5
Head, bowled by Peto	3	bowled by ditto	1
J. Stanford, bowled by ditto	2	caught by Trimnell	0
W. Stanford, not out	2	caught by ditto	0
Wood, bowled by Peto	0	caught by Peto	4
Byes, &c.	31	Byes, &c.	16
Total	—92	Total	—70

MONTPELIER.	1st inn.		2d do.
Mr. Rowed, caught by Longley	2	bowled by Wood	2
Challis, bowled by Scott	5	caught by Chapman	7
G. Whyting, bowled by Wood	2	caught by Wood	16
Peto, caught by Cheal	0	bowled by Wood	0
Foulds, bowled by Scott	7	caught by Wood	1
Trimnell, bowled by ditto	4	caught by W. Stanford	5
Lewis, bowled by Wood	3	not out	11
C. Whyting, caught by Longley	0	run out	14
Baker, bowled by Wood	4	caught by Hooker	15
Williams, not out	0	bowled by Wood	0
Dawson, caught by Cheal	2	bowled by Wood	7
Byes, &c.	7	Byes, &c.	8
Total	—36	Total	—86

Jul 1st - "Cricketting" is once again on the front page and despite no advertising of the match the week before, there is a report on Montpelier v Chertsey played at the BeeHive, Walworth on Tuesday. The scores were: Montpelier first innings 163 (Mr Elt scored 35, C. Whyting 34, Challis 16, Lewis 11, Peto 15, Baker 14 & c) Chertsey 40 and 35.

Jul 8th - There is again little of local interest except statistics of Montpelier v Lingfield played at Walworth. Montpelier scored 88 and 80 and Lingfield 40. The newspaper reported "The Lingfield having to obtain 128 runs, and losing one of their wickets for four, at eight o'clock resigned the match."

Jul 15th - There are four more columns of cricket reports and Montpelier feature twice. Initially there is mention of their forthcoming match against Chertsey at Woolger's ground, Chertsey on Thursday the 19th and then "on the Wednesday following, the 25th inst. the Montpelier expect the pleasure of meeting the Copenhagen Club and ground at the Bee Hive, Walworth."

Jul 22nd - "The return match of the Chertsey Loyal and Montpelier Clubs was played on Thursday last at Chertsey and ended with daylight as follows. Chertsey first innings 100, second ditto 118; Montpelier first innings 92 second ditto 43-3. We regret not having space for the full score."

July 29th - Although it was not advertised the previous week, there is a full match report on Montpelier v Copenhagen at Walworth on Wednesday. Copenhagen scored 68 and 45 and Montpelier 223 (Baker 95) but again there are no other reports of matches in the locality.

Aug 5th - "A match will be played on the Beehive Cricket Ground, Walworth on Wednesday next week between 11 butchers and 11 bakers of the neighbourhood of Walworth."

Just below these match details the newspaper tells "A man in the employ of Messrs. Hawkes and Co., brewers of Bishops Stortford, after making a run at cricket, momentarily rested on his bat and then fell down a corpse. A Coroner's jury returned a verdict of "Died by Visitation of God." He has left a widow and two children."

Aug 12th - Four columns are given to cricket under "Cricket Register", three contain full match reports, which should be applauded and these include Montpelier v Kingsland at the Beehive ground, Walworth on Thursday last. Montpelier scored 146 and the opposition 242-8 (Mr Cater 99 not out). The newspaper reported “The Kingsland did not finish their first hands, as it was getting dark, and time was called.” Shame indeed for Mr Cater, stuck one short of a century.

Sep 9th - “The return match between Kennington and Ponders End will be played at Kennington Common tomorrow (Monday) the wickets to be pitched at half past nine, and the game played out. The parties will afterwards partake of one of Mrs Davey’s well known good dinners, at the Cock Tavern, Kennington Green.”

This season saw hardly any reporting of lower level matches, yet prominent fixtures from around the country were often covered in depth. As mentioned earlier Roger Packham pointed out that club secretaries often had to pay the local newspaper for their matches to be featured. This may explain why between 1828-1838 there was a different slant of matches advertised and matches reported on, and why some clubs seem to be featured more than others. This season in particular has seen a sharp drop in lower-level local matches being reported, although match reports for the Camberwell Clarence Club are more evident. It is a shame that other club details, such as years of formation, club President and club members are not featured, but again perhaps it came down to economics or perhaps *Bells Life* was not interested in these quirky details.

On the other hand, details of the location of the various club’s grounds did get into print along with some details of members for which we must applaud the staff who compiled these match details. We should add further thanks for the journalists who saw fit to include such long articles about the opening of pavilion, pre and close-season meals and other pieces of cricket-trivia. It allows me to illustrate the style of reporting in the Georgian and Victorian eras much more graphically.

Montpelier Gardens Plate.

This fine plate depicting Montpelier Gardens is currently to be found in the Cuming Museum in the Old Town Hall in Walworth Road, Southwark, not far from where Montpelier played. It is a shame that it does not illustrate the cricket ground itself, but it is still a valid connection with the topic of this book.

My thanks go to the staff of the Cuming Museum, London Borough of Southwark, for allowing publication of this photograph.

1839

Mar 31st - Under "Cricketer's Register" is news that "The gentlemen of the Montpelier Club meet at Starling's Ground, Walworth, on Tuesday next April 3rd, to commence the season with a day's play - The Bee Hive new Thursday's Club of amateurs will commence their career on Thursday, the 25th of April with a day's play on the above ground."

This year was the first season that I was able to gain access to *The Era*, but it sees very few mentions of cricket in the newspaper and none for our club and what is featured, is often hidden in a column with no title or sub-title.

We have been used to seeing cricket reported on late in the year, but so far, not as early. This report is a gem as it is the first mention of Starling's ground, which is in fact the Beehive ground, named after landlord William Starling. He held the post from 1833 until his death in April 1835, whereupon the license passed to his wife Catherine, who held it until October. George Sousidison then held it until November 14th, whereupon it passed to William Carter. Thus the reporter is referring to a ground by a title that would have expired over three years previous. For the record, Isaac Bryant took over the licence in July 1842 and remained landlord until the Montpelier's lease was terminated.

Jun 9th - The front-page headline this week concerned discussions about the introduction of a "Penny Post" system. The newspaper reported "The Duke of Richmond presented several petitions in favour of Penny Postage. His Grace said that he was quite sure that the revenue would be best protected by fixing the postage at the lowest possible rate ..... otherwise the legislative would act against the very principle of Mr Rowland Hill, which was to induce and encourage letter-writing."

Amongst a healthy amount of match reports from around the country is to be found brief mention of the recent Dulwich v New East Surrey Club. Dulwich scored 177 and 83-6 and the visitors 60, before rain and dark skies brought an early end to the match. This is an interesting inclusion as it shows that the East Surrey Club is now back on the scene, albeit precluded by the word "New", yet to date there has been no other mention of its re-birth (or even the demise of the original East Surrey Club).

Jun 23rd - Under a sub-title of "South London Club" (whose first mention this is in *Bell's Life*) it is reported that "a match was played on Thursday last at the

BeeHive, Walworth between eleven married and eleven single of the Club, which was won by the eleven former with 11 wickets to go down." The scores were: Single 38 and 78 and Married 115 and 2-0.

Under a sub-title of "Montpelier Club" is "The members of this club play their first match this season (on their ground Bee-hive, Carter-street, Walworth) tomorrow (Monday) against the gentlemen of the Lingfield Club and as the parties are exceedingly well matched, a most interesting contest may be anticipated. The club also anticipate meeting very shortly the following clubs - The Bramshill, Godstone, Albion and the Canonbury." Lingfield now appear to be regular opposition for Montpelier, whose opponents have by now settled down into a familiar pattern.

Although brief and irregular, these short reports are most valuable. This one ties the club to a ground and shows the distances that teams travelled to fulfil matches. It is also interesting to note how their address was referred to in the press, as now. we type the first letter of street in capitals, but back then it was different.

Jun 30th - There is a full match report on Montpelier (141 and 98) v Lingfield (70). The newspaper also reports that "On Wednesday a match was played at Hall's Ground, Camberwell, between the East Grinstead Victoria and the Camberwell Clarence Club. Camberwell scored 70 and 38 and the visitors from Sussex 47. "The day closed in upon them before the match was played out."

Jul 14th - The newspaper reports briefly the return match between Lingfield and Montpelier "played at Dormans Land on Monday last (see below). Lingfield beat their opponents in a single innings with 20 runs to spare. Their score in their only innings amounted to 134 ..."

MONTPELLIER VERSUS LINGFIELD.—The gent from town seem destined to be outdone by the countrymen, for in this match, which was likewise a return match, and came off at Dorman's Land on Monday last, Lingfield beat their opponents in a single innings with 20 runs to spare. Their score in their only innings amounted to 134. The Montpellier eleven were sent to the right about the first hands for 12; they then went in upon the runs, and succeeded in scoring 102, which left them still 20 runs in a minority. We know not to what we are to attribute the bad success of the Montpellier Club, unless to the bowling of Martingell against them, which was splendid. He is a most promising bowler, and, we understand, is about to visit Marylebone, where, we have no doubt, he will meet with that patronage which he so richly deserves.—From a Correspondent.

July 14th 1839

Jul 28th - Under a sub-title of "Upper and Lower Camberwell" it is reported (see below), "this interesting match was played on Monday at the Royal Veteran Ground, Coldharbour Lane." This is a very important short report as it gives the location of this ground on its first mention in the newspaper. It was to this ground that the Montpelier Club would re-locate when they left The Oval some six years later.

Also reported is "On Thursday last the Chertsey Loyal and Montpelier Walworth Clubs played a match at Chertsey. Chertsey scored 30 and 83, total 113 and Montpelier 61 and 53-4 total 114, the Montpelier winning with six wickets to go down."

In a good week's cricket reporting by the newspaper, it reports "A return match will be played at the BeeHive Ground, Walworth on Monday between eleven gentlemen of Clapham and eleven of the South London Club." This is the second mention of the latter club this season, but it is a shame that more details about it are not forthcoming and the club grew over the next few years.

UPPER AND LOWER CAMBERWELL.—This interesting match was played on Monday at the Royal Veteran Ground, Cold Harbour-lane, when the gents of Lower Camberwell came off victorious by a majority of 447. Score: Lower Camberwell, first innings 77, second ditto 62; total 139. R. Thimbleby marked 16 and 7, Spinks 2 and 5, Morris 5 and 11, Bennington, Jun., 0 and 9, Connell 3 and 12, May 0 and 0, W. Thimbleby 16 and 2, Osman 16 (not out) and 1, Farmer 0 and 2, Buesell 0 and 5, Bennington, sen., 1 and 1; byes 10 and 3, wide balls 8 and 4. Upper Camberwell 50 and 42, total 92. Beagley scored 25 and 21, D. Sanders 0 and 0; and Messrs. E. Sanders, Kettle, R. Thimbleby, E. Sanders, sen., Bennett, Collingbourn, Heckford, Bades, and Thomas, minor numbers. The bowling of Messrs. Connell and R. Thimbleby was excellent, and the batting of several others was also very good. The return match will be played on the above-named ground on Monday.

CHERTSEY AND MONTPELIER.—On Thursday last the Chertsey Loyal and Montpelier Walworth, Clubs played a match at Chertsey. Score—Chertsey 30 and 83, total 113; W. Taylor scored 0 and 16, R. Moire 3 and 2, G. Taylor 11 and 0, Brackwell 0 and 31, G. Howard 1 and 2, Joseph Moire 1 and 6, James Wallis 0 and 1, H. Moire 1 and 2, James Berryman 0 and 0 (not out), James Hall 2 and 0, W. Howard 0 (not out) and 4, byes, &c. 11 and 13. Montpelier 61 and 53, total 114; G. Whyting scored 18 and 9, Chalens 1 and 3 (not out), Wilde 0, Lewis 0 and 3, Baker 13 (not out) and 14 (not out), Trimnell 0 and 3, Wood 1, Peto 7 and 9, C. Whyting 1, Garrett 1, Locknell 6, byes 16 and 12. The Montpelier winning with six wickets to go down. The return match is fixed to come off at Walworth on the 20th August.

Aug 18th - "The return match between the Hampton Court Union and the Montpelier Clubs will be played at Hampton on the 5th September" and "The Montpelier play at Walworth on Tuesday against the Chertsey Loyal."

Aug 25th - There is a match report on the Montpelier v Chertsey match played at Walworth last Tuesday (see next page) which saw the home team lead by 50 runs on first innings scores; 92 runs to 42. In their second innings Montpelier scored 24 when the day's play closed. There is an interesting letter about the quality of opposition beaten by the Montpelier Club written by "a Cricketer", who also gives his opinion on fixtures against the Clarence Club. This is to be found under the match report

Also reported was "A match between the junior members of the Montpelier Club and Edmonton was played on Thursday at Edmonton, which ended as follows: Edmonton 137 and Montpelier 31 and 72 total 103. The Edmonton winning in one innings with 34 runs to spare."

Sep 8th - There are full statistical details printed of the Hampton v Montpelier match played at Hampton last Tuesday which saw, Hampton win by 10 runs.

Also briefly reported on is "The return match between eleven junior members of the Montpelier Club and the Invincibles came off on Wednesday at Vincent Square, Westminster, as follows: Invincibles 94 and 95 total 189, Montpelier 59 and 90, total 149. The Invincibles winning by 40."

It is a shame that there are no details given about The Invincibles, who, prior to this date had not come to notice.

Oct 6th - There are full match statistics are shown for a match in Vincent Square, Westminster on Monday last between Pimlico Victoria 104 and 19-5 and Walworth Amateurs 162. The newspaper reports "At this point of the game "dark" was called, or there is little doubt it would have been a single-handed match." Heath scored 52 for the Walworth Amateurs (their first mention).

Oct 13th - Full match statistics for the match between Montpelier (91 and 75) and Invincibles (51 and 39) on Wednesday played at the Beehive ground are given.

25/8/39.

MONTPELIER AND CHERTSEY.

The return match between the Montpelier and the Chertsey Loyal Independent came off on Tuesday last, at Walworth, as follows:—

MONTPELIER.		CHERTSEY.	
G. Whyting, bowled by G. Howard	1	W. Taylor, ct C. Whyting, b Coltson	6
Challis, bowled by ditto	2	G. Howard, bowled by Lewis	0
Coltson, bowled by ditto	3	Bliss, bowled by C. Whyting	0
Trimnell, run out	2	Brockwell, bowled by ditto	0
Lewis, ct Bliss, b Brockwell	6	Wallis, bowled by Lewis	1
Baker, ct G. Taylor, b G. Howard	15	J. Moir, bowled by ditto	0
C. Whyting, ct J. Hall, b by ditto	8	G. Taylor, bowled by ditto	22
Peto, not out	4	R. Moir, hit wicket, b C. Whyting	0
Wilde, leg b wicket, b Brockwell	13	H. Moir, run out	2
Garrett, bowled by Bliss	1	Berryman, bowled by Lewis	3
Lochner, ct Brockwell, b Bliss	6	J. Hall, not out	2
Byes 9, wide balls 22	31	Byes 6, wide balls 10	16
Total	92	Total	42

In the second innings of Montpelier, Challis scored 12; Coltson, 1; Trimnell, 9 (not out); byes, &c., 12; total, 24; when the day closed.

Montpelier Club.—Mr. Editor—It has been my good fortune, being a great admirer of the game of cricket, to see it played most efficiently in every point by the gentlemen forming the Montpelier Club; I have witnessed with much pleasure numerous matches played by them on their ground at Walworth, in all of which they have come off victorious. But I must say that on more than one occasion the parties they contended with, although what may be considered a good country eleven, were not sufficient players to have anything but a poor chance of winning a match when pitted against the Montpelier; the consequence was they only came off second best, and without affording the amusement expected by the numerous admirers of the game, who came far and near to give it their patronage and support. I know it is the wish of many gentlemen (friends to both parties) resident in and about Camberwell, that they should contend for the Championship with a strong efficient Club, I, therefore, recommend to their notice the Clarence Club, held at Hall's Ground, Camberwell, and although my opinion is that it would be a neck and neck race for a time, yet that the Montpelier would carry away the "wedge," and again I am convinced that it would be a most sporting and slap up match. I remain your obedient servant, a Cricketer.—Camberwell, 20th Aug. 1839.

1840

Reports are much improved this year in *The Era* which has two or three columns of cricket reports each Sunday, but does not cover as many matches as *Bell's Life* and the round-up section below the full match reports is far shorter too. There is some overlap in the matches covered, but the geographical area of those covered is much smaller and the style of reporting is more agreeable, although it too occasionally lapses into the familiar "A match was played at …."

May 17th - Under a sub-title of "The Union Club, Kennington", (their first mention in the newspaper) the newspaper reports "The members of this newly formed club held at the Horn's Tavern, Kennington met the first time for play on the common on Wednesday last."

May 24th - In the weekly round-up columns is reported "We are informed that at the opening dinner of the Montpelier Club, a silver snuff-box was presented to Mr G. Mattam, the president, as a mark of respect entertained for him by his brother members. A long account has been sent us of the dinner, but as it took place on the 5th inst, it cannot now be interesting."

This is another example of harsh comments by a reporter about an event whose inclusion would have been of interest. Under a sub-title of "South London Club" is reported "A match will come-off tomorrow (Monday) at the Bee Hive, Walworth between the married and single members of the club."

Jun 7th - A short report giving scores of Montpelier v Edmonton played at the Bee Hive, Walworth. Edmonton scored 139 and 86 and the hosts 60 and 55-3.

Jun 21st - *The Era* - Full match report on Montpelier v Canonbury and "The following is the result of the match played at the Beehive, on Friday, June 12th viz: Montpelier 110 and 144-9 and Canonbury 84." It carried on, "Leaving the Montpelier on 170 in advance and one wicket to go down, when the darkness of the evening put an end to the game."

Jun 28th - "The New East Surrey and Edmonton Clubs - These clubs played a match on Thursday at Staton's (late Hall's) ground of which the following is a brief account of the scores, we not having space for its insertion at length. New East Surrey 69 and 45 and Edmonton 59 and 56-3."

Jul 5th - "The Montpelier Club having taken up the gauntlet thrown down by the Beaconsfield club in our column a few weeks since, a match took place at Starling's, BeeHive Ground, Walworth on Wednesday. Montpelier first and second innings 237, Beaconsfield first innings 67, the Montpelier leading their opponents 170 with five wickets to go down. The play was excellent…"

Jul 5th - *The Era* - Full match report on "Montpelier v Beaconsfield - on Wednesday last a match took place at Starling's Beehive ground, Walworth between eleven of the Montpelier Club and eleven of the Beaconsfield Club. The scores were; Montpelier 133 and 104-5 and Beaconsfield 67 … the return match will be played at Beaconsfield on an early day."

Below this was "The Canonbury Cricket Club intend playing the return match with the Montpelier Club on Wednesday next, the 8th inst., on the Canonbury ground."

Jul 12th - Full match report on Canonbury v Montpelier played at the ground of the former, in which there is a nice turn of phrase concerning how the match was eventually rained off (see below).

12/7/40

CANONBURY v. MONTPELIER.

The return match between these clubs took place at the Canonbury ground on Wednesday last. The Canonbury scored 75 in their first innings, when the Montpelier took the bat, and had obtained 45 with the loss of but two wickets, and the two men in (Messrs. Williams and Coltson) in excellent play, when an unexpected interruption to the game took place from the appearance on the ground of Aquarius, who dispensed the contents of his waterpot so liberally as completely to prevent any resumption of the game. It was stated, however, that Murphy was about to be enrolled as a member of the Canonbury, which will enable them in future to guarantee their antagonists a fine day. The score was as under:—

CANONBURY.

Couch, run out	0	Swain, caught by Challis	2
Hill, bowled by Lewis	2	Peto, bowled by C. Whyting	4
Slade, bowled by Lewis	5	Sanderson, stumped by Coltson	0
Froggett, bowled by Lewis	2	Tuck, not out	5
Garratt, bowled by Coltson	23	Byes, &c	28
Dewdney, caught by Elrick	3		—
Pobjoy, bowled by Lewis	1	Total	75

MONTPELIER.

Challis, bowled by Swain	7	Byes, &c	19
G. Whyting, caught by Pobjoy	6		—
Williams, not out	8	Total	45
Coltson, not out	5		

Jul 12th - *The Era* - Full match report on Canonbury 75 and Montpelier 45-2 and the report states "… the remaining players were bowled out without a run - by the weather - which set at nought all attempts to play out the game …. It was in vain, however, to contend with the weather, the reign of cricket was over, while that of St Swithuns was commenced. The players therefore, adjourned to the Pavilion, to console themselves with "warm with" for the prevalence of "cold without" and after spending a very pleasant evening separated, hoping for better luck next time."

Jul 19th - The newspaper reports that "The Montpelier and Mitcham clubs played a match at Mitcham which was won by the Albion in one innings and 49 runs. Score: Mitcham 171 (Asprey 73), Montpelier 71 and 51."

The second report of local interest concerns Montpelier v Invincibles. "This match took place on Friday week at Walworth which after a close struggle was decided in favour of the Invincibles by seven runs. Score: Montpelier 60 and 120, Invincibles 104 and 83."

It is most infuriating that this newspaper does not give the reader a clue as to who the Invincibles are, or where they hail from. However we are redeemed as *The Era* does solve the problem below:

Jul 19th - *The Era* - Full match report on Montpelier v Invincibles - "A match took place on Friday 10th inst at the Beehive ground between the second eleven of the Montpelier, and eleven gentlemen assuming the above title (among whom were several members of the Montpelier); the result was as follows: Montpelier 60 and 120 and Invincibles 104 and 83." Although again brief this match report tells us the make-up of the opposition and also clarifies that our team had a second eleven, something that to date has not been mentioned or reported on.

Aug 2nd - There is a brief mention of Beaconsfield v Montpelier - "The clubs met on Monday last when the score at the close of the day stood as follows: Beaconsfield 69 and 66, Montpelier 107".

Below this is a short report "The Upper and Lower Camberwell elevens played a match on Monday at White's Ground, Coldharbour lane, Brixton when the residents of Lower Camberwell won with eight wickets to go down." Is this the same ground as the Royal Veteran Ground, earlier mentioned (July 28th 1839)?

Aug 9th - "The BeeHive and Hampton clubs played a match on the BeeHive ground, Walworth on Tuesday. Scores: BeeHive 119 and 98, Hampton Court 89, when night put an end to the game. The parties afterwards dined together at Mrs Starling's." The Beehive Club are thus back after no mention in the newspaper for a while of the Beehive Victoria Club.

Aug 9th - *The Era* - "The return match between the gentlemen of the Montpelier Walworth Club, with ten gentlemen of the Mitcham Club with Sheppard given was played at the Beehive Ground, Walworth, on Friday. The play on both sides was first-rate. Being a day's play it was decided in favour of the Montpelier on the first innings. The following is the score; Montpelier 99 and 88-3, Mitcham 93."

Aug 16th - "The return match between Montpelier and Mitcham Albion took place on Friday the 7th inst. at the BeeHive Club and, from the defeat experienced by the Montpelier at Mitcham, excited much interest. Montpelier 99 and 88-3, Mitcham 91." And again "Night put an end to the game." The newspaper continues "The return match between Montpelier and Invincibles was played at Starling's BeeHive ground, Walworth on the 5th inst. and after a close contest terminated in favour of the former club ….. Montpelier 180 and 57 (Saggers 22 and 0 and Jarvis 46 and 1), Invincibles 167 (Peto 65)." Again the newspaper tells "Night put an end to the game." The Invincible's Peto is probably the same player who often played for Montpelier.

Aug 23rd - "The Edmonton and Montpelier clubs played a match on Thursday at the former place which was won by Edmonton with nine wickets to go down. Score: Montpelier 65 and 49 (Peto 1 and 14), Edmonton 85 and 33-1."

This year's reports are laid out much neater in the newspaper and most come under a sub-title which highlights the two teams, thus making the finding of reports with a local interest a little easier. However we still have only repetitive and basic grammar used to report matches, for example "a match was played on" and "a match will be played between."

Aug 30th - *The Era* - In the round-up is "The return match between Edmonton and the Montpelier Walworth club, was played on Friday, in Starling's Beehive grounds, Walworth. There not being time to play the match out, it was decided in favour of the Montpelier on the first innings."

Sep 6th - The return day's play between Montpelier and Edmonton came off at Walworth on the 28th inst. Scores; Montpelier 92 (Peto 28, Elt 17), Edmonton 89 and 55."

1841

May 2nd - "The Union Club (Beehive) Walworth intend having a day's play on Wednesday next, and any friends wishing to join them will receive a hearty welcome …" and continues its local vein "The Kennington Union Club (their first mention) will commence their season on the 12th inst and the opening dinner will take place in the week after, at the club-house, the Horn's Tavern."

The newspaper's good early season coverage of local teams carries on with "The New East Surrey club have met for the season at Hall's ground, Camberwell, which is, we hear in very excellent condition."

May 9th - "On Thursday next a match will be played at Hall's ground, Southampton Street, Camberwell between the Clarence Vauxhall and Camberwell Victoria Clubs. Many of the Camberwell Clarence being members of the Vauxhall Club, the strength of the Camberwell will be reduced."

"The Montpelier Club commences the season on Tuesday next the 11th inst. with a day's play and the members and friends will afterwards dine together at the beehive, Carter street, Walworth." The newspaper again manages to cover three local teams when it reports that "The South London Club, BeeHive, Walworth, meet for a day's play Thursday next when they will be happy to see any of their friends to join them …. The return match between this club and the Ickham (near Canterbury) will be played at the BeeHive ground on Monday the 24th inst."

It appears from these reports that the Beehive ground was home for the Kennington Union, the Montpelier and the South London Clubs.

May 16th - *The Era* - "At Hall's, the headquarters of the New East Surrey club, several matches will be played during the season; and we hear that one or two new club's are to be formed to play here …."

May 30th - "The Kennington Albion club will be happy to make a match with any other junior team within 20 miles of London. A line addressed to the secretary at The Swan, Kennington will meet with immediate attention."

Jun 6th - Two columns of cricket reports but just a mention of the forthcoming Montpelier v Mitcham match to be played at the BeeHive on the 11th inst..

Jun 6th - *The Era* - Full match report on South London Club v Ickham at the Beehive ground on Monday May 31st. South London scored 149 and the visitors 97 and 117-3. The match was watched "by a large concourse of spectators" and Montpelier and Surrey's E. Garland played for the home team.

Jun 27th - Match statistics and a three-line report on Montpelier v The Albion, Islington played at the BeeHive ground Wednesday and Thursday last. At the close Montpelier had scored 170 and 62-5 and the visitors 75.

Jul 11th - There are full match statistics and a two-line report for Mitcham Union v Montpelier played on Mitcham Green on Thursday. The hosts scored 168 and Montpelier 89.

Jul 11th - *The Era* - Full match report on Mitcham v Montpelier at Mitcham Green "on Thursday played their return match" and the scores were; Montpelier 89 and Mitcham Green 168.

Jul 18th - "The Montpelier and Edmonton clubs played their return match at the BeeHive ground on Friday last .... Montpelier scored 52 and 127 (Elt 9 and 22) and Edmonton 53 and 44-8 ....when night put an end to the game."

Aug 15th - "The Islington Albion and Montpelier Clubs play a match on the 25th inst. at Garratt's Fields."

Aug 22nd - Briefly reported was "Montpelier v Lingfield played a match on Monday at Lingfield. Scores; Lingfield 91 and 59, Montpelier 105."

Aug 29th - There is a full match report on Vauxhall Clarence v Reigate played on Kennington Common (see next page), which includes memoirs of the "ground".

Also reported is "The Walworth Montpelier and Islington Albion clubs played their return match on Wednesday and they stood as under at the close of play. Albion first innings 79, Montpelier 42-4." Sadly no venue is again given.

Aug 29th - *The Era* - Full match report on Islington Albion v Montpelier - "The return match between the Islington Albion and Montpelier, came off on Thursday at Copenhagen House, as follows; Islington Albion 79, Montpelier 42-4."
"The return match with the Lingfield gents will take place on Monday, the 20th, at the Beehive ground, Carter-street, Walworth."

VAUXHALL, CLARENCE, AND REIGATE CLUBS.

Very many years have elapsed since Kennington Common, the ground on which the return match between these clubs was on Tuesday and Wednesday last played, has presented such a scene of animation and pleasure as was exhibited on this occasion. Indeed, it brought back to our recollection "days gone by"—a time when there were as many clubs on the Common as there were days in the week—a time when if the citizen and the west-ender took his walk or his ride to this "lung of the metropolis," he would see, in addition to the club whose "day" it was, with their wickets on the best part of the ground no fewer than 20 or 30, or even more, different wickets pitched. Then scarcely a week passed in the season without one or two matches being played on Kennington Common; whilst now, for several years, if it became the "battle field" of two contests during the cricketing months, great, indeed, was the astonishment of the neighbourhood. This may be accounted for by the numerous private grounds which have been established. Each club was formerly known by the day on which it met, and certainly a personal knowledge of all of them for a very lengthened period enables us to state that for upwards of 25 years no match has drawn so large a concourse of spectators as the present, save and except one that took place between the old "Wednesdays" and the Mitcham with the celebrated Lambert, given to Kennington, about 23 years ago. On walking round the vast ring on Tuesday, we thought we recognised some faces which had graced that contest by their presence, and greatly gratified did they, as well as those of the present generation of gazers, appear to be as the operations were going on. We should say that the numbers who had collected to see this match could not have been fewer than 6,000 on each day. "Play" was called at twelve on Tuesday, and the work was commenced by Martingell and Lanaway going in on the part of Reigate. As on the former occasion, the bowling of Day and Salmon, of the Vauxhall, and of Martingell, Killick, and Scott, for Reigate, was of the finest and first-rate description. In the fact of no one man getting what is termed a score, clearly proves its character, the more so, too, when it is remembered that many of the players are the best hitters of the county of Surrey. The Reigate, from the subjoined account, scored in their first innings 66 runs off of 114 balls bowled by Day, and 112 by Salmon, in all 226 balls. In their second hands they made (Martingell being absent) 43 from 80 balls bowled by Day and 77 by Salmon, in all 157 balls. The Vauxhall in their first scored 76, from 120 balls bowled by Martingell, 123 by Killick, and 24 by Scott, making a total of 267 balls; whilst in their second they had one wicket only down for 22 runs, for which 122 balls were bowled, namely, 62 by Killick, and 60 by Scott. As will be easily imagined the play was very fine. The Vauxhall headed their opponents by 10 in the first hands, and had one wicket only down at the close of the play on the second evening, leaving ten wickets to get the remaining 10 runs to win. Of course the Reigate upon this gave up the match. It is scarcely possible to offer too much praise to Watkins, of the Goat's Head, in the Wandsworth Road, by whom the match was got up, for the exertions he bestowed and the money he expended in providing every requisite for the occasion. He had as many as five large booths, one of immense extent, in which the players and their friends, to the number of 80, we believe, sat down on each day to as excellent a dinner, and as well laid out, as any one could have desired. All was good humour, satisfaction, and gratification. The following is the score:—

REIGATE.	1st inn.		2d do.
Martingell, c by Day, b by Salmon	0	absent	0
Lanaway, bowled by Day	11	run out	1
Nichols, c by Knight, b by Salmon	1	c by Day, b by Salmon	2
Caffyn, bowled by Day	6	c by Heath, b by Day	12
Chadband, bowled by Day	8	bowled by Salmon	1
Pa[illegible]ey, bowled by Salmon	1	c by Knight, b by Day	2
Kent, bowled by Salmon	0	bowled by Salmon	1
Lambert, bowled by Salmon	4	bowled by Salmon	6
Scott, bowled by Day	2	bowled by Salmon	0
Killick, not out	5	not out	11
Relf, bowled by Day	16	bowled by Salmon	0
Wide, &c.	12	Wide, &c.	7
Total	—66	Total	—43

VAUXHALL CLARENCE.

Bennett, bowled by Martingell	6	Brockwell, c Lanaway, b Martingell	10
Heath, c by Nichols, b by Killick	1	Hammond, c Killick, b Martingell	11
Day, bowled by Killick	0	Whaite, not out	13
Salmon, c Martingell, b Martingell	8	Weeks, bowled by Killick	0
Bryant, bowled by Killick	2	Wide, &c.	22
Pobjoy, bowled by Martingell	6		
Knight, c Nichols, b Killick	3	Total	76

In the second innings of Vauxhall, Day scored 16 (bowled Killick and Whaite 2 (not out); wide, &c., 4—total 22.

Sep 5th - Full match report on Montpelier v Lingfield played "on Monday last" (see below) and also reported is that the Montpelier Club will play a match with the Eltham gentlemen tomorrow (Monday) at the Beehive ground, Walworth."

Sept 5 1841

MONTPELIER AND LINGFIELD.

The return match between the above clubs took place on Monday last, on the Bee Hive Ground, Walworth, as follows :—

MONTPELIER		LINGFIELD	
George, run out	19	Chapman, sen., b by Coltson	2
G. Whytind, bowled by J. Stanford	5	W. Stanford, caught by Lewes	25
Coltson, bowled by Cheal	16	Cheal, run out	32
Fookes, bowled by J. Stanford	20	G. Pickering, Esq., c Fookes	50
Trimnell, bowled by Cheal	4	C. Head, caught by Trimnell	7
Lewes, run out	19	J. Stanford, run out	14
Baker, not out	31	Chapman, jun., b by Baker	2
Peto, bowled by Chapman, sen.	10	Wood, jun., bowled by Baker	3
Challez, b by Chapman, sen.	8	G. Head, not out	0
Jarvis, bowled by J. Stanford	0		
Garrett, bowled by J. Stanford	0		
Byes 12, wide balls 10	22	Byes 13, wide balls 9, no ball 1	23
Total	154	Total	158

Sep 5th - *The Era* - Full match report on Montpelier v Lingfield at the Beehive ground. Montpelier scored 154 and the visitors from Surrey 158-7.

Sep 12th - There are full match details printed for Montpelier; 187 against Eltham; 40 and 55 played on Monday at the Beehive ground.

Sep 12th - *The Era* - Full match report on Eltham v Montpelier at the Beehive ground, Walworth although no date is shown for the fixture. Montpelier scored 187 and the visitors 40 and 55

Sep 26th - "The carpenters of Bermondsey played a match last week at the BeeHive ground, Walworth under the title of Jack planes and Saws. The following is the score; Jack planes 108 and 110, total 218. Saws 136 and 141, total 277. The parties afterwards partook an excellent supper at Mr Shanklie's, Old Kent road and spent a pleasant evening."

"The Montpelier Club intend meeting for a day's play on the BeeHive Ground, Walworth, Carter street, Walworth on Tuesday next. Wickets to be pitched at eleven o'clock when they will be happy to see as many friends as can conveniently attend."

Oct 3rd - In the round-up comes the first mention in the newspaper of the Vauxhall Clarence Club (held at the *Goat's Head*, Wandsworth Road) who played Westminster Union (held at the *King's Arms*, Upper Ebony Street, Pimlico) on

Kennington Common on Wednesday. Westminster scored 69 and Vauxhall 40. This is another example of a helpful report, as it is one of the few that tells which public-house (if any) a club was connected with.

1842

Jun 5th - "The Lower Clapton and New East Surrey Clubs play a match Wednesday next, at the Rosemary Branch Ground, Peckham." It is the first mention of the latter playing at this ground as previously they had played home matches at Halls/Hampton's ground in Camberwell.

Jun 12th - "The Montpelier and Lingfield Clubs play a match tomorrow (Monday) on the BeeHive Ground, Walworth."

Jun 12th - *The Era* - Full match report on The East Surrey v Lower Clapton at the Rosemary Branch, Peckham. The home team scored 137 and 104 and the visitors 53.

Jun 19th - "The Montpelier and Lingfield Clubs had a day's play on Monday last, on the BeeHive Ground, Walworth. Scores Montpelier first innings 226 (Lewis 68, Coltson 52 and Foulds 29) and Lingfield first innings 136-3."

Jun 19th - *The Era* - Full match report on Montpelier Beehive Club v Lingfield - "The club had a day's play at the Beehive Cricket-ground, Carter-street, Walworth. The Montpelier gents went in first and scored 226 runs out of which Lewis got 68 …. The Lingfield gentlemen, at the close of the day, had obtained 136 runs, with three wickets to go down …"

Jul 10th - Under a heading of "Montpelier and Lingfield Clubs" the newspaper went on to report "The return day's play between these two clubs took place on Monday last at Lingfield. Scores, Lingfield 76 and 108, Montpelier 83 and 10-4."

Jul 31st - "The Chislehurst and Montpelier Clubs had a day's play on Monday at the former place, and at the close the score stood as follows. Chislehurst 56 and 93, total 149 Montpelier first innings 103 Spenceley 24, Lewis 17 and Baker 17 (not out) …. In their second innings Coltson obtained 14 and Elt 7 (not out) when the play ceased, the Montpelier having 25 runs to get to win, with 9 wickets standing."

Aug 21st - "The South London and Etonian Clubs play their return match tomorrow at Bryant's BeeHive Ground, Walworth, tomorrow, Monday."

This report shows that the Beehive ground was now in the hands of a Mr I. G. Bryant It is also interesting to note that to date this season, there has been no mention of the Beehive Club, nor Hall's ground in Camberwell.

Sep 4th - "The Epsom and Montpelier Clubs played a match at Epsom on Monday last, one innings each, which terminated in favour of Epsom with 51 runs to spare. Score Epsom 100 of which H. Richardson scored 35. … Montpelier 49 of which Spenceley obtained 8, Dawson 8 and Baker 6 … the return match will be played on the BeeHive Ground, Walworth on the 14th inst.."

"The Montpelier and Epsom Clubs will play their return match on Wednesday next, the seventh inst, at Mr I. G. Bryant's, the BeeHive Ground, near the Surrey Zoological Gardens, Walworth. Wickets to be pitched at ten o'clock."

Although these two reports feature in the same newspaper, they give a different date for the return match, although the newspaper should be complimented for giving such a detailed address in the lower report for the match.

Sep 11th - There is a full match report on Montpelier v Epsom match played at Beehive Ground which resulted in a very tight finish (see below).

Sep 11th 1842

EPSOM AND MONTPELIER CLUBS.

These clubs played their return match on the Beehive Ground, Walworth, on Wednesday, which terminated in favour of Epsom by one run. Score :—

EPSOM.		MONTPELIER.	
C. Chadband, b Hill	7	Houghton, b H. Richardson	6
A. Chadband, b Hill	40	Sagger, b H. Richardson	7
G. Richardson, b Lewis	0	Foulds, b A. Chadband	56
H. Richardson, b Baker	23	Coltson, b A. Chadband	17
Churchill, b Hill	1	Wood, b H. Richardson	4
G. Moore, run out	0	Lewis, c Lemon	18
H. Miller, b Hill	17	Peto, b Chadband	11
J. Buggs, c Baker	20	Baker, not out	19
T. Lemon, c Hill	19	Finch, b H. Richardson	8
T. Richardson, b Coltson	19	Garratt, b H. Richardson	0
Crisp, not out	6	Hill, b Richardson	19
Byes, &c.	43	Byes, &c.	44
Total	191	Total	190

Sep 11th - *The Era* - In the round-up is "Epsom v Walworth Montpelier - An excellently contested match was played on Wednesday at the Beehive, Carter-street, Walworth between the above-named clubs, when, after some very scientific play on both sides, the Epsom gentleman were declared the winners by one run, the former scoring in two innings 191, and the latter 190."

After an improvement in 1840, there is little cricket reported in *The Era* this summer; sometimes the tally for the week amounts to but one column.

Sep 18th - Under a heading of "Match at South Lambeth" is reported "Five from Hampshire and an equal number of the Vauxhall Clarence Club played a match on the 15th inst. on Mr Price's Meadows, South Lambeth. Score Hampshire 9 and 7, Clarence Club 51 …. the parties afterwards retired to Watkin's The Goat's Head, Wandsworth road, and the "spread" was all that could be desired."

This report highlights another local ground, not far from The Oval.

"The Montpelier Club played against Eleven Players at the BeeHive Ground, Walworth on Monday when the Players won by 44 runs. Scores Montpelier first innings 95 … Players first innings 139." Note that scores are given as "first innings" despite it being a one innings match.

Sep 25th - In the weekly round-up "Parsons Green v Beehive, these clubs on Wednesday last played their return match at the former place which ended by the Surrey gents coming off victorious by nine runs." This is the first mention of the Beehive Club in the newspaper this season.

William Baker

(1808-85)

Born at Kennington he played for the Montpelier Club for at least fourteen years. His first reported match for the club was against Windsor and Eton on August 4th 1834. The match features in *Bell's Life*, and although no scores are mentioned, the opposition won by seven wickets. The match was played at Montpelier Gardens which is interesting, as between 1831-44 the home ground for the club was normally the Beehive ground. In the same team for this match and featured in other pen pictures were Coltson and Lewis.

On July 25th 1838 he scored 95 for Montpelier against Copenhagen at the Beehive ground and 83 against Chelsfield on July 12th 1843 at the same ground. His last reported match for the team was against Croydon on July 19th 1848 at Coldharbour Lane, Brixton and it features in *Scores and Biographies* (volume three). Between his first and last match there are records showing him playing for the club every season except in 1836 and 1840. He also played for South London Club on June 13th 1844 against Watford at Watford, debuted for the Surrey X1 on July 13th 1846 against Marylebone at Lord's and played for Surrey Phoenix on September 3rd 1849 against Surrey Paragons at Kennington Oval (and then played for Surrey against Camden the next day).

He normally played as a lower-order batsman and his first-class career consisted of seven matches, all for Surrey between 1846-53. He played five matches at Kennington Oval and two at Lord's, both against M.C.C. and scored 118 runs at 9.83 and held 2 catches.

He died at Lambeth in his late seventies, not far from his birthplace.

Charles Coltson

(1813-52)

Born in Lambeth the first report of him playing for the club is again in *Bell's Life* dated August 4th 1834 when he too played against Windsor and Eton. He batted normally at number three or four and played for the club every season until 1848, for Mr Foulds X1 against Mr Houghton's X1 at The Oval in May 1845, for the Surrey X1 between 1846-50, Gentleman of Surrey and for Surrey Phoenix on September 3rd 1849 (and for Surrey the next day). In *Bell's Life* there is a report for this last match, and below it a shorter one on the Surrey v Walham Green match stating; "C. Coltson of the Montpelier Club plays for Walham Green "in order to perfect the eleven."" It also tells that he was a member of both the Surrey Club and Walham Green clubs, as well as playing for Surrey Phoenix the previous week.

Cricket records show him as "an occasional wicket-keeper". Playing against Islington Albion on August 18th 1845 (see *Scores and Biographies*) he kept wicket and made one stumping in both innings, and also took two wickets. One was caught by Garland (perhaps E. Garland who features later?) who appeared to be a substitute fielder, as the scorebook read "c Garland (for), b Coltson 23" and one was bowled. In the Surrey v Streatham match on June 11th 1850 he dismissed three Streatham batsmen in the first innings and stumped one. In the second innings, he took three of the four wickets lost. Baker, Denison and Garland also played in this match. In the same season on September 8th and 9th he played for Twenty Gentlemen of Surrey against Eleven Players of Surrey at the Oval and scored 6 and 7 in totals of 48 and 122.

He played 13 first-class matches, his first being for Gentlemen against Players at Lord's in 1843. Batting at number five he was dismissed without scoring and did not bat in the second innings as his side won by an innings and 20 runs. His other twelve matches were for Surrey and were played between 1846-51 at Kennington Oval, Petworth Park, Hyde Park Ground (Sheffield), and Brunswick Ground (Hove). In 23 innings he scored 162 runs at 7.71 with a top score of 24 not out and held 7 catches.

He was invited to be one the founder committee members for the new Surrey C.C.C. but died at Kennington prior to his fortieth birthday.

William Denison

(1801-56)

Born at South Lambeth, London he is first reported playing for the Montpelier Club against East Surrey in Walworth in *Bell's Life* on May 28th 1835. He played at least three more times for the club in July and August that season and scored 13, 0, 0, u/k, 5 and 160.

He played for the Kennington Saturday Club eleven on the local common on September 20th 1834 prior to making his debut for the Montpelier Club the following season. He played a few times in 1836 after which his name appears to fade away, but in the 1830s and 1840s he wrote about cricket for *The Times*.

On August 1st 1844 he played for Surrey against Mitcham (non first-class) at Mitcham and scored 5 runs, and in his only first-class match for Surrey, against M.C.C. at Kennington Oval in May 1846, he scored 2 runs and 1 run at number eleven aged 45, and also held a catch. This match saw Baker, Lewis and Spenceley make their first-class debuts and Coltson was also in the team.

He also played for Mr Houghton's X1 against Mr Foulds X1 at The Oval in May 1845, and the same season for Gentlemen of Surrey against Players of Surrey, which Gordon Ross in his Surrey C.C.C. history book (page 17) describes as "the first (match at Kennington Oval) officially connected with the Surrey Club.."

Towards the end of his career he played for Surrey against Streatham at Kennington Oval on June 11th 1850, but failed to score at number eleven in a match they lost. Baker, Coltson and Garland also played for the county side.

He played eight first-class matches between 1832-47 and scored 34 runs at 3.77, took 30 wickets at 12.41 and held a catch. Six of these matches were for Gentlemen of England (all against Gentlemen of Kent), one for M.C.C. and one for Surrey and they were played at five different grounds.

His nickname was "Stick 'em up" and his name appears again when the Surrey Club emerges as he was elected Hon. Secretary between 1845-48. He died at Lee, Kent, which is now in southeast London, and is buried in Nunhead Cemetery in a grave now unmarked.

Edward Garland

(1826-82)

Another player whose exact date of birth has been lost in the passage of time; although we do have the year. He was born and christened in Kennington, so was another local boy. The first report of him playing for the Montpelier Club came in *Bell's Life* on July 28th 1845 when he scored 0 and took 5 wickets, away to Upper Clapton. Montpelier scored 52 and 27 and the home team 83. He played again away to Upper Clapton on June 16th 1846 who this time won by 40 runs on first innings scores.

He played for the Gentlemen of Surrey against Players of Surrey at Kennington Oval on August 21st and 22nd 1845, and as opener with Charles Whyting scored 23 and 16 runs. He also took three wickets in the Players' first innings.

The first of his two first-class matches came for Surrey against Kent on June 25th and 26th 1846 at Kennington Oval. He scored 0 and did not bat in the second innings as Surrey won by ten wickets.

Bell's Life contains a report of the Surrey against Streatham match at Kennington Oval on June 11th 1850 and he opened the batting and scored 5 runs and took two wickets in the first innings and one in the second. The match was drawn.

His second and last first-class appearance was for Surrey against M.C.C. on July 21st and 22nd 1853 at Kennington Oval when he scored 3 and 3 and took 5 wickets as Surrey won by three runs.

On Tuesday August 11th 1856 he played in Montpelier's win against Blackheath Dartmouth in a friendly at The Oval. In his team's total of 231 he scored 9 and witnessed the opposition being shot out for just 37. A few weeks later, on September 3rd he played at the same ground against Surbiton and scored 1 as opener in Montpelier's total of 115 and held a catch, as they won by an innings and 15 runs.

Seventeen years after he came to notice he played for Surrey against South Wales C.C. at Kennington Oval on July 21st and 22nd 1862. He scored 0 not out and 0 and took 1-36 and 3-31 as the visitors won by two wickets. In the opposing team were two of the Grace brothers; Edward and Henry.

In this brief first-class career, he scored 6 runs at 2 and held a catch. He died at Kennington in September 1882.

1843

Jun 4th - "Matches to come on the Walworth Ground - a single wicket match between a gentleman of the Montpelier Cricket Club and a gentleman of the Islington Albion for £50 a side will take place on the 19th inst. at Isaac G. Bryant's Ground, the Beehive, Carter-street Walworth wickets to be pitched at 11 o'clock. Also on Tuesday the 6th June, a match will come off between the Montpelier and Dartford Clubs, and on Thursday, the 8th June a match between the South London Club and the East Sheen Club, at the above ground."

I am very grateful to find this report, as it ties clubs to grounds so early in the season.

Jun 4th - *The Era* - In the round-up is "South London v East Sheen Club - a match has been made to come off Thursday next, on Bryant's Beehive ground, Carter-street, Walworth between the following two elevens of the above-named clubs ..." The South London Club included E. Garland and Lewis; familiar names for our club.

Jun 11th - There are two columns of cricket reports although nothing of local interest. To put matters into perspective, there are two columns of boxing reports, one of pedestrianism (a form of long-distance, endurance race-walking), one of wrestling, two on aquatics which in the main is about sailing, five on horse-racing and a further two on horse-racing "on the continent". All considered, the newspaper covered a wealth of different sports and in detail.

In the round-up below is the result of South London v East Sheen. The former scored 96 and 126 and the latter 79.

Jun 11th - *The Era* - In the round-up is a report on the rain-affected Dartford v Montpelier. "A match was commenced between these clubs on Tuesday, at the Beehive ground, Walworth, but owing to the unfavourable state of the weather, the parties being obliged to fly their tents for shelter from the showers, the game could not be played out. The Dartford Club went in first, and scored 126. The Montpelier had scored 44 runs, with seven wickets to go down, when night put an end to the play."

"Matches at Bryant's Ground, Beehive, Walworth - On Monday (tomorrow) a match between a gentleman of the Montpelier Club, and a gentleman, a member of the Islington Albion for 50 sovs-a-side. On Tuesday the Montpelier gentlemen play a match with the Clapton club." Sadly there are no details of the participants for this one-a-side match.

Jun 18th - "The South London and Montpelier Clubs play a match on Wednesday next, at Mr Bryant's Beehive Ground, Carter-street, Walworth." The Middlesex v Surrey match due to be played at Garratt's Ground, did not take place until Monday "Owing to the extreme badness of the weather." Surrey scored 43 and 74 and Middlesex 49 and the newspaper reported "few runs could be obtained owing to the heaviness of the ground."

Jun 18th - *The Era* - In the round-up is "Matches at Bryant's Ground, Walworth - The South London and Montpelier Clubs will play a match on Wednesday next, at the Beehive ground, Carter-street, Walworth. The Upper Clapton and Montpelier match is postponed to Monday, the 17th July, in consequence of the wet on Tuesday." Immediately below is "Dartford and Montpelier Clubs - The return match between these clubs will take place on Monday week, the 26th inst, on Dartford Brent."

Jun 25th - "The Montpelier (Walworth) and Clarence (Putney) Clubs played a match on Finch's Ground, Putney which we hear is to be fitted up in grand style for the approaching regatta." The scores were; Montpelier 141 and 87, total 228 and Clarence 109.

The South London team for the forthcoming match against East Sheen to be played Monday (tomorrow) at the East Sheen ground is listed as: Messrs Hill, Lewis, E. Garland, W. Garland, Heath, W. Edwards, Davis, White, Buck, Waters and Bucket.

I have been unable to establish if the South London team drew players exclusively from other local teams or whether they could stand alone as a team. Garland and Lewis are familiar names so I expect that there was some form of cross-over between teams.

"The Montpelier Club and South London Clubs played their match at the Bee Hive, Walworth on Wednesday inst. Scores, Montpelier 98 and 35, total 133, South London 82 and 90, total 172."

Jun 25th - *The Era* - In the round-up is South London - a match came off on Wednesday at Bryant's ground, Beehive, Walworth, between two nines selected from the above clubs … South London scored 82 and 90, total 172 and Montpelier 98 and 35, total 133 and six wickets to go down." This match was played at a ground that was home to both clubs and who became frequent oppositions for each other.

Jul 2nd - "The Montpelier (Walworth) and Dartford clubs played their return match on Thursday last at Dartford Brent. At the end of the day the scores stood, Dartford 105 and 60-6, Montpelier 105 ….. we regret not having room for the full score."

"Surrey and Middlesex - on Monday (tomorrow) a match will be played on the Rosemary Branch ground, Peckham between two elevens from the above counties, wickets will be pitched at half-past nine."

Jul 9th - "Surrey and Middlesex played their return match at the Rosemary Branch ground, Peckham for the benefit of Brockwell the bowler to the ground, which terminated in favour of Surrey, Scores, Middlesex 79, Surrey 213-7 (Heath 68, Brockwell 4 and byes & c 56)."

Jul 9th - *The Era* - In the round-up is "Matches at the Beehive Ground, Walworth - a match will be played on Wednesday next, between eleven of the Chelsfield Club and eleven of the Montpelier Club. On Tuesday week, the Upper Clapton Club meet the Montpelier and from the success of the former during the present season (they having beaten eleven at Lord's, the Dartford & c &c) and the Montpelier ranking as one of the strongest amateur clubs, some very fine play will no doubt take place."

Jul 16th - There are innings scores printed in full for Montpelier v Chelsfield at the Beehive ground, Walworth on Wednesday. Montpelier scored 214 (Baker 83) and the visitors from near Orpington, Kent 101. In Denison's *Cricketer's Companion* which shows many early cricket scores, this match is shown as a Montpelier win by 105 runs, which is slightly different from the above outcome.

Jul 23rd - There is a full match report (see next page) on Montpelier v Upper Clapton played at Beehive ground, which saw the home team beat the East London visitors by 86 runs on the first innings.

Jul 23rd - *The Era* - Full match report on "Montpelier v Upper Clapton - This long talked of match between two crack amateur clubs of London came off at the Beehive ground, at Walworth on Wednesday. The game as far as it proceeded, was decided in favour of the Montpelier, as the annotated score will show. The play throughout was of first-rate order, and the display of both batting and fielding, has seldom been surpassed." Montpelier 156 and 99-5 and Clapton 79.

MONTPELIER AND UPPER CLAPTON CLUBS.

This match, between two of the best amateur clubs of London, took place at the Beehive Ground, Walworth, on Wednesday last, the 19th inst. Great interest was manifested in this match, and the ground was well attended. The play was throughout of first-rate order, and the batting and fielding of the Montpelier gentlemen elicited frequent applause. The Clapton gentlemen, although unsuccessful, played with great skill, energy, and good humour, and the day passed off altogether pleasantly. Score :—

MONTPELIER.		UPPER CLAPTON.	
Baker, b Austin	14	Burrowes, b Gardner	0
Wood, b Austin	6	Cloves, c Wood	15
Spenceley, c Gordon	13	Craven, c Peto	14
Coltson, not out	51	Gordon, c Wood	14
Challis, b Craven	0	Nicholson, b Hill	0
Lewis, c Nicholson	4	Austin, b Hill	6
Foulds, run out	39	Gibson, run out	0
Peto, b Burrowes	6	Key, c Peto	2
Gardner, b Austin	6	George, c Gardner	11
Hill, b Burrowes	0	Fox, b Hill	3
Garrett, b Austin	0	Cooper, not out	1
Byes 3, wide balls 12, no ball 1	16	Byes 5, wide balls 8	13
Total	156	Total	79

In Montpelier's second innings, Challis scored 2 (b Austin), Baker 1 (b Burrowes), Spenceley 5 (c Cloves), Wood 29 (b Austin), Coltson 22 (not out), Foulds 15 (b George), Lewis 3 (not out); byes 10, wide balls 12—total 99. At eight o'clock, when the stumps were drawn, the Montpelier were 176 ahead, with five wickets to go down.

July 23 1843

Jul 30th - "The Montpelier and Putney Clarence Clubs played their return match on the Beehive Ground, Walworth on Wednesday last. The scores stood as follows when night put an end to the contest, Montpelier 172 and 103, total 275, Putney Clarence 121."

Also mentioned in the round-up were Kennington Royal Standard Club (their first mention in the newspaper), who lost to Clapham Star on Clapham Common. I presume that this was a match between two pub teams, but someone thought fit to let the newspaper know about it. It also illustrates another, albeit minor cricket team from the Kennington area.

Jul 30th - *The Era* - In the round-up is "Montpelier (Walworth) and Putney Clarence Clubs. A match was played on Wednesday, on the Beehive ground, Carter-street, Walworth between an eleven of the Montpelier club and eleven of the Putney Clarence …. Scores Montpelier 172 and 103 and Putney Clarence 124."

Aug 6th - *The Era* - In the round-up is "Montpelier v Chislehurst. A match was played on Chislehurst between an eleven of the Walworth Montpelier and eleven of the Chislehurst Clubs which, after an excellent day's play terminated the Montpelier beating their opponents in one innings, by 47 runs." Sadly there were no scores to accompany this report and this was the last Montpelier report to grace to newspaper this season.

Aug 20th - In the round-up is mention of West Surrey (whose first mention in the newspaper this is) v Chertsey played at West Surrey's ground in Wandsworth Road near the *Goat's Head Inn*. West Surrey scored 91 and 65, total 156 and Chertsey 42 and 16 total 58. This is the first mention of this club from the opposite side of the county. Credit to the newspaper too that they pinpoint the club's home ground, which is not too distant from Kennington. *The Goat's Head Inn* also featured in a report on October 3rd 1841 as the home of the Vauxhall Clarence Club, so again we have evidence of clubs sharing a venue, or moving in when another has left.

Sep 3rd - "Montpelier and South London Clubs versus Eleven Chosen Players. This match, for the benefit of Messrs Heath and Mortlock, two well-known and respected cricketers came off on Monday at the Beehive ground, Walworth. We regret we have not room for the particulars sent, and can only give a brief account of the score. Gentlemen first innings 84 (Colston 23, W Garland 12 and E Garland 1), Players first innings 125-4 (Heath 35, Brockwell 4)."

It is interesting that the newspaper refers to them as Gentleman and Players. Brockwell was the bowler at the Rosemary Branch ground and played for Surrey in the match reported on July 9th.

Sep 24th - "Essex and Montpelier - The annual match between the county of Essex (with F. Pilch and Martingell given) and the Montpelier Club, will take place at the White Hart Ground, Abridge, on Friday next, the 29th inst.."

If this was an annual match it is the first time that is has been reported in the newspaper, although it illustrates another county into which the club ventured.

Oct 1st - Full match report on West Surrey (with A. Mynn) v Islington Albion at their ground in Wandsworth Road, shows the home team's batting order as; Buckett, Brockwell, Chester, Heath, Day, A. Mynn, Sewell, Bennett, R. Noyes, Beagen and Druce. None played for the Montpelier Club.

1844

The previously mentioned *Surrey Cricket - Its History and Associations* by Alcock and Alverstone contains some worthwhile details about this season. They comment (on page 345); "As it happened the "Beehive" ground was not long at their disposal. Its position made it attractive, particularly so for building purposes. As a result, the members of the Montpelier Club found themselves without a local habitation in the early months of 1844."

Also of relevance is a letter taken from Denison's *Cricketer's Companion* for the 1843 season which outlines some unpleasantries in an East Surrey v Montpelier match.

> Many years ago it was the practice where the contending parties could not spare *two* days in succession to play a match, that a third day should be named for the purpose of " playing out " the ends of the original, and the return matches. This was the almost universal rule, but one which was broken through, and led to unpleasant results, in a match between the EAST SURREY and MONTPELIER CLUBS, two clubs which in those days were second only to the MARYLEBONE, whether in regard to their strength of play, or in the number and respectability of their members. The former met at Hampton's Ground, Camberwell, the latter at the Bee Hive, Walworth. Upon this match betting had taken place to a considerable amount, and at the termination of the play for the day, bets were claimed by the one party on the ground that the match was determined by the *first* innings. To this doctrine the losing side, at that period of the game demurred, alleging that the custom with their club was to "play out" their matches in the manner already mentioned. In the second innings, it chanced too that they had made a very " long hands," and so bid fair to become the victors. Eventually the bets were not paid, and ill blood, having been thus generated, continued to exist to a painful extent between the clubs for very many years.
>
> This affair became a topic of discussion amongst most of the clubs in the neighbourhood of London, and from that period it has, when not specially arranged otherwise, become the usage, and indeed the rule, that all matches to which *one day* only is devoted shall be decided by the *first* innings if the *two* are not played.
>
> 3, Portland Terrace,
>
> Wandsworth Road, Surrey.
>
> April, 1844.

Apr 14th - *The Era* - "Beehive Club .... The Montpelier Club also commenced their season on this ground on the Tuesday in the preceding week, and will continue to practice on Tuesday and Fridays until the end of the season."

Apr 14th - "The South London Club commenced their season on Thursday April 11th at the Beehive ground, Walworth with some very excellent play and spent a very pleasant evening afterwards."

This rather uninformative reporting was followed by:

"The West Surrey club commenced play for the season on Monday last at Watkin's Ground, Wandsworth Road." Whether this ground is the one in the same road, termed "Bennett's" in 1851 is not known.

Apr 28th - *The Era* - "Beehive Ground, Walworth - the members of the South London Club will meet at the above ground ... after the play they will dine together in their club-room at the Beehive Tavern."

May 5th - "South London Club - Beehive Walworth - the sixth anniversary of this club was celebrated on Thursday, by a day's play between the members who afterwards sat down to one of Briant's excellent dinners. Mr A Mynn and several other friends were visitors on the occasion."

May 12th - "The Montpelier Club commenced their season at the Beehive ground, with a day's play between two elevens of the members, which ended in a tie. They afterwards adjourned to their club room and partook of a very excellent dinner and spent the evening in the pleasantest manner."

May 12th - *The Era* - "Beehive Ground, Walworth - The Montpelier Club commenced their season on Tuesday, on their ground, with a day's play between two elevens of its members, which after some very excellent batting and bowling terminated in a tie, each side scoring 72. They afterwards partook of an excellent dinner at the house, and spent a very pleasant evening." It is interesting to note that despite it being mid-May, by which time now the season would be well under way, the club are still playing "in-house" matches in preparation for their forthcoming season.

Jun 2nd - *The Era* - Full match report on Putney Clarence v Montpelier (Walworth) - a match was played at Finch's ground, Putney between two elevens selected from the above-named clubs. The weather was exceedingly cold and unfavourable to cricket, but nevertheless the play was exceedingly good. At the close of play, the Montpelier gentlemen were declared the winners, with seven wickets to go down…" Putney 19 and 67, Montpelier 50 and 37-3.

Jun 16th - In the round-up is "Lingfield and Montpelier - these excellent clubs again contended on Wednesday last at Lingfield, Surrey, which after some excellent play, the match terminated in favour of the latter by the first innings. Score Montpelier 104 and 97, total 201 (Lewis 35 not out), Lingfield 87."

Jun 16th - *The Era* - In the round-up is "Lingfield v Montpelier Cricket Club (Walworth) - these ancient rivals met again in honourable contention on Wednesday, at Lingfield, Surrey, which terminated in favour of the Montpelier Club, in one innings, played in excellent style. Scores: Montpelier 104 and 97, total 201." Both newspapers agree that the play in this match was of a good standard, however *The Era* does list some of the player's individual scores (which total 87) but the Lingfield team total is not shown!

Jun 23rd - *The Era* - In the round-up is "Upper Clapton and Montpelier (Walworth) Clubs - these crack metropolitan clubs played their annual match on Thursday last, the 20th inst. at Clapton, when after some splendid play in the batting … terminated in favour of the Montpelier, on the first innings by 53. Score Montpelier 136, Clapton 83."

Jun 30th - Innings scores shown for Montpelier v Putney Clarence at Bryant's Beehive ground, Walworth on Wednesday last. Montpelier scored 154 and 11-5 and the visitors 86.

"The Montpelier and South London clubs will play their annual match on their own ground (the Beehive, Walworth) on Friday next July 5th, when the play it is expected will be first rate."

Jun 30th - *The Era* - In the round-up is "Montpelier (Walworth) and Putney Clarence - these clubs played their return match on Wednesday, on the ground of the former, at Bryant's, the Beehive, Walworth when the Montpelier again proved successful, they having won every match they have been engaged in this season. The score stood thus: Montpelier 154 and 11, total 165 … Putney Clarence 88."

"The Montpelier and South London Clubs play their annual match on Friday next, at the Beehive, Walworth."

"Lingfield v Montpelier - the return match between these two elevens is to be played at the Beehive ground, Walworth on Wednesday next. Much speculation has taken place as to the result of this match 6 to 4 being freely laid on Lingfield. The Montpelier in the first match were the winners by 17 runs and will no doubt muster all their strength on this occasion."

Jul 7th - "Lingfield v Montpelier - the return match between these two clubs came off on Wednesday last at Bryant's Ground, Beehive, Walworth and terminated again in favour of the Montpelier who won by 75 runs. Scores, Lingfield 113, Montpelier 188 (Coltson 27, George 25, Foulds 24 and Spencely 12)."

Jul 21st - "Bromley and Montpelier clubs - this match was played on Friday the 11th inst at the ground of the latter, the Bee Hive, Walworth. The batting on both sides was very effective, but the superiority in fielding was on the part of the Montpelier. Montpelier scored 121 (Driver 24, Coltson 20), Bromley 133 (Wigsell 65) .... The return match will be played at Bromley on the 7th of August."

"Montpelier v South London - the match between these two clubs came off on their own ground the Beehive, Walworth on Wednesday last. The score when the stumps were drawn was Montpelier 140 and 88, total 228, South London 49 and 40, total 89 with eight wickets to go down."

Perhaps the match scheduled for July 5th was postponed?

Jul 21st - *The Era* - In the round-up is "Montpelier v South London - the match between these clubs came off at their own ground, the Beehive, Walworth on Wednesday. They score stood as follows; Montpelier 140 and 88, total 228, South London 49 and 49, total 89 with eight wickets to go down."

Jul 28th - "Montpelier and Clapton - these clubs played a match at the Beehive Ground, Walworth on Tuesday last and the weather proving extremely fine, there was a numerous muster of spectators. The play was very good on both sides. Scores, Montpelier 183 and 61, total 244, Clapton 94."

Jul 28th - *The Era* - In the round-up is "Beehive Ground, Walworth - a match has been made to come off at this ground on Wednesday next, for the benefit of T. Mortlock, umpire of the ground, between two elevens selected from the Montpelier and South London Clubs and eleven players chosen by Mortlock."

Aug 4th - Full match report on Players v Montpelier match played at the Beehive Ground (see next page) for the benefit of Mortlock, the umpire at Bryant's (Beehive) Ground. The report refers to the Montpelier Club as "Gentlemen".

MATCH AT THE WALWORTH GROUND.

The match for the benefit of Mortlock, the umpire at Bryant's Ground, Beehive, Walworth, was played on Wednesday last, between eleven of the Montpelier and South London Clubs and eleven Players chosen by Mortlock. The Gentlemen were the victors, as will be seen by the following score :—

PLAYERS.		MONTPELIER.	
Brockwell, c White, b Gardner	0	Challis, b Plank	15
Barton, b Garland	1	Garland, hit wicket	17
Edwards, st Driver, b Gardner	5	C. White, b Plank	10
Paul, c Whyting, b Garland	1	C. Coltson, b Plank	57
Plank, b Gardner	0	C. Whyting, c Mortlock, b Hunt	10
Hunt, b Gardner	0	Lewis, not out	41
Field, b Garland	1	Gardner, b Barton	1
Dogell, run out	0	Peto, b Plank	1
Hinton, b Gardner	0	Driver, b Plank	4
Mortlock, not out	3	Saggers, hit w, b Plank	4
Page, c Coltson, b Garland	0	Griffiths, c Hunt, b Plank	0
Byes	2	Byes 17, wide balls 22	39
Total	13	Total	199

Paul 12, Hunt 1, Brockwell 3, Edwards 3, and Barton 3 wide balls.

Aug 4 1844

Aug 25th - "The Montpelier and South London clubs play their return match on Tuesday next, at Bryant's Ground, Carter-street, Walworth. The wickets are to be pitched at ten precisely."

Aug 25th - *The Era* - In the round-up is "Montpelier and South London - These clubs play their second match of the season on their own ground at the Beehive, Carter-street, Walworth on Tuesday, the 27th instant."

Sep 1st - "The Montpelier and South London clubs played their return match at Bryant's Ground, Beehive, Walworth on Tuesday last when the South London proved victorious, one innings each being played, Scores Montpelier 50 (Trimnell 13, Saggers 8 and Blenkairn 5), South London 121 (Page 41, W. Garland 19, Driver 16 and Edwards 13).

Sep 1st - *The Era* - In the round-up is "Montpelier v South London - an eleven of these clubs met on Tuesday at their ground, the Beehive, Walworth to play their return match, which was decided in one innings as follows: Montpelier 50, South London 121 … the latter club winning by 71 runs."

Oct 6th - "New East Surrey Ground, Peckham - George Brockwell's benefit on Tuesday last between eleven gentlemen chosen by Mr Brockwell and eleven by Mr Barton." Both sides totalled 40 in their innings and the newspaper reported

"The ball was far too good for the bat ... and ...We were sorry to see that the lateness of the season had anything but a beneficial effect."

Earlier I mentioned Montgomery's *The History of Kennington and its Neighbourhood* and within it and relevant to this season is; "This brings us to the origin and growth of the Surrey Club. A meeting of the old Montpelier members was held in 1844: among the names of those present I find C.H. Hoare, W. Baker, T. Lewis, C. Coltson, J. Burrup, junr., W. Pickering, W. Houghton, N. Felix and W. Denison. Old Mr. Ward (a household name among Cricketers in those days) presided, and it was agreed to found a County Club. In the autumn of the same year (1844) a dinner was given at the Horns to collect members and start the Club in good earnest. The Hon. F. Ponsonby (now Lord Bessborough) came over expressly from Ireland to be present and to take the chair: and about 70 members of the Montpelier Club enrolled themselves in the County Club."

Montgomery rounds off by telling "For a year or two the Club did not prosper much: There were internal jealousies, and dissensions, and dissatisfaction with the management, and above all the money was not plentiful. At the beginning of the season Mr. Denison (the Secretary) announced that the debt had amounted to £70 before any of the yearly expenses were considered: and that it seemed impossible to play any first-class matches, that many of the members were retiring from the Club. The meeting almost decided to break up the Club, and I suppose had such a vote been carried, the Oval would have been at once built over and some very happy memories of Kennington would never have exposited at all. It is to the present Lord Bessborough that we owe the continuance of Cricket upon the Oval. He was Vice-President at the time and suggested that the £70 should be paid off by allowing six gentlemen to become Life members by paying down £12 a piece. A gentleman present next said "who will pay £12 to be Life member of a bankrupt Club?" "I will" said Old Mr. Cressingham, one of the oldest members: and "I will" said five others, of whom Mr. Ponsonby was one. Lord Besborough, in writing of this memorable meeting, adds - "looking back to that distant day I fear I have been a bad bargain to the Club by becoming a Life Member for £12." But we may add upon the other side - "Had you not spoken up on the occasion I would have been a still worse bargain for the Club.""

On page 173 he writes "In 1844 the Bee-Hive Ground in Walworth, was taken for building purposes, and the Montpelier Club obtained the lease of the Oval. The late Mr Baker of Kennington Road, a very fine all-round Cricketer, entered into negotiations with the Duchy, as the owners would not transact business at that time with a Club as such. A lease was obtained for 31 years, at £120 per annum, and the taxes amounted to about £20 more. The 3½ acres of the ground were turfed; and the remaining 9-acres were sown. Mr. Houghton came forward, as President of the Montpelier Club, and became proprietor of the ground, whilst eight gentlemen of the Montpelier Club guaranteed the rent in case of any failure in getting the money in other ways. The first Secretary was Mr. W. Denison, a well-known man in Cricketing circles in those days. It must be confessed, however, that the first years were by no means prosperous for Cricket here. First, the old Montpelier Club suffered. They played matches here for about two years, but Houghton by degrees tried to confine them to one corner of the ground: the result was that they left the Oval and took a ground where Coldharbour Lane now stands. Here they played for a year or two, but finally the club was merged in the County Club and broke up."

The story surrounding the club leaving Kennington Oval so shortly after their arrival is covered in more detail in 1848 by way of three letters recently found in *Bell's Life*, which perhaps have not been seen since their appearance in the newspaper. They are all well written, very illuminating and quite turgid.

1845

I was unable to find any copies of *The Era* for this year earlier than Sep 28th and the reports in October contained no reports of Montpelier matches either. This of course was the season when the club moved from the Beehive ground to The Oval and it would have been interesting to see if *The Era* was able to outline more fully the reasons for this move, apart from what has been reported elsewhere that their ground was needed for building on.

In *Off and On the Field* written by Surrey player Henry Leveson-Gower (on page 80) he states "Try to imagine yourself entering the ground in the year 1845. In the spring of that year the first sod of turf was laid on the present ground; 10,000 turves cut from Tooting Common were brought there. A year previously the ground had been a thriving market garden, but when in early 1845 the famous Montpelier Club had to vacate its ground adjoining the Beehive Tavern, Walworth, which had been sold for building purposes, the members decided to trek to the Oval. The treasurer of the Club, Mr. W. Baker, a fine all-round cricketer, was chiefly responsible for the decision to acquire the ground, and a lease of thirty-one years was taken from the Otter family…."

On page 345 of Alcock and Alverstone's authoritative tome the link between the Montpelier Club and the new county team is mentioned; "Mr. Baker, who made himself immortal in cricket history by securing the first lease of the Oval as a cricket ground, a very fine all-round player; Hayter Reed, a good wicket-keeper; E. Garland, for some years on the Committee of the Surrey C.C.; C. Lewis;

A.K. George; and Brockwell, uncle of the excellent all-round Surrey cricketer of today, were prominent members of the Montpelier Club at the time."

Details taken from *Surrey Cricket - Its History and Associations* by Alcock and Alverstone and Montgomery's *The History of Kennington and its Neighbourhood* book are included at the start of the entries for the 1844, 1845 and 1847 seasons and describe the formation of the Surrey County Cricket Club from the Montpelier Club well. One could therefore be excused for thinking that 1845 marked the demise of the latter club. Not so.

Apr 27th - "South London Club - The members of this club intend meeting on Thursday next, the 1st of May on the Beehive Ground, Walworth for a day's play and opening dinner when a strong muster is expected."

May 18th - Full match report on Mr Fould's side v Mr Houghtons side (see below) which it mentions "the Montpelier club assembled for the first time this season to enjoy a day's play on the new Surrey Ground …"

May 18th 1845

THE MONTPELIER CLUB.

On the 13th inst., the Montpelier Club assembled for the first time this season to enjoy a day's play on the new Surrey Ground, Kennington Oval. The sides were chosen by Messrs Foulds and Houghton, and after most excellent sport, interrupted occasionally by a few heavy showers, the members and their friends, to the number of fifty, retired to the Horns Tavern, where a first-rate dinner was provided by Mr Briant, in the large concert room. The chair was taken on the occasion by the worthy president of the club, Mr Houghton. The following is the score:—

MR FOULD'S SIDE.		MR HOUGHTON'S SIDE.	
T. Phillips, Esq, c Peto, b Gardner	0	Pretyman, Esq, st Foulds, b Coltson	0
W. Fould's, Esq, c Spencely, b Burrup	26	C. Whyting, Esq, b Foulds	8
J. West, Esq, l b w, b Gardner	0	Busher, Esq, run out	5
C. White, Esq, b Gardner	6	J. Burrup, Esq, c White, b Coltson	11
Earnshaw, Esq, b Gardner	0	W. Houghton, Esq, b Coltson	8
Burnett, Esq, c Pretyman, b Burrup	1	Spencely, Esq, b Coltson	3
C. Coltson, Esq, c Whyting, b Burrup	18	H. Gardner, Esq, not out	8
J. Peto, Esq, b Burrup	8	B. Driver, Esq, b Coltson	0
Blenkarn, Esq, not out	0	Tuelock, Esq, b Coltson	1
J. Smith, Esq, run out	0	J. Clark, Esq, b Foulds	0
J. M'Kenzie, Esq, b Gardner	0	C. Leach, Esq, c White, b Burnett	0
Bye 1, wide balls (Gardner 2, Burrup 1) 3	4	Byes 6, wide balls (Burnett 13, Coltson 8, Foulds 3) 18	24
Total	63	Total	67

Jun 1st - "The New East Surrey Club and the Lower Clapton Clubs play a match at the Rosemary Branch, Peckham on Wednesday, 4th of June."

Jun 29th - "Montpelier and South London - These clubs played a match on Thursday the 20th inst, at the Beehive Ground, Walworth. Scores Montpelier 127 and 84 total 211, South London 101 and 42 total 143."

"The Montpelier and Islington Albion clubs play a match at Copenhagen House Islington on Thursday July 10th."

Jul 13th - "The Montpelier and Upper Clapton Clubs will play their annual match on the Surrey ground, Kennington Oval, on Thursday next, the 17th instant, and from the celebrity of these two strong clubs, a great treat is expected. The ground is in fine condition." Below this is "The Montpelier and South London Clubs play a match on the Surrey ground, Kennington Oval on Wednesday, the 20th inst."

Haygarth states that the first match at The Oval was on July 17th 1845 between the Montpelier Club and Clapton and W.W. Read agrees with this, although Montgomery does not. In the latter's *History of Kennington and its Neighbourhood* book he states the primary fixture was between the Montpelier Club and Mitcham on September 24th 1845. Alcock mentions these differences in his book and adds that the first actual game at The Oval was on May 13th 1845!

Montgomery then relates that "The River Effra, which ran on the south side of the Oval, must have overflowed its banks and caused this destruction (he is commenting after the death of a local porter found drowned in the creek near Kennington Oval). The Effra now is safely stowed away in a large drain made in 1880, to obviate any further annoyance; but the river has sent up to the surface a substitute. The high terraced banks, which are so much appreciated by sight-seers in the Oval, are composed of soil dug out of the place where the river now runs. It was a great boon to the Contractors to have a place so near to shoot earth, and they consented in return for this favour, to make the banks in the Oval, which are now concreted terrace, and turf them free of charge. If ever there was a mutual benefit to two contracting parties, this was the one: and if ever there was needed a reason to bless the Effra on its departure it is afforded every time the inhabitants of Kennington have obtained a good seat for a great match."

Jul 20th - The Montpelier v Upper Clapton match at "the New Ground, Kennington Oval on Thursday last" is briefly reported on (see next page). In a one innings match which ended at eight o'clock, the home team scored 70 and the visitors 143. Below this is mention of the Islington Albion v Montpelier match "played at the Copenhagen Ground in Islington on Tuesday the 10th inst. Islington scored 215 runs and Montpelier had reached 104-5 when stumps were drawn."

In the round-up is "The Montpelier and Bromley clubs will play a match on the Kennington Oval Ground, on Wednesday next. Each club will play their strength."

July 20 1845

Upper Clapton and Montpelier Clubs.—A match, which excited considerable interest, took place between the above clubs on Thursday last, at the New Ground, Kennington Oval. Some fine play was exhibited on both sides, and though at the termination of the game the friends of the Montpelier gentlemen were backing them at odds, yet from the steady bowling and fielding of their opponents, the game was by no means won. The following was the score at eight o'clock, when the wickets were drawn, it being only one day's play: Clapton first innings 133; of which Anth. Gibson Esq scored (run out) 2, T Craven Esq (c Coltson, b Garland) [illegible], C Gordon Esq (b Garland) 9, E Cooper Esq (b Gardener) 18, J Walker Esq (c Peto, b Lewis) 8, A K George Esq (b Gardener) 1, W Davies Esq (c Davis, b Gardener) 13, W Nicholson Esq (b Lewis) 28, S Lancaster Esq (b Garland) 13, G Bode Esq (c Garland, b Lewis) 5, G Trist Esq (not out) 4; byes 11, wide balls 23. Montpelier first innings 79; of which H Gardener Esq obtained (c Walker, b Craven) 23, J Grove Esq (run out) 0, Spenceley Esq (run out) 31, C Colston Esq (hit wicket) 11, C Whyting [illegible] (not out) 1; byes 4, wide balls 9.

King's College and St Paul's Schools.—This match came off on Saturday.

The Islington Albion and Montpelier Clubs [illegible] on the Copenhagen Ground, on Thursday, the 10th inst., and some very scientific play was exhibited by both of these celebrated clubs. On reference to the score it will be seen that the Albion obtained in one innings 213 runs, by good batting, and when time was called the Montpelier had obtained 104 runs, with the loss of five wickets, leaving 109 runs to be got by six wickets. The return match is looked forward to with some anxiety. Score:—Islington Albion, first innings 213; Rogers obtained (c Peto, b Whyting) 51, Thompson (b Gardner) 8, Scarr (b Gardner) 18, Anthony Gibson (c Whyting, b Colston) 23, Tildesley (run out) 5, Luckhurst (b Gardner) 23, Alf. Gibson (c Baker, b Colston) 2, Cox (c Peto, b Gardner) 6, Paul (b Colston) 9, Dewdney (not out) 18, Hillyard (b Lewis) 15; byes 11, wide 23.—Montpelier 104, with five wickets to go down; Gardner scored (b Paul) 10, George (b Scarr) 33, Spenceley (c Thompson, b Scarr) 33, Colston (c Hillyard, b Rogers) 19, Whyting (run out) 1, Lewis (not out) 0, Peto (not out) 0; byes 7, wide 7.

Jul 27th - The Montpelier and Lingfield Clubs play a match tomorrow (Monday) on the Surrey Ground, Kennington Oval. This match excites much interest both on account of the admirable matches that have been played between these clubs for many years, and also for the opportunity it affords of seeing what the cricketers of the lower part of the county can do."

Aug 3rd - There are two full match reports featured; Montpelier v South London (see below) and Montpelier v Upper Clapton.

MONTPELIER VERSUS SOUTH LONDON.

A match between these clubs came off on the Surrey Ground, Kennington Oval, on Wednesday last; but, owing to the unfavourable state of the weather, only one innings a side was played. The following is the score:—

MONTPELIER.		SOUTH LONUON.	
Challis, c Holt, b Grey	11	Edmed, b Smith	17
C White jun, b Grey	14	W Hester, b Smith	3
Winder, b Elt	0	Davis, absent	23
Day, b Elt	5	R Harris, b Smith	0
Trimnell, leg b w	1	T Elt, run out	4
Lambert, c Davis, b Grey	0	Grey, c Houghton, b Smith	5
Saggers, b Grey	6	Holt, leg b w	0
Capt Smith, not out	5	Field, b Lochner	11
Lochner, b Elt	1	Page, not out	9
Houghton, b Grey	4	H Hester, run out	3
Reman, c Holt, b Elt	1	Paul, b Smith	0
Byes 9, wide balls 5	14	Byes 5, no balls 6, wide 19	30
Total	64	Total	101

Below these is "Montpelier and Lingfield Clubs - This match was played on the Surrey Ground, Kennington on Monday last. Scores Lingfield 62 and 79-3 total 141, Montpelier 146" and "The Montpelier and Reading Clubs play their return match at the Beehive, Walworth on Friday next."

Aug 17th - "Montpelier and Reading Clubs. This match was played at Reading on Friday the 8th inst. Montpelier 159 and 45-5 total 204, Reading 73"

"Enfield and Montpelier. These two clubs played their return match at Kennington Oval on Tuesday last. Scores Montpelier 104 (E. Garland marked 39), Enfield 106."

"The Montpelier and Islington Albion clubs play a match tomorrow (Monday) on Kennington Oval."

Aug 24th - Full match report on the Gents and Players of Surrey match, played at Kennington Oval, watched "by a vast amount of spectators." In the Gents team were some familiar names; C. Whyting, E. Garland, C. Coltson, N. Felix, C.H. Hoare, W. Denison, T Courtnay (who was in fact Thomas Courtney Lewis) and W. Baker. The Montpelier Club is mentioned in the report (see next page).

"The Montpelier and Putney Clarence Clubs play a match in Finch's Ground, Putney on Monday Sept 1st.

GENTLEMEN AND PLAYERS OF SURREY.

This match was played at the new ground, Kennington Oval, on Thursday and Friday, and was witnessed throughout with much interest by a vast number of spectators. It was got up by several influential cricketers, as the first step towards the foundation of a Surrey club, of which the object will be to collect the criketing strength of the county, and then bring it forth. The gentlemen in this match were unexpectedly deprived of the assistance of the Hon F Ponsonby and Mr Randolph, by their unavoidable absence, and members of the Montpelier club were brought into requisition. The great press of cricketing and other sporting events reluctantly compels us to omit the particulars of the play; but we subjoin the state of the score when the stumps were drawn on Friday:—

THE GENTLEMEN.	1st inn		2d inn
C Whyting, Esq, c Bucket, b Blackwell	0	c and b Chester	0
E Garland, Esq, run out	23	leg before wicket, b Chester	16
C Coltson, Esq, hit wicket, b Shearman	11	b Chester	9
N Felix, Esq, b Shearman	11	c Shearman, b Chester	1
W Foulds, Esq, b Shearman	39	b Chester	3
T Courtnay, Esq, b Shearman	0	c Chester, b Islead	0
C H Hoare, Esq, b Shearman	0	run out	14
W Denison, Esq, b Blackwell	4	not out	15
H Gardner, Esq, not out	13	b Shearman	7
W Baker, Esq, b Chester	8	c Chester, b Islead	1
B N Driver, Esq, c Chadband, b Chester	6	c Islead	11
Byes 2, wide (Blackwell 1, Chester 2, Islead 3, Shearman 4) 10	12	Byes 4, wide 1	5
Total	—127	Total	—82

THE PLAYERS.	1st inn		2d inn
W Sewell, run out	0	b Denison	6
Cressell, c Hoare, b Denison	38		
Richardson, hit wicket, b Garland	0		
Blackwell, c Williams, b Garland	21	c Lewes, b Denison	0
Heath, c Driver, b Garland	37		
Chester, st Foulds, b Denison	0	not out	3
Chadband, st Foulds, b Denison	2		
Islead, c Davis, b Denison	4		
Bennett, not out	9	not out	7
Buckett, c Felix, b Denison	4		
Shearman, b Denison	5		
Byes 10, wide (Gardner 3, Garland 5, Coltson 5) 10, no ball (Denison) 1	21		
Total	—150	Total	—16

Aug 31st - "The Montpelier and Lingfield Clubs played their return match at Lingfield on Tuesday last. Scores Montpelier 78 and 70 total 148 (Peto obtained 24 and 0) one player was absent. Lingfield 65."

There is also a short report about "a determination to form a county club", a proposition that emanated from W. Denison (see below).

SURREY CLUB.—We are delighted to find that the result of the late important match at the Oval Cricket Ground, Kennington (decidedly the finest in the neighbourhood of London), has led to a determination to form a "Surrey Club." This proposition emanated from Mr W Denison, after a dinner which took place after the match, at the Horns tavern, Kennington. The resolution was seconded by Mr Felix, and was carried unanimously, and the following gentlemen were named as a committee to carry the proposition into effect (with power to add to their numbers):—The Hon F Ponsonby, the Hon S P onsonby, W Bolland Esq, J Bonsor Esq, C Coltson Esq, W Denison Esq, N Felix Esq, G Hoare Esq, C H Hoare Esq, W Houghton Esq, H Pickering, Esq, and W Pickering Esq.

Sep 7th - "Montpelier and South London Club's - a match will be played on Monday the 15th instant on the Beehive Ground, Walworth between the gentlemen and players of the above clubs, for the benefit of T. Mortlock, umpire to the ground when we hope he may have a bumper."

"The Reading and Montpelier Clubs play their return match on the Kennington Oval ground on Tuesday next."

Sep 14th - Putney Clarence and Montpelier Clubs - a match between these two clubs came off in Finch's Ground on Monday the 1st of September .... one innings alone being played and decided in favour of Putney by 31 runs. Putney 128 Montpelier 97 .... The return match is fixed for Wednesday next, at the Oval, Kennington."

1846

Although cricket reports begin on April 12th, the first of local interest does not appear until May 3rd when under a sub-title of "South London Club, Walworth" the newspaper reported "On Thursday the members of this club, and their friends met at the Beehive, Walworth for a day's play, and to have the opening dinner. Among the visitors were Messrs Felix, A and W Mynn, Sharp, Spenceley & c as well as some players of note ... the parties afterwards dined together at the Beehive, the hosting serving up an excellent liberal entertainment."

This report is of great assistance as history records that the Montpelier Club had to leave the Beehive ground when it was sought by builders for development. The club may well have moved out, but the ground was still being used.

There are noticeably less full match reports this season in *The Era* and our club, having moved from the Beehive ground to Kennington Oval, do not feature until well into the season. It is also the first year that the newly formed Surrey county team played their home matches at The Oval.

May 17th - Under a title of "The Surrey Club" it is reported "The committee held a meeting on Wednesday evening at the Oval, Kennington, the Hon F. Ponsonby in the chair, when the following matches for the season were appointed:

Thurs Aug 27, The Gentlemen of Surrey agst the Montpelier Club".

In the round-up below "The Walworth Union and Kingston Albion Club's play a match on the Beehive Ground, Walworth on Tuesday next."

Jun 7th - *The Era* - Full match report on Surrey v Mitcham at The Oval "in front of a large assemblage of spectators" which saw Surrey post 96 and 168 and the visitors 144 and 9-1. Montpelier's C. Coltson played for Surrey and scored 11 and 2 and Peto scored 0 and 0 for the same eleven.

The Montpelier Club are now scheduled to play their matches at Kennington Oval, but it was an arrangement that would not last long.

In "Matches to Come" is listed: "August 27th; The gentlemen of Surrey against The Montpelier Club. At the Oval."

Jun 21st - There are many university match reports but in amongst them is a full match report on Clapton v Montpelier - "This match was played at Clapton on Tuesday, and it being one day's play, the Clapton won by 40 runs on the first innings. The bowling on the part of the Montpelier Club was very good, but in consequence of the hardness of the ground and the pace of the bowling the byes were numerous." The home team scored 98 and Montpelier just 58 and in the second innings Clapton scored 53-2.

Jun 28th - Full match report for South London Club v Montpelier game - "A match was played at The Oval on the Surrey Cricket Ground, Kennington on Wednesday last between these two powerful provincial clubs, and after a display of good batting ended in favour of the South London by 19 runs …." South London scored 161 and Montpelier 142.

In the round-up below is "The Surrey club will play a match with the Montpelier Club on the Surrey Ground, Kennington Oval on Thursday next." Here is a case of the new playing the old, and at a ground that was home to both.

Jul 5th - "Beehive Club - an interesting match was played on the Wednesday last on the Ipswich ground, between eleven married and eleven single gentlemen of the Bee Hive Club, which terminated in favour of the Benedict's with two wickets to go down. There was a large display of beauty and fashion on the ground, comprising most of the elite of the neighbourhood." The Single's scored 71 and 24 and the Married's 66 and 30.

On March 31st 1839 the newspaper had reported "Starling was landlord (of *The Beehive* pub) from 1833 until his death in April 1835, whereupon the license passed to his wife Catherine, who held it until October. George Sousidison then held it until November 14th, whereupon it passed to William Carter." Isaac Bryant took over the licence in July 1842 and remained landlord until the Montpelier's lease was terminated." Ipswich must therefore be the name of the new lease-holder for *The Beehive* pub.

The newspaper continues "The Surrey and Montpelier Club's played a match on the Surrey ground, Kennington Oval on Thursday last. Score Montpelier 197 and Surrey 103-3."

In the round-up is reported "Montpelier and Clapton Club's, these club's will play their annual match on the Surrey ground, Kennington Oval on Thursday next, when an excellent match is expected to take place, as each club will play to their strengths. The Montpelier players are listed as: W. Baker, G. Barton, C. Coltson, A. Earnshaw, W. Foulds, H. Gardner, N. Garland, T. Mill, C. H. Hoare, T. C. Lewis, J. Spenceley."

This week's reports are the most varied and detailed appertaining to local clubs that have appeared in the newspaper before and are valuable in establishing where each club was playing this season.

Jul 5th - *The Era* - Full match report South London v Harrow Town "This match was played on Tuesday at the Beehive Ground, Walworth and was the means of bringing forth some very fine play on the part of Mr Long, the Hon. R. Grimston and Mr Commerell, on the Harrow side and by Mr Hinkley on behalf of the South London. Scores; Harrow 121 and 83, South London 48." T. Lewis played for South London and scored 3 and E. Garland played for the same eleven and scored 9.

Jul 12th - There is an advert for Marylebone v Surrey at Lord's "tomorrow and Tuesday" which lists the Surrey eleven as W. Baker, C Coltson, N. Felix, A. M. Hoare, T. Lewis, W. Pickering, W. Strahan, Hayley, Brockwell, Ilay and Sewell. Baker, Coltson and Lewis are familiar Montpelier players.

Baker, Coltson and Lewis played at Lord's for Surrey and then at The Oval for Montpelier respectively in the space of a week. Coltson also managed to play for the Gentlemen against the Players at Lord's which commenced "on the 20th inst".

There is a full match report on Hartley Row v Montpelier at Hartley Row "on Tuesday last, the Montpelier Club bearing off the honours by 51 runs." The home team scored 47 and Montpelier 98. There another full match report on Montpelier v Clapton played at the Oval "on Thursday last, Clapton proving victorious by 12 runs." Clapton scored 116 and the home team 104.

Jul 12 - *The Era* - Full match report on Surrey v Montpelier "A match between these two clubs was played on the Surrey ground, on Thursday the 2nd inst. The following was the result; Montpelier 197, Surrey 103."

Full match report on Montpelier v Upper Clapton "A match was played at the Surrey Cricket Ground, on Thursday last, the 9th inst, between the above clubs. The following is the score: Upper Clapton 116 (five wickets for Garland, four for Lewis and one for Hoare) and Montpelier 104."

In the round-up is "A match will be played on the Surrey Cricket Ground, Kennington-oval on Wednesday next, the 15th inst. between the Montpelier Club and Islington Albion Club."

Jul 19th - *The Era* - Full match report and large detailed report (see next page) on Montpelier v Islington Albion at Kennington Oval "Wednesday last" which saw the home team score 88 and the visitors 168.

Jul 26th - Under the heading "Further matches to come" it is reported "The West London and Charlton Club's play a match on the Beehive, Walworth on Thursday next. A good day's play may be expected, as the gentlemen are well known to the cricketing world as first-raters."

It is interesting to see from the above report that the Beehive ground was still staging matches and was made available to teams from well outside the local area.

Aug 9th - There are adverts for Montpelier v Enfield on Monday August 17th and v Chertsey on Monday August 24th, both to be played at The Oval and Kent v South London Club Monday August 24th to be played at Canterbury.

Aug 16th - *The Era* - In the same column as the full match reports is an advert for a forthcoming match: "A match will be played at the Surrey Cricket ground, Kennington Oval, on Monday, August 17th 1846 between the Montpelier and the Enfield Club." The Montpelier Club is listed as; W. Baker, C. Coltson, H. Gardner, H. Garrett, C.H. Hoare, T.C. Lewis, J. Peto, F. Saggers, J. Spenceley, C. White and J. Wood.

ISLINGTON ALBION v. THE MONTPELIER CLUB.

This excellent match was played on Wednesday last, on the Surrey Ground, Kennington Oval, and there not being time to play out the first innings, it was considered a drawn match, though it must be very evident upon reference to the score, that the Albion gentlemen were in the ascendant. We must put in our veto against losing so much time in one day matches, and here is an instance in point. Several gentlemen on the Montpelier side were not ready to go in when called, one taking fully twelve minutes before he appeared at the wicket. True it is that by the laws of the game, a wicket can be claimed after two minutes have elapsed; but in what is termed a friendly match, such a proceeding would be misplaced, and we believe in this case, was offered, and very properly refused; at the same time we think that when a match is played for the sake of gentlemanly amusement, and a friendly trial of skill, no impediment that can well be avoided, should be allowed to exist. The Albion commenced their innings by placing Mr. Goldham and Paul, at the wickets, the latter of whom scored four threes, five twos, and singles to the amount of 23, but was at length caught by Mr. Lewis, off his own bowling. Mr. Goldham also contributing 9 runs, when he was caught by Mr. White, off Mr. Garland, who, by the way, we consider to be one of our very fastest bowlers, as regards the rate of delivery from the hand. Mr. Anthony Gibson soon appeared, and was hitting very finely, when a change of bowling was tried, and Mr. Gardner came on, but without staying the progress of the score, until after obtaining a four, five threes, a two, and singles to the amount of 28, Mr. Gibson was caught by Mr. Lewis off his own bowling. Mr. Rogers then came in, and hit the ball away for fives, fours, and threes, and Mr. Mackworth on assuming the bat played in a very scientific manner, and quickly added seven to the general account, when he was bowled by Mr. Garland. Mr. Luckhurst was run out for 2, and Mr. Garland, at this period, resumed bowling, Mr. Thompson bringing in his bat, and resisting the bowling, until Mr. Lewis dismissed him with six appended to his name. Mr. Alfred Gibson now wielded the willow, and effected ten runs, when Mr. Gardner found his wicket, and he was replaced by Mr. Dewdney, who was not long in obtaining 13 runs, and that in very good style. Another change was now made in the bowling, Mr.

Lewis being withdrawn, and Mr. Garland put on, and not without effect, for he shortly took Mr. Rogers's wicket, though not before, by dint of determined and yet cautious hitting, he had obtained 43 runs, without giving a palpable chance. Mr. Cox now appeared, and hitting Mr. Gardner to the leg for four, the ball was overthrown, and a seven was scored in consequence, which, with three singles, gave him 10 runs, when he was caught by Mr. Challis off Mr. Lewis, and succeeded by Mr. Hillyer, who had only time to make a fine leg hit for four, when Mr. Dewdney was bowled by Mr. C. Orr, the Albion having thus obtained 168 runs.

On the part of the Montpelier, Messrs. Gardner, Spencely, C. Orr, and White obtained good scores, but the bowling of Paul and Mr. Luckhurst was too good to make much off it. Time, too, pressed hard, and owing, partly to the circumstance we have alluded to at the commencement of our observations, the game was put an end to, the Montpelier having obtained 88 runs, with two wickets to go down, with which they required to obtain 81 runs to win. Press of matter precludes a more extended notice of this match, but we cannot conclude without awarding much praise to the fielding of both parties, which was animated, and all but faultless. We trust the remarks we have felt called upon to make may be taken in the proper spirit, inasmuch as they are induced by a desire to promote the kind and gentlemanly feeling that ought to characterize our favourite game, and promote its interests to the extent of our ability.

Aug 23rd - *The Era* - Full match report on South London v Putney Clarence - "This match was played at the Beehive, on Tuesday. Scores as follows: South London 121 and 11-4 and Putney 52." In the South London eleven were Montpelier players E. Garland and Lewis.

Below this is an advert for Kent v South London to be played at Canterbury next Monday and Tuesday and in the South London team are; E. Garland, W. Garland, T.C. Courtenay (T. C. Lewis) and C. H. Hoare. Clear evidence then, as if any more was needed that some players played for a variety of teams in the locality. C. H. Hoare would later captain the Surrey County eleven.

Aug 30th - There is a brief match report on Montpelier v Chertsey played at The Oval "on Monday last" which saw the hosts score 57 and the visitors 86.

Under the heading "Further matches to come" is "The Montpelier and West Hackney Club's play a match on the Surrey Ground, Kennington Oval on Wednesday next."

Aug 30th - *The Era* - Full match report on Montpelier v Enfield - "On the 17th inst., a match was played on the Surrey Cricket Ground, Kennington-oval, between the Montpelier Club and the Enfield Club. Scores Montpelier 164 (C.H. Hoare 21, Lewis 1, Saggers 3 and Coltson 0) and Enfield 37."

Full match report on Montpelier v Chertsey - A match was played on the Surrey Cricket Ground, Kennington-oval August 24th, between the Montpelier and Chertsey Clubs. Scores Chertsey 86 and 26-5 and Montpelier 57."

In the round-up is "A match will be played on the Surrey Cricket Ground, Kennington-oval between the Montpelier Club and the West Hackney Club." However the newspaper fails to include a date for this forthcoming match!

Sep 6th - Full match report from the Copenhagen ground which saw Islington Albion beat Montpelier by 125 runs to 80. The newspaper noted "The Albion have not lost a single match either in their first or second eleven contests, although they have played some very strong clubs including Bishop Stortford, Rickling, Montpelier, the Guard & c, & c ..."

In the round-up "Montpelier and West Hackney Clubs, a match was played on the Surrey Ground, Kennington Oval on Wednesday last between the above clubs. Scores, West Hackney 65 and 52-8 total 117, Montpelier 172 (G Yates 60)."

Sep 6th - *The Era* - Full match report on Islington Albion v Montpelier - "The return match between these two clubs was played at Copenhagen House, on Monday last, when after some very excellent play, the Albion gentlemen were victorious. It is somewhat singular, that during the whole season, the Albion have not lost a single match … we subjoin the score of Monday's match: Islington Albion 125 and Montpelier 80 (Lewis 28)."

Sep 13th - *The Era* - In the "Matches to Come" column is: "Sept 16th Islington Albion v South London Club at the Beehive, Walworth and Sept 21st Twenty-two Gentlemen and Players, for a Gold Cup, and two other prizes at the Beehive, Walworth." Therefore this famous local ground was still available for use for proper matches.

Sep 20th - Under "Further matches to come" is "The Montpelier Club will play their final match this season on Wednesday next, at the Surrey ground, Kennington Oval, on which occasion the first eleven will play against the next twenty members."

It is re-assuring to read that despite their forced move to The Oval, the club still has strength in numbers.

Sep 27th - "On Thursday next a grand match will be played at the Beehive ground, Walworth between two elevens selected from the Gentlemen Players of the Surrey, Montpelier and South London Club's and will include some of the finest batsmen in the county - being the last match of the season."

Although the club are now playing at Kennington Oval, there is no surprise to find that they still have impressive fixtures and are clearly still a force to be reckoned with.

Oct 4th - *The Era* - Full match report on The Gentlemen v The Players "at the Beehive last Thursday" for the benefit of Mortlock "one of the Surrey umpires." The Gentleman scored 135 and the Players recorded 35 and the former included the familiar names of C. Hoare, E. Garland and J. Spenceley from the Montpelier Club.

1847

Montgomery's book gives some interesting comments about this season; "Mr. Burrup, who became Secretary in 1847, saw that the only way to save the ground was to get rid of the proprietor, Mr. Houghton. But how could this be done if Houghton was unwilling to depart? Mr. Burrup brought forward and carried a motion that the Club should play no matches at all upon the Oval: and then Houghton was driven to part with his right to the field. The lease then fell into the hands of the Surrey Club who have kept it ever since. The new lease given to the Club was granted by the Duchy of Cornwall in the names of C.H. Hoare, A. Marshall and H. Marshall, for a term of 7,14 or 21 years. The arrangements in those early days were, that players were paid £3 a match if they were beaten, and £4 if they won. Entrance to the ground was never more than 6d."

May 2nd - The newspaper reports with regards to the Surrey Club that "a general meeting of this influential club was held at the Oval, Kennington on Wednesday last and numerously attended .... their finances were not so flourishing a condition as could be wished, but their prospects were most cheering...."

In the round-up is "The Montpelier and Dorking clubs play a match on Friday the 14th inst. at Kennington Oval." which although very brief does tell us where the Montpelier were playing their home matches.

May 9th - "The South London Club commenced playing for the first time this season at Kennington Oval, on Thursday last, which event was celebrated by the members afterwards dining together. The secretary announced that the funds of the club were in prosperous condition, and there was every hope of their having a brilliant season, as several matches were already made."

Kennington Oval was therefore home to at least three clubs at this time.

May 16th - "New East Surrey and Blackheath Phoenix - the clubs hitherto playing under these names have now united their force, and will in future play on the Rosemary Branch Ground, Peckham under the name of St George's Camberwell Cricket Club, and meet every Monday and Thursday, at five o'clock. The new club is under the management of Messrs Kiddle (president), Bevington (vice president), Corbett (treasurer) and Northcott (secretary).

This is a very valid report, although it would have been more helpful if it had included a reason for the amalgamation. It was a comprehensive re-naming of these two clubs. The local church, called St George's next to the canal is still there, although the ground is now covered by a large housing estate.

May 23rd - *The Era* - In the round-up is "Montpelier and Dorking - a match was played at Kennington Oval on Friday, the 14th inst between these two clubs, in which, as will be seen by the scores both the batting and bowling of the Montpelier was found too powerful for their opponents. The scores stood as follows; Montpelier 167, Dorking 62 and 34."

May 30th - "Montpelier and Dorking Clubs - the return match between these two clubs came off on Tuesday last, on Cotmonadene, a piece of ground not at all adapted for cricketing purposes, it being so hilly as to prevent many of the fieldsman being seen. Scores Dorking 51 and 57, Montpelier 32 and 64-6. Dorking won on first innings."

May 30th - *The Era* - In the round-up is "Dorking and Montpelier. These clubs played their return match on the Dorking Cricket Ground on Tuesday the 25th inst., when some fine play was witnessed on both sides. The formidable Montpelier club, on this occasion were headed in the first innings by nineteen runs, which is a credit to their youthful opponents … Dorking 51 and 57 and Montpelier 32 and 63."

Jun 6th - "The Gentlemen of Kent and Surrey play a match on Thursday and Friday next, on the grounds of the White Hart Hotel, Bromley. The Surrey team were listed as C. Coltson, W. Denison, B. Driver, A. Earnshaw, E. Estridge, N. Felix, W. Foulds, C. F. Hoare, C. H. Hoare, H. Mortimer and C. Randolph." The first two are linked with the Montpelier Club, Felix should need no introduction and C.H. Hoare was Surrey captain from 1846-50.

Also reported is "South London and Putney, the return match between these will be played at the Oval ground, Kennington on Monday 14th inst.", and "The Montpelier and Hartley Row clubs play a match on Monday and Tuesday the 7th and 8th inst. at Hartley Row" and "Montpelier and Reading, a match between these clubs is fixed to come off on Wednesday the 16th inst. at the Oval ground, Kennington."

Jun 13th - Full match report on Hartley Row v Montpelier which saw the home team score 101 and the visitors 20 and 50, and the newspaper goes on to say "We wish the vanquished better success, for, as the members of the Hartley Club observed, a pleasanter set of cricketers never entered the field."

Jun 20th - Full match and decent length report on King's College v Montpelier on the 12th inst. although as none of the names are at all familiar and the match was played on Blackheath, then it is most likely to be Blackheath Montpelier (who were mentioned in the newspaper on July 27th 1828) and Montpelier v Reading "This match came off on Wednesday last at the Oval Ground,

Kennington but the weather proving so unfavourable for cricket, it raining nearly all day. The Montpelier were unable to finish their innings and the game was in consequence drawn." Scores Reading 100 and Montpelier 70-6.

Jun 27th - Full match report for Montpelier v Harrow at the Oval "This interesting match attracted a goodly muster of spectators to The Oval Ground, Kennington on Thursday last, where some fine play was witnessed." Montpelier scored 167 and the visitors 113-7. Also reported was their match against West Hackney "On Monday last, at the Oval Ground, Kennington the above clubs played a match in which Montpelier came off victorious, scoring in their first innings 140, Challis exhibiting some excellent batting, as did also Lochner, Seymour, Beeman and Yates. Scores West Hackney 71 and 73 total 144, Montpelier 140 and 5-0."

Jul 4th - Under a sub-title of "Montpelier and Richmond" is "The clubs played an excellent match on Wednesday last on Richmond Green, which terminated in favour of Montpelier with seven wickets to go down. The play on both sides was admirable. Montpelier 216 and 51, total 167 (clearly a misprint) and Richmond 65 and 100, total 165."

Jul 11th - "Montpelier and West Hackney - the return match between these two clubs is arranged to be played on the ground of the latter, at Shacklewell, on Wednesday next."

Jul 18th - Full match report on West Hackney v Montpelier played at Shacklewell " … the Montpelier team was very weak, and the bowling against them being good, but few runs could be obtained … the innings amounted to 61. West Hackney then went to the wicket, but the Montpelier fielded extremely well and the innings terminated in a tie. Montpelier again handled the timber, but such was the havoc played with their wickets, that half an hour saw them all out, for a score of only 21."

Below this report is "Reading v Montpelier - played at Reading on Monday last. It was rather a one-sided affair, the Reading club carrying away the laurels in one innings and nine runs to spare. Montpelier 45 and 26, Reading 80."

Jul 25th - Full match report on Montpelier v Richmond played at The Oval "on Wednesday last, the Montpelier proving victorious, the first innings deciding it, as the game was not played out." Montpelier scored 69 and 150-9 and Richmond in their lone innings scored 45.

Jul 25th - *The Era* - In the round-up is "Montpelier v Richmond - the return match was played on Wednesday last, on Kennington Oval, victory declaring in favour of the former. Scores; Richmond 45, Montpelier 69 and 15. It was decided on first innings."

"Montpelier v Hartley Row - a match will be played at Kennington Oval on Wednesday and Thursday next, the 28th and 29th inst.."

Aug 1st - There is a good length report on Hartley Row v Montpelier "This return match was played at the Oval ground, Kennington on Wednesday and Thursday last, and terminated in favour of Hartley Row with three wickets to go down. The game was well contested and it was rendered very interesting from the fact that five or six of the Hartley Row eleven were left-handed players. Montpelier scored 82 and 57, total 139 and the visitors 61 and 79-7, total 140."

Aug 29th - *The Era* - Full match report on Harrow Town v Montpelier played at Harrow on Monday during which "some very fine cricket was exhibited in the course of the game. The Montpelier won the match upon the first innings by 42 runs. The score stood as follows; Montpelier 103 and 41 and Harrow 61." No venue was shown for the match however.

Sep 5th - A match report on South London v Montpelier Club states "This friendly match between the above clubs came off on Thursday last at the Surrey Ground, Kennington Oval which terminated in favour of the Montpelier by 10 runs. It was a well contested game, one innings each only being played." Scores Montpelier 95, South London 85.

Sep 5th - *The Era* - Full match report on Montpelier v South London "This match between the second eleven of these clubs, was played on the Surrey Ground, Kennington-oval on Thursday last, and was decided by the first innings in favour of the Montpelier by 13 runs, the South London playing a man short… Scores: Montpelier 95 and 104-4, South London 82." The Montpelier team was; Houghton, Seymour, Newman, Baker, Burrup, Lambert, Winder, Bennett, Lawson and Driver and from this list they also appear to have been a man short! This is the second report of a Montpelier second eleven match (the first was back in 1840), which again shows the depth of the club. Their opposition is familiar and the venue too.

There have been as many Montpelier matches featured in the newspaper this year as has been the norm since 1843 and they have shown the opposition to still be of a good standard.

Chapter Six

Montpelier Quit Kennington Oval

I had intended to filter into the last chapter three letters published in *The Era* outlining the reasons for the club quitting The Oval. However they are worthy of a chapter to themselves and provide a break from page-upon-page of details gleaned form *Bell's Life* and *The Era.* As mentioned before, the fact that the Montpelier Club left The Oval had been briefly touched upon in books appertaining to the history of Surrey C.C.C. although the clearest reason for this event comes in Montgomery's *The History of Kennington and its Neighbourhood* when he writes "First, the old Montpelier Club suffered. They played matches here for about two years, but Houghton by degrees tried to confine them to one corner of the ground: the result was that they left the Oval and took a ground where Coldharbour Lane now stands."

I feel that the letters are best included verbatim and not edited or otherwise interfered with, as they tell of the events as they occurred and are written in the language of the period. The first letter appeared on May 21st (on page 13) and was written by Montpelier player and Secretary Thomas Lewis and makes the reasons for this move very clear. Unfortunately it is located in the first column, close to the spine of the newspaper and with a whole year's worth of the newspaper bound together, it proved impossible to lay the heavy volume flat on the photocopier.

The letter as could be expected, generated an equally lengthy and severe reply from W. Houghton (of Surrey C.C.C.) during which he casts doubt on the authenticity of the writer. On June 11th a second letter from Thomas Lewis answers Houghton's reply, and again it is another lengthy one and equally as forceful. It is quite possible that these three letters have not been seen before by modern day cricket historians.

THE MONTPELIER CLUB AND THE SURREY CRICKET GROUND.

TO THE EDITOR OF THE ERA.

Sir,—Considerable surprise having been expressed at the secession of the above Club from the ground which they instituted, and various incorrect versions of the circumstances which led to the adoption of that step being in circulation, the members have justly considered it due to their position in the cricketing world thus to place on record a true statement of the case. In making the explanation, they desire to avoid acrimonious comment, their object being less to reprobate the repudiation of engagement by others than to show that a contrary spirit has animated themselves. This will be most effectually done by "a plain, unvarnished tale."

The Montpelier Cricket Club had been in the habit of playing at the Beehive Ground, Walworth, where they had two club nights per week (Tuesdays and Fridays), on which evenings, from four o'clock till dusk, they had the exclusive use of the ground; on other nights they had the privilege of practice in common with other parties.

At the close of the season of 1844 an intimation was received that the ground would be required for building purposes, and that it was a matter of uncertainty whether the season of 1845 could be completed without interruption. In this dilemma the active spirits of the Montpelier Club were instantly upon the look-out for another eligible plot of ground, and one of them obtained information that the Kennington Oval (then a nursery ground) was to be let. Mr. Baker, the Treasurer of the Club, was deputed to make further inquiries, and he ascertained that the ground would not be let to a body of persons, but to an individual only. He at once placed himself in such a position as to secure the first option, and immediately called a Committee Meeting to arrange the best mode of carrying out the desired object. At this period, Mr. Houghton (the present proprietor of the Oval) was the President of the Montpelier Club, in which office he had, throughout a considerable period, deported himself in such a manner as to secure the confidence and respect of all. It being necessary that some one should be forthwith nominated as lessee of the ground, the first proposal was made to Mr. Houghton, as senior officer of the Club, accompanied by offers of considerable pecuniary assistance from certain members, which would, in effect, have made the speculation a joint-stock one. These proposals Mr. Houghton at first entertained, but at the next meeting, after courteously thanking those gentlemen who had come forward, he elected to take the ground as his own private venture, a course which the Club immediately assented to, their object being to secure a good ground, and not pecuniary profit. Mr. Houghton made it a *sine qua non* that the Club should remove to the Oval *instanter*, and not remain at the Beehive for the season of 1845, very fairly insisting that, in an undertaking of such magnitude, it was essential to secure a revenue as early as practicable. To this the club also readily assented, although they feared that the Oval would not be in a condition to play upon, and that they were laying themselves open to a charge of acting unhandsomely in quitting the Beehive Ground *before* it became absolutely imperative to do so. *Mr. Houghton distinctly undertook to secure to* the Montpelier Club upon the Oval, all the privileges they were then enjoying upon the Beehive Ground; they, on their part, undertaking to promote the interests of Mr. Houghton so far as they could do so. In this spirit every member endeavoured to introduce a friend as a subscriber to the Club and ground, and the numbers of the M.C.C. were thus increased from fifty to very nearly one hundred. A sum of £30 was also voted from the Club funds to Mr. Houghton, to enable him to increase the area of turfed ground. In the same season, the project of a County Club was mooted, and a match was got up for the purpose of developing the cricketing talent of Surrey. A sum of about £18 was required to pay the players engaged in this match, which amount was collected by Mr. Baker, the Treasurer of the Montpelier Club, in donations, almost exclusively proceeding from its members. Mr. Houghton, of course, received all the entrance money taken at the gate, besides the money spent in the house and on the ground.

About thirty members of the Montpelier Club also enrolled themselves in the County Club, for the express purpose of affording increased support to Mr Houghton in his new undertaking. In two successive years Mr. Houghton made an application to the Surrey magistrates for a license, in support of which many members of the Club used the most strenuous exertions privately, while the Club, in its collective capacity, lent its aid by a strong memorial.

All went on smoothly until the season of 1847. The Montpelier Club had never asked Mr. Houghton for a written agreement, and herein lies their only subject for regret; they had not demanded it, because his conduct, at present, had always been such as to prevent a suspicion of bad faith. Last season some squabbling took place between Mr. Houghton and one of the members of the M.C.C., owing to the latter having pitched his stumps on a practice night upon the edge of the centre turf, which had, by common consent, been held sacred to matches, but which had been similarly violated by a member of the Surrey Club without reproof or remark. This invasion was occasioned by Mr. Houghton having introduced additional parties upon the ground contrary to covenant, and the made ground being only of limited extent, there was not room to play safely without trenching upon the forbidden centre plot.

This matter having tended to disturb the good understanding previously existing, it was naturally considered that it would be more satisfactory to all parties to have the terms upon which the Montpelier Club used the Surrey Cricket Ground distinctly defined in a written agreement. As a matter of courtesy, it was left to Mr. Houghton to present to the Club what may be termed its new constitution at his convenience, and this he distinctly undertook to do at a winter meeting of the Club in January last, but *failed to redeem his promise*. The heads of the agreement entered into with Mr. Houghton with the Montpelier Cricket Club had been, in the autumn of 1847, reduced to writing, and handed to him, with an intimation that any reasonable modification would be favourably considered, provided that he could show his pecuniary interests to be involved in any desired alteration. Nothing was done on his part until the first week in March, when the Montpelier Cricket Club met to elect their officers, and then he came forward with a string of proposals utterly subversive of every privilege previously enjoyed by the Club, *and depriving them of the exclusive use of the ground on both their Club nights*. Great surprise, mingled with indignation, was naturally felt, and it was communicated to Mr. Houghton that his proposals could not for a moment be entertained. Subsequently. in order, if possible, to accommodate matters, and avoid a rupture, it was intimated to Mr. Houghton that the Committee of the Montpelier Club would meet him in a liberal spirit, and *would concede every point to him but one*, viz, that they must insist upon one independent Club night, with the exclusive use of the ground. This was absolutely indispensable, for, according to Mr. Houghton's plan of allocating the turfed portion of the ground, had another club been playing at the same time, as he proposed, the respective balls would have been continually hit across each other's play, and, possibly, an unpleasant collision would have resulted from it.

Mr. Houghton permitted the Club to commence their season on the first Tuesday in April, and made no communication during the progress of business that evening. On the following Thursday, as the President was leaving the house, a person ran after him and handed him a letter, in which Mr. Houghton coolly expressed his determination "not to enter into any engagement with the Montpelier Club for the present season!" At the next meeting this letter was read, when resolutions were unanimously passed, "That the Club do now adjourn to the Horns' Tavern;" and "That a new ground be forthwith instituted."

The latter resolution has been carried out, and an excellent field engaged in Cold Harbour-lane, Brixton, where play will commence in about three days from this date.

In conclusion, the Montpelier Club do not desire to impute motives, but, they think they may fairly ask their friends whether Mr. Houghton's tactics do not denote "a foregone conclusion," and whether their own overweening confidence has not made them the easy victim of a piece of discreditable jockeyship?

I am, Sir, your obedient servant,

THOMAS COURTENAY LEWIS,

Secretary of the Montpelier Cricket Club.

Horns' Tavern, May 19th, 1848.

THE SURREY CRICKET GROUND AND THE MONTPELIER CLUB.

TO THE EDITOR OF THE ERA.

Sir,—A letter appeared in your paper of Sunday last, signed "Thomas Courtenay Lewis," which professes to give "a plain unvarnished tale." Had it done so, I should not have intruded myself upon your notice; but the facts are so clouded by fictions, that, in justice to myself, I must make a reply. The writer, who, from the style of the composition, is evidently not Mr. Thomas Courtenay Lewis, states that one of their members "obtained information that the Kennington Oval (then a nursery ground) was to be let." That "Mr. Baker, the treasurer of the Club, was deputed to make further inquiries, and he ascertained that the Ground would not be let to a body of persons, but to an individual only." This statement is inaccurate. Mr. Baker was not deputed by the Club to make inquiries, neither did he ascertain that the Ground would not be let to a body of persons, but to an individual only. The simple fact is, that one of the members of the Club, seeing a board in front of the premises stating that they were to be let, called, with Mr. Baker, on the agent, to make inquiries as to rent, &c., and afterwards met three other members of the Club, and myself (the then president), for the purpose of consulting whether it would be practicable for the Club to take it The six members were unanimously of opinion that it would be impracticable for the Club to do so. I then said that if I could obtain the Ground upon proper terms, I would become the lessee. It was not offered to me "as senior officer of the Club." It was an offer on my part as a private speculation. It was never decided to make it a joint-stock speculation, neither did I receive "offers of considerable pecuniary assistance" (though three members offered me a loan of fifty pounds each at interest, which, as stated, I afterwards declined). I never made "it a *sine qua non* that the Club should remove to the Oval instanter." I admit that the Club were to be admitted to the Ground upon the same terms, and to enjoy the same privileges, as they had upon the Beehive Ground—which privileges they enjoyed for three years—but then it was, in both cases, an engagement only from year to year, which, at the end of a season, either the Club or the proprietor of the Ground could terminate. The increase in the number of their members is not to be attributed to their exertions only, but principally to the great advantages the Club derived from the New Ground. The statement that at the match got up to develop the cricketing talent of Surrey I received the money spent in the house and on the ground is also wrong. The house was not then opened as a house of business, and the dinners and refreshments on the Ground were supplied from the Horns Tavern.

It is then stated, that "about thirty members of the Montpelier Club also enrolled themselves in the County Club, for the express purpose of affording increased support to Mr. Houghton in his new undertaking." You, sir, and the public can judge whether such was their object, when I inform you that they stipulated that they should be allowed to join the Surrey Club at ten shillings per year each less than any other member, such ten shillings being the amount paid by the Surrey Club to me for each member; so that I received no direct pecuniary advantage from the members of the Montpelier Club joining the Surrey Club, while they participated in all the advantages the Club afforded.

Again, when the South London Club joined the Ground, the Montpelier did all they could to induce me not to receive them; and such members of the Montpelier Club who were also members of the South London Club, claimed a similar reduction of ten shillings each per annum as I had granted to them in the Surrey Club; and upon my refusing to allow it, they all immediately sent in their resignations to the South London Club. So much for their great professions of patronage and liberality.

The letter also states, "That last season some squabbling took place between Mr. Houghton and one of the members of the M. C. C. (for M. C. C., read Montpelier Club) owing to the latter having pitched his stumps, on a practice night, upon the edge of the centre turf, which had, by common consent, been held sacred to matches." Why lay the blame upon one member, instead of stating the fact that it was three members. Besides which, it was not upon the *edge* of the turf; and the wickets were ~~also~~ placed there for the express purpose of annoying a party of gentlemen who were playing on the ground. It is also stated that I failed to present to the Club my terms for the present season in proper time. That I deny. It was arranged that the terms of an agreement with me should be discussed on the second Tuesday in January. ~~I attended the meeting that night~~ and was prepared with my proposals. Neither the president nor vice-president was present, and no business was transacted. I had previously reminded Mr. Lewis, the secretary, that

~~was placed there for the express purpose of annoying~~ a party of gentlemen who were playing on the ground. It is also stated that I failed to present to the Club my terms for the present season in proper time. That I deny. It was arranged that the terms of an agreement with me should be discussed on the second Tuesday in January. I attended the meeting that night and was prepared with my proposals. Neither the president nor vice-president was present, and no business was transacted. I had previously reminded Mr. Lewis, the secretary, that the discussion was to come on upon that evening, and he replied that he would not have it entered into until he called a general meeting. It is, therefore, his fault that the Club was not earlier in possession of my proposals, and if there was any jockeyship it was on his part and not on mine.

At that general meeting I presented my proposition, which was so liberal in its nature that I am now very glad the Club did not accept it. That I permitted a few members of the Club to practise on the Ground on the first Tuesday in April, was a mere matter of courtesy on my part; and afterwards finding that it was not likely that any engagement could be made and carried out to our mutual satisfaction, and knowing that some in authority in the Club had said that if they agreed to my proposals they would play no matches on the ground, that they would not have any refreshments from the house, and having experienced a course of overbearing and ungentlemanly treatment from some of their members, I deemed it quite time to put an end to a connexion which could only be continued to my injury and serious loss—to the injury of the Surrey County Club, and the practice of cricket on this ground; I, therefore, declined to enter into any engagement with them. I trust I have shown that the Montpelier Club did not institute the Ground—that they have not seceded from it—but that I have declined to receive them in consequence of the annoyances to which I have been subjected, and that I have honourably fulfilled all my engagements with them.

I have the honour to be, sir, your obedient servant,

William Houghton.

Surrey Cricket Ground, Oval, Kennington,
May 26th, 1848.

CRICKET GROUND.

TO THE EDITOR OF THE ERA.

Sir,—I am so well aware that you can employ your columns more profitably than in perpetuating this controversy, that I should have hesitated to intrude further upon your space, had not Mr. Houghton been so imprudent and unmannerly as to impugn my veracity. This leaves me no other course to pursue than to join issue with him, and I adopt it with alacrity.

Mr. Houghton tries hard to "make the worse appear the better reason." His reply is an odd compound of sophistry and swagger—he attempts a tone of confidence, but it sits uneasily upon him, and he continually subsides into characteristic casuistry. He doubts his powers of bravado, and finally tries the effect of an *ad misericordiam* appeal. When ingratitude is exposed, no artifice is more common than for the injurer to assume the character of the injured. The stale device shall not succeed in this instance.

Mr. Houghton charges me with deliberately "clouding my facts with fictions," in other words, with designedly manufacturing falsehoods; he must not complain, therefore, if he finds this communication still less palatable than he did my former one, in which I strove to publish truth untarnished by personality or vituperation. I throw back his imputation with scorn, and it shall go hard but I will show who is veracious, and who is not.

Mr. Houghton is naturally anxious to prove that the Montpelier Club did *not* institute the ground of which they blindly made him the master—he asserts that the gentleman who first obtained his information that the Oval was to be let, derived such knowledge from a board publicly exhibited. I have referred to this gentleman. Hear what he says—"I repeat, that I derived my information from a private source, and the board was not put up until the lapse of several days. Feeling that, in such a matter, caution and privacy were desirable, I consulted two or three only of the leading members of the Club, and *Mr. Houghton, at that time, was in ignorance of the project.*" Now for Mr. Baker's statement on this point.

"Immediately that the party had obtained the information, he called upon me, and we, on behalf of the Montpelier Club, had an interview with the surveyor. At that meeting nothing could be done, as Mr. Vigors was in treaty for the place to build upon; but, at a subsequent interview, *we got the refusal of the ground in my name for the Montpelier Club.* We then immediately set about getting a few influential members together at the Horns Tavern. Amongst others, Mr. Houghton (as President of the Club) was invited to attend. At that preliminary meeting the facts produced proved that the ground was as good as engaged by the Montpelier Club, and a debate ensued whether it would be better to make it a joint-stock affair, or whether an individual member of the Club should become lessee. The latter course was considered the preferable one, and pecuniary assistance to the amount of £300 was guaranteed to any member who would come forward in that capacity. Mr. H. then said that, upon these conditions, he would take the ground. There were other members present who were ready to occupy that position; but, as Mr. Houghton had made the first offer, they did not interfere. Mr. H. then put himself in communication with the surveyor, *who refused to have anything to do with him until released from his engagement to me;* whereupon Mr. H. came directly to my place of business, and induced me to go with and introduce him as the party selected by the Montpelier Club to take the ground.

I think these facts, "*un*clouded by fiction," are sufficient to convince any impartial mind, that the Montpelier Club *did* originate or institute the Surrey cricket ground."

All this Mr. Houghton must well recollect, were he disposed to do so; but I fear that he is one of the *non mi ricordo* genus, the crafty class who take refuge in a conveniently defective memory.

The first part of Mr. Houghton's reply is a series of verbal quibbles. For example—"Mr. Baker was not *deputed by* the Club," the real question being whether he was acting *for* the Club, and whether he did not secure the refusal of the ground. I pass over the evasions, and come to what looks like a bold assertion, although I am half inclined to suspect that, in this instance, he is only questioning words, and not facts," He says, "I never made it a *sine qua non* that the Club should remove to the Oval *instanter.*" In rejoinder to this, I assert that, at a special general meeting, held January 28th, 1845, after thanking the members present for their kindness, he called upon them to use their influence to induce the Club to remove to the Oval *in the ensuing season*, promising that the Ground should be fit for their reception, and offering to confirm all their then existing privileges without any reservation. Mr. Houghton now condescends to a miserable shuffle, and says that the agreement was only from year to year. In the absence of a written contract we must reason upon probabilities; and I ask whether it is at all likely that the Montpelier Club would have placed Mr. Houghton as lessee of the Oval, would have offered him loans of money, would have given him £30 towards the formation of his Ground, would have subscribed £18 to pay the expenses of his first match, would have laboured earnestly to procure him a license, if they had imagined that he possessed, *or desired to possess*, the power of turning them off the Ground of their own creation at the end of the very first season, or whenever he thought proper to take advantage of their *laches* in not binding him by black and white?

I come now to another quibble, which I notice only to show how consistently an accusation of "clouding by fiction" comes from Mr. Houghton, and how hardly driven he is to make out a case. He says, referring to the first match, "The statement that I received the money spent in the house, and on the ground, is also wrong. The dinners and refreshments were supplied from the Horns Tavern." He suppresses the fact that he received a commission from the proprietor of the Horns, and says nothing about the money taken at the gate, nor the £18 which we raised for him.

I asserted in my former letter, and I now repeat, that about thirty members of the Montpelier Club enrolled themselves in the County Club, for the express purpose of affording increased support to Mr. Houghton in his new undertaking. Upon this Mr. Houghton remarks, "You, Sir, and the public can judge whether such was their object, when I inform you that they stipulated that they should be allowed to join the Surrey Club at 10s per year less than any other member, so that I received no direct pecuniary advantage from the members of the Montpelier Club joining the Surrey Club." Now, what confidence can be placed in Mr. Houghton's statements, when I declare that *the proposition emanated from himself*, and that I have now lying before me a circular of his to that effect? He says that he "derived no *direct* pecuniary benefit." Did Mr. Houghton never hear of "giving a sprat to catch a herring?" What became of the 30s which each member of the Montpelier Club *did* pay to the funds of the Surrey Club? What are the resources of Cricket Clubs expended upon but matches for the benefit of the grounds to which they are attached? Mr. Houghton well knew the importance of the Montpelier Club to him in forming the nucleus of a county club, although it now suits his tactics to disavow it.

Mr. Houghton has thought proper to drag the South London Club most unnecessarily into the controversy, with the gentlemanly object of embroiling the Montpelier Club with that Society, and at the same time currying favour with the latter. Here is another instance of his shifty policy. In the early part of 1845, I was a member of the South London Club, and attended a meeting at which it was proposed to remove to the Oval, a step which I opposed, simply because I knew that there was not accommodation for them. I received Mr. Houghton's thanks for the part I took; and he subsequently, on several occasions, assured me *that he should decline to receive that Club upon his ground!* Let them look to their position, and secure it.

Mr. Houghton pretends to deny that he failed to present his proposals at the period agreed upon. Let me refresh his debilitated memory upon this point. He says that he had reminded me prior to the second Tuesday in January, that the discussion was to come on upon that evening. This is not true. Mr. Houghton never mentioned his proposals until about a week before I called the ordinary general meeting in March, when he asked my private opinion upon them, which I had no difficulty in at once delivering, to the effect that I considered some arbitrary, others silly, and the whole perfectly inadmissible. I beg to remind Mr. Houghton that, as stated in my former letter, an agreement was presented to him by the Vice-President in December last, with an intimation that any reasonable modifications would be favourably considered. He undertook to return this agreement with his remarks, on the second Tuesday in January, *but this he failed to do.* If, as he states, he was prepared with a draft of his own, and meant to act candidly, ought he not to have shown them to me on that day, and so have given me an opportunity of calling a special general meeting, which I undoubtedly should have done, seeing that the interests of the Club were so seriously compromised? The "simple fact" (as Mr. Houghton says) is, that it suited him to keep his proposals *in petto.* He knew that they never would be accepted, and proves, in his letter, that I was right in saying that his tactics denoted "a foregone conclusion," by admitting that he had made up his mind to "to put an end to the connexion." In the same spirit he pocketed all his grievances, that they might serve at a future time as plausible pleas to cover his contemplated treachery to the Montpelier Club.

He says that his proposition "was so liberal in its nature, that he is now glad the Club did not accept it." This is rich—"the force of" impudence "can no further go." The Club had previously enjoyed two club nights per week, with the exclusive use of the Ground. Mr. Houghton's proposition went to deprive them of the exclusive use of the Ground on *both* nights, besides other arbitrary and absurd alterations. Verily Mr. Houghton's liberality is like his gratitude, so attenuated as to be visible to nobody but himself.

The pharisaical self-complacency with which Mr. Houghton winds up his effusion is highly diverting. He "trusts" that he has achieved the impracticsble feat attempted by the old ladies in the fable, when they tried their soap upon the blackamoor, and if he can still think so I shall not seek further to disturb his comfortable conceit. He says that the Montpelier Club did not secede from the Oval Ground, from which it is intended that the public should infer that he subjected them to the indignity of a dismissal. Here the honorable gentleman attempts to prove too much for his own reputation. He blinks the acceptance of the £30 towards making his ground, but he is anxious to have it believed that he kicked the donors. He asserts that he was subjected to "ungentlemanly and overbearing conduct," if so, why do we hear of it now for the first time? Why was no appeal or remonstrance made? There were many gentlemen in the Club as warm friends of Mr. Houghton as of peace and order. If there were any truth in the accusation, was it just, silently to sacrifice his friends for the thoughtless *escapades* of the young and the *fast?* It is, evidently, a mere pretext, and were it not so, it affords no justification to Mr. Houghton in taking advantage of the non-existence of a written contract to quibble away his engagements with us, or in kicking down the ladder which raised him, the moment he fancied that it would answer his purpose to do so.

I now take my leave of the disagreeable subject, and have only to offer my apologies for having been so diffuse.

I am, Sir, your obedient servant,

THOMAS COURTENAY LEWIS.

Secretary of the Montpelier Club.

Montpelier Club-room, Brixton, 1st June, 1848.

Chapter Seven

Bell's Life and *The Era* Match Reports

(1848-58)

1848

This season witnessed the club move from Kennington Oval to a new ground in Coldharbour Lane, Brixton, a few miles south. The ground was called the Royal Veteran ground and also the Royal Victoria ground, so perhaps there was a Royal Victoria pub in the road and close to the ground? No reason for this move appears in the newspaper, although there are brief reasons given as to why this occurred in other books about Surrey C.C.C..

Apr 30th - "South London Club - the first day's play and opening dinner of the season will take place on Thursday next at the Kennington Oval Ground."

May 21st - "Montpelier Club - The members for this excellent club open their new ground in Cold Harbour lane, Brixton, on Tuesday next, with a day's play. They have engaged Hinkley for the season as their bowler."

May 28th - "Montpelier Club - The members for this club opened their season on Tuesday last, on their new ground, Cold Harbour lane, where forty sat down to dinner. They are now quite ready to meet any of their old opponents in the field" Above this report was mention of Surrey to play Blackheath "Dartmouth" Club "on the Oval, Ground, Kennington on Tuesday next."

From the previous report we can see that although the club's tenure at Kennington Oval is now finished, they are still keen to retain their regular fixtures.

May 28th - *The Era* - In the same week as Houghton's reply the round-up section reported "Montpelier - Tuesday last was the first field day of the above, on which occasion, there was a good muster of the members and some excellent play, after which forty of the members sat down to dinner at the Horn's Tavern, Kennington and passed a very pleasant evening. The club will be very happy to hear from any of their old opponents. Any letters addressed to the secretary, either at the Royal Veterans, Cold Harbour-lane, Brixton, or the Horn's, Kennington will receive immediate attestation."

This is a worthy report as it shows that the club now use *The Horns* pub for their meals instead of *The Beehive* (see report dated May 12th 1844) and that they can be contacted at either of two addresses.

Jun 4th - *The Era* - In the round-up is "Montpelier Club - this club met for a half-day's practice at their new ground, in the Brixton road, on Tuesday. The play was not of the character to call for the especial notice or critical mark. The ground is now in excellent condition, and the arrangements for several very interesting matches are all but completed." The club's new ground, although described as "in the Brixton road" was in Coldharbour Lane, although it does lead to Brixton.

Jun 18th - *The Era* - In the round-up is "Montpelier - the above club play the Dorking club at Dorking, on Monday June 19th, the Bramshill Club at Bramshill on Monday June 26th, and the Chertsey club, at Chertsey on Monday July 3rd."

There is also a full match report on Surrey v Marylebone at the Oval "on Thursday and Friday last" and C. Coltson scored 0 and 4 for Surrey.

Jun 25th - "Montpelier and Chertsey - a match will be played on Garrard's ground, Chertsey Bridge on Monday July 3rd, between the Montpelier Club (with Hinkley) and Chertsey (with Chester)."

Jun 25th - *The Era* - In the round-up is "Montpelier v Dorking - this match commenced on the new cricket ground, Dorking, on Monday last, but, owing to the unfavourable state of the weather, there was not time to play it out. The play on both sides was excellent, and the following was the score; Montpelier 53 and 25 … Dorking 35 and 33-3"

Jul 2nd - There is a full match report on Bramshill v Montpelier played in the grounds of Sir John Cope which resulted in an easy win for Montpelier (see next page).

Jul 2nd - *The Era* - In the round-up is "The Montpelier v Bramshill, these clubs met on Monday last in the beautiful park of Sir John Cope, Bart. A prettier spot or a more existite piece of turf it would be impossible to find. The match was too unequal to be highly interesting. Some good play was exhibited …. Bramshill 23 and 44 and Montpelier 137 (H. Gardner 56)."

July 2nd 1848

THE MONTPELIER AND BRAMSHILL CLUBS.

This match was played on Monday last, in the park of Sir John Cope, Bart. A more delightful locality for the game is not to be found in England; and the gentlemen of the Montpelier were no less gratified by the beauties of the spot than they were by the urbanity of their honourable opponents. The game, as will be seen by the subjoined score, was rather too much on one side to be very interesting. Mr Parfett's *à la* Clarke bowling, which proved teazing and effective on a former occasion, was now patiently met and successfully played. Hinckley's bowling on the Montpelier side was deservedly admired, as was the first-rate batting of Mr. Gardner. The best bats of the Bramshill were unlucky on this occasion. In the return match the chances are that we shall have a stronger taste of their quality. Score:

BRAMSHILL.	1st inn		2d inn
May, Esq, b Hinckley	0	st Driver, b Lewis	5
Wombwell, Esq, run out	2	not out	7
Lord Paget, b Gardner	1	b Hinkley	0
Payne, c Gardner, b Hinkley	2	c Saggers, b Lewis	4
F. Paul, b Hinkley	0	run out	2
Capt Parry, hit w, b Gardner	2	b Lewis	8
Waterer, b Hinkley	3	b Lewis	4
White, not out	10	b Hinkley	7
Sir H. Mildmay, c Saggers, b Hinkley	0	b Lewis	7
Mildmay, Esq, b Hinkley	0	c and b Lewis	0
Parfett, Esq, b Hinkley	0	st Driver, b Hinckley	0
Byes	8	byes	0
Total	—23	Total	—44

MONTPELIER.

B. Driver, Esq, b Waterer	17	C. Beman, Esq, c Payne, b Parfett	[illegible]
A. Earnshaw, Esq, b Parfett	4	J. Pete, Esq, b White	[illegible]
F. Saggers, Esq, c Sir H. Mildmay, b Parfett	0	J. Hurrup, Esq b White	[illegible]
H. Gardner, Esq, b Waterer	56	W. Baker, Esq, not out	[illegible]
J. Spencer, Esq, run out	0	Byes 2, wide balls (Waterer) 7	[illegible]
Hinkley, b Waterer	16		
T. C. Lewis, Esq, b Waterer	0	Total	137

Jul 9th - "Montpelier and Chertsey - these clubs met on Monday last at Chertsey, but owing to the unfavourable state of the weather, only one innings on each side was played. The very slow bowling of Mr J Moir sorely tried the patience of the Montpelier players, although they proved the victors. Montpelier 91, Chertsey 56. …. On Wednesday the 19th inst, the Montpelier play the return match with the Dorking club on the Montpelier Ground, Cold Harbour lane, Brixton and on

Wednesday the 26th play a match with the Croydon Clarence Club also on the Montpelier ground."

Jul 9th - *The Era* - In the round-up is "Montpelier v Chertsey. This match came off at Chertsey on Monday last. The weather was most unpropitious, and only one innings could be played on each side. The slow bowling of Mr J. More was at once puzzling and annoying. Some people would say that it is courtesy to call it cricket, but with the Marylebone Club patronizing the style, we most naturally expect to find imitators throughout the country … the following is the score; Montpelier 91 (Coltson 23) and Chertsey 56." It is a shame that the newspaper did not elaborate on Mr More's style of bowling, which so offended their reporter.

Jul 23 - *The Era* - In the round-up is "Return match. Montpelier v Dorking - the clubs contended on Wednesday, when the play on both sides was of a superior kind, and gave great satisfaction. Scores; Dorking 52 and 41, Montpelier 62."

Jul 30th - *The Era* - In the round-up is "Montpelier v Croydon Clarence, in consequence of the very unfavourable state of the weather on Tuesday and Wednesday last …. play was not proceeded with sufficiently to require especial remark."

Jul 30th - In the round-up is "Montpelier v Croydon Clarence, in consequence of the very unfavourable state of the weather on Tuesday and Wednesday last …. play was not proceeded with sufficiently to require especial remark."

Aug 6th - "Montpelier and Croydon Clarence - this return match will not take place on the 9th inst but on Wednesday, the 23rd inst, owing to the Montpelier gentlemen having engagements with other clubs to attend to.

Aug 13th - There is a detailed match report on Peckham v Montpelier, the first ever match between these two clubs which was played on Peckham Rye (see next page).

Aug 13th - *The Era* - Full match report and long report on the Surrey v England match played at the Oval on August 7th which saw the home team score 131 and 76-5 (C. Coltson 17 and 6) and England score 129 and 77.

Under "Further matches to come" is "Surrey Paragons (their first mention in the newspaper) and St Bartholomew Clubs play a match on the Surrey Ground, Kennington Oval on Tuesday next."

Aug 13 1846

PECKHAM v MONTPELIER.

The first match between the above clubs was played on Peckham Rye, on Saturday, the 5th inst, when the former, by the first innings (it being but a one day's match), proved the victors, owing to the excellent slow bowling of J. Andrews, Esq, who contributed to the taking of fifteen wickets; nor must we forget to mention the bowling of — Peto, Esq, on behalf of Montpelier. The batting on the side of the Peckhamites by Messrs T. Morris, P. Spurling, W. Fry, and N. Morris, was much admired; as also of their opponents Messrs B. Driver, Teats, and Peto. The score stood thus when time was called: Montpelier 63 and 67—total 129; Saggers Esq marked 7 and 7, Powell Esq 9 and 7, B. Driver Esq 33 and 0, Beman Esq 0 and (not out) 4, Baker Esq 0 and 9, Howell Esq 5 and 0, Peto Esq 2 and 12, Prettyman Esq (not out) 1 and 3, J. Teats Esq (absent) 0 and 18, &c; byes &c 1 and 5. Peckham first innings 99; T. Morris Esq scored 38, P. Spurling Esq 15, W. Fry Esq 10, N. Morris Esq 6, Jaman 8, &c; byes &c 14.

Aug 20th - "Montpelier and Croydon Clarence - on Wednesday next a match will be played on the Fairfield Ground, Croydon, between the Montpelier and Croydon Clarence Clubs commencing at ten o'clock."

Aug 20th - *The Era* - In the round-up is "Montpelier v Bramshill - this match was played on Thursday, at Bramshill, and the following is the score; Montpelier 96 and 25, Bramshill 70."

Aug 27th - *The Era* - In the round-up is "Montpelier and Croydon Clubs - the return match between the above parties was played on Wednesday, at Croydon. Montpelier who went in first scored 111. Against this, Croydon set in 72. The ground was discontinued before seven, at which time three wickets of the Montpelier were down for an additional eight runs."

Sep 3rd - "The Montpelier and Peckham Rye clubs play a match on Saturday the 16th inst at Brixton", and "The Montpelier and Wimbledon Clubs play their return match on Thursday next at Brixton." Two lines below the latter report is "Wimbledon Clarence and Montpelier Brixton clubs play their return match on the Royal Victoria Ground, Brixton, on Thursday next." (On July 28th 1839 the ground was referred to as the Royal Veteran's Ground" - perhaps it was re-named a few years after the accession of Queen Victoria?

It is interesting to note in the above report that the club are now being referred to as Montpelier Brixton.

Sep 10th - "Montpelier v Wimbledon "This return match was played at Brixton on Thursday last, when it was decided by the first innings in favour of Montpelier, there not being enough time to play it out. Scores: Montpelier 88 and 83, total 171 (with five wickets to go down), Wimbledon 46."

There is not as much of local interest reported as in previous years, and there is no mention of the St George's Club, Camberwell; the re-named New East Surrey Club. There is no mention either of the Beehive ground, and less of the Montpelier Club, although they do feature often in *The Era* newspaper. It is interesting however to note that the Oval is used by a variety of teams.

Sep 10th - *The Era* - In the round-up is "Montpelier v Wimbledon - the return match was played on Thursday at Brixton. Scores; Montpelier 88 and 83, Wimbledon 46.

Thomas Lewis

(1816-82)

Although his date of birth is not known, we do know that he was born in Holborn, London and was christened at the local St Andrew's Church on March 2nd 1816. The first report of him playing for the Montpelier Club again came in *Bell's Life* on August 4th 1834 and he played for the club in the same era as Baker, Coltson, Denison, Peto, Spenceley and Whyting. He also occasionally played under the name Courtney.

He played two first-class matches, the first for Gents v Players in 1837 at Lord's when in the first innings he batted at number sixteen (sixteen in the team) but was shown "absent hurt" for the second innings. The Players, who had eleven in their side won by an innings and 38 runs. The Gents managed only 42 in their second innings and Whyting, with 12 runs was the only player to score double figures. His second match came nine years later, for Surrey against M.C.C. in 1846 at Kennington Oval and his team included Baker, Coltson, Denison, Felix and Spenceley. He batted at number two in the first innings and scored 4 runs and in the second batted at eight but failed to score. He did not bowl in the first innings but dismissed four of the first six M.C.C. batsmen in the second, although the bowling figures have been lost. M.C.C. won by 48 runs however.

On June 25th 1848 when playing for Montpelier against Bramshill at the ground of Sir John Cope, he failed to score in his team's total of 137 and failed to take a wicket in the home team's first innings. But in their second innings he dismissed six of their batsmen to send them to defeat by an innings and seventy runs.

There are records of him playing for the Montpelier Club every season from 1834 until 1849 and he batted in many different positions up and down the order and was an occasional bowler. He was also elected Secretary of the club, although the dates that he held this post are not known. It is known that he was awarded a sliver tankard when club secretary in 1843 however, so this offers us a clue. He took the chair at a number of committee meetings of Surrey C.C.C. and also became a printer and produced prints of cricketers from his company in Cheapside, London.

On October 12th 1851 *Bell's Life* featured a match between "Australians and Europeans" played on Hyde Park ground, Sydney, N.S.W. earlier in the year on May 27th. At number ten in the European's eleven is a Thomas Lewis who scored 2 not out and 5. To date there is no written or family evidence that Lewis travelled to Australia, but his absence from the London cricket scene after 1849 makes this an interesting theory.

He died at Sandown on the Isle of Wight.

John Peto

(1810-74)

Born in Goldalming he is first shown playing for the Montpelier Club in a report in *Bell's Life* dated May 28th 1835, against East Surrey at the Beehive ground. He played for the club until 1849, usually as a lower-order batsman and was also an occasional bowler (he took three wickets in the match against Lingfield on June 18th 1838 and on June 26th took six wickets against Chertsey) and there are records of him playing for the club every season except 1840. His last reported match was against Islington Albion at Brixton on August 22nd 1849, a match featured in *Scores and Biographies* (volume three) and he scored 17 runs batting at number nine in a total of 132 after the visitors had scored 83. He also held two catches in the match.

He played just one first-class match; for Surrey against M.C.C. in 1847 at Kennington Oval. Batting at number ten he scored 7 in a first innings total of 197 and at number nine was undefeated on 5, as his side totalled 101 in the second innings. In the second innings of M.C.C. he stumped Samuel Dakin who top-scored with 64, off the bowling of Felix, but despite them following on 106 runs behind, they won by 9 runs.

He died at Guildford.

J Spenceley

(18??-??)

Possibly James Spenceley (1820-80)

History has been unkind to us and not left us his first name or any dates or places of birth or death. A check on the website www.freebmd.org.uk which covers births, deaths and marriages in England and Wales after 1837 shows only one J. Spenceley to have died in the London area after this date; a James Maudlon Spenceley, aged 59, whose death was registered in the first quarter of 1880 in Stepney, East London. There are a high percentage of people with this surname shown residing in the Bradford and Leeds areas in the era of his birth, so perhaps he came south when young?

The first record of him is in *Bell's Life* on September 4th 1842 for a match between Epsom and Montpelier at Epsom on August 29th. The home team scored 100 and the visitors 49 of which he scored 8 runs. In the return match at the Beehive ground the following week which Epsom won by one run, he did not play. Records show that he normally batted at number three, but on occasions at six, seven and as low as nine.

He played two first-class matches; in 1846 for Surrey v M.C.C. at Kennington Oval when he scored 5 runs and 3 runs as opener, as his side were beaten by 48 runs and in the same fixture in 1848 at Lord's. In this match he batted at eight in the first innings and scored 1 run and opened in the second innings and failed to score. Again his side lost, this time by seven wickets.

His surname crops up regularly in match reports and he played for the club every season from 1842 until his last reported appearance, against Islington Albion on August 5th 1850 which is to be found in *Scores and Biographies* (volume three). He scored 3 runs in their only innings and held a catch, as the match ended in a draw.

Charles Whyting

(1812-66)

Again history has left us to guess his exact dates of birth and death, although he was christened in 1812, so I shall guess that he was born that year too. He was born in Newington, southeast London, so again very close to Kennington Oval.

He played for Putney Victoria against the Montpelier Club on June 16th 1836, and again on June 30th. It is not clear if he was a "given man" to balance the teams, or lent to make up the Putney numbers. Perhaps he played for them prior to Montpelier?

He is first reported playing for the Montpelier Club in *Bell's Life* on June 28th 1837 against Mitcham at the Beehive ground, a match that was drawn. His name was misspelt but he scored 0 and 7 as opener and took 2 wickets, or maybe 3, as Hicks' dismissal is shown "–Whyting", so perhaps the other Whyting in the team took the wicket? This is the match about which Haygarth laments that he was unable to obtain the scorebooks of either team "as they played many good matches about this time."

He played for the Gentlemen of Surrey against Players of Surrey at Kennington Oval on August 21st and 22nd 1845, and as opener with Garland recorded a pair. He appeared for the Montpelier club every season until 1850, so, like many of the others about whom I have written some notes, he enjoyed a long and rewarding spell playing cricket, although he did not make any first-class appearances.

In the *Bell's Life* report dated September 16th 1855 concerning Peckham Rye Standard and Brixton's return match the previous Wednesday, there is a C. Whyting in the Brixton eleven. The match was played on Peckham Rye and Brixton scored 79 and 43 against Standard's 88.

He played for Montpelier on Tuesday August 11th 1856 against Blackheath Dartmouth in a one-day friendly match at The Oval and scored 8 in his eleven's total of 231. The Blackheath side were then dismissed cheaply for 37. He also played for the same team at the same ground on September 3rd 1856 against Surbiton and scored 16 in his team's total of 115 as they won by an innings.

There is a G. Whyting who also played for the Montpelier Club between 1837-39 and who, like him also played for Putney Victoria against Montpelier on June 16th and 30th 1836. By examining the www.freebmd.org.uk website the only G. Whyting whose life was around this period was a George H. Whyting whose death aged 64, is recorded in the first quarter of 1872 in Romford, Essex. I will assume that the two were brothers.

1849

Apr 1st - "Surrey CCC General Meeting at Oval Ground, Kennington on Monday last the 26th inst. to receive a report a report from the committee for the present." The newspaper continued "The ground is in first-rate condition, a billiard room and additional dressing room have been added to the former accommodation of the establishment."

Apr 8th - "South London Club - A meeting of the members of this club took place at their club house, Surrey Ground, Oval Kennington on Wednesday last … it appears that the club is in a very flourishing condition."

May 13th - *The Era* - In the columns set aside for cricket news is "Montpelier Club - On Tuesday the 8th inst., this long established club met in their new ground, in Coldharbour-lane, Brixton, for a day's play, but owing to the very unpropitious state of the weather, the muster in the field was by no means so great as it would have been had the day been fine and warm, but in spite of wind and weather sides were made by Messrs Lewis and Driver and the play was continued until rain put a stop to the game. The members afterwards retired to the Royal Veteran, to partake of a good dinner, provided by Mr Collis, the landlord. The chair was taken on this occasion by John Peto Esq., who has kindly undertaken the office of president of the club and under the auspices of so good a cricketer, the club must prosper. The ground is in first-rate condition, no expense having been spared to make it so, and very great credit is due to the worth president, who has bestowed so much time and attention in the improvement of it. The club now mustering nearly 90 members, look forward to a very pleasant season, and hope to meet many of their old opponents for a friendly game.The first match at present arranged to be played will be at Dorking against the gentlemen of the Dorking Club, on the 12th of June."

No doubt that the Lewis was Thomas C. Lewis, a Montpelier player of many years and Peto is the one of that name who plays for the club in the next match against Dorking.

Jun 17th - There is a match report on Betchworth Park v Montpelier (with Paul) at Betchworth Park Ground and the newspaper reports "Being a one-day match it was decided in the first innings, the Montpelier winning by 25 runs. Score:- Montpelier 93 and 34-5, Dorking Club 68." There seems to be some confusion about the name of the opposition.

Jun 17th - *The Era* - Full match report - Montpelier v Betchworth Park (Dorking) "The match was played on Tuesday the 12th instant, at Dorking, on the Betchworth Park Cricket Ground. The weather was very agreeable for cricket. Being only a one day match, it was decided on first innings, the Montpelier winning by 25 runs. The batting of Messrs Peto, Whyting and Gardner on the part of the Montpelier Club was very good … the score; Montpelier 92 and 34-5, Dorking 68."

Jul 1st - "Montpelier and Peckham Rye Club - These clubs will play a match tomorrow (Monday) at the Montpelier Ground, Cold Harbour lane, Brixton." It is interesting to note that the ground now takes the name of the club whose home it is.

Jul 1st - *The Era* - Full match report for West Hackney v Montpelier "An interesting match was played at Brixton on Thursday last, between eleven of the West Hackney and eleven of the Montpelier Club. The match could not be played out, the hades of evening preventing the West Hackney from concluding their second innings. Scores; West Hackney 108 and 81-2 and Montpelier 87."

Jul 8th - "Montpelier v Peckham Rye - A match was played on Monday last between these clubs on the ground of the former, at Cold harbour lane, Brixton which was decided in favour of the Montpelier, they being 28 runs in advance on the first innings. Score: Montpelier 129 and 47-8, Peckham Rye 101." The newspaper continues "The following match are fixed to come off with the Montpelier: - 12 July (at Copenhagen Ground, Islington), the Islington Albion v Montpelier; 25th July (at West Wickham), West Wickham v Montpelier; 1st August (at Cold Harbour lane, Brixton) return, Dorking v Montpelier; 9th August (at Wimbledon); Wimbledon v Montpelier." In a good week for local cricket, the newspaper continues "West Hackney v Montpelier - These clubs met for a day's play on the ground of the latter at Brixton on Thursday week, when after a pleasant game it was decided in favour of West Hackney by the first innings by 21 runs. Scores: West Hackney 108 and 8-3, Montpelier 87"

These reports show that the club did manage to keep many of its old fixtures.

Aug 5th - "West Hackney v Montpelier - The return match between these two clubs, was played on the ground of the former at Shacklewell, on Wednesday last, when, after a spirited contest, West Hackney won by 26 runs on the first innings … night putting an end to the game. Score Montpelier 46 and 68-7, West Hackney 72."

Aug 5th - *The Era* - Full match reports for Gentlemen of Surrey v Players of England played at the Oval on Monday and Tuesday last. Coltson scored 15 and 1 and Hoare 1 and 4 as the Surrey eleven totalled 141 and 71 and the England team 138 and 44.

Sep 2nd - "Montpelier and West Wickham - These clubs played a match on Tuesday (at Brixton) we presume but neither the day nor the ground is named by our correspondent. Montpelier proved victorious by 14 runs scoring first innings 59, West Wickham 45. Montpelier scored 58-4 in their second innings."

Sep 2nd - *The Era* - Full match report on Waltham Green v Surrey at Waltham Green on Thursday. The home team scored 86 and the visitors for whom Coltson scored 49, recorded 145.

Sep 9th - Full match report on Surrey Paragons v Surrey Phoenix at Kennington Oval, (see next page) which was a "well-contested match" and ended as a draw. W. Baker and W. Miller played for the former and W. Houghton and C. Coltson for the latter.

In the round-up below is mention of Surrey v Walham (sic) Green. Coltson of the Montpelier Club plays for Walham Green "in order to perfect the eleven." It goes on to state that he was a member of both the Surrey Club and Walham Green clubs, as well as him playing for Surrey Phoenix last week.

Sep 23rd - "Wimbledon and Montpelier Clubs - The return match between the Wimbledon Clarence and Montpelier Clubs was played on the Wimbledon ground, on Monday, the 17th inst. (one innings each), when the former won. On the part of the Montpelier the bowling of Powel (one 'l'), Lambert and Driver was certainly good, but the batting of their opponents was far superior, Withem scoring 60, Hossack 17….. Scores: Wimbledon 125, Montpelier 45."

Sep 23rd - *The Era* - A short report on Surrey v Croydon Clarence at the Oval on Monday. C. Coltson scored 3 in Surrey's 43 and Croydon amassed 185.

Perhaps Coltson's regular appearances for Surrey is evidence of the rapid demise of the Montpelier Club, whose matches, if there were many this season, have hardly been covered in the newspaper.

Oct 28th - South London Club - This club held their closing annual dinner on Thursday week … the secretary stated the funds to be in a flourishing condition, and had much improved on that of last year. The evening was then spent very convivially."

SURREY PARAGON v SURREY PHŒNIX CLUB.

This well-contested match was played on the Oval Ground, Kennington, on Wednesday last. Some excellent batting was displayed on both sides, and good scores obtained. The Phœnix obtained 141, and in the commencement of the innings of the Paragon, fortune appeared to be in their favour, they getting runs fast, Mr Baker batting beautifully, and for the loss of five wickets they had obtained 113 runs; but alas, for the chances of cricket, the next four wickets were lowered for six runs, and, instead of an anticipated easy victory, defeat appeared to be inevitable, when just as the last man was going in, "time" was called, thus leaving the game unfinished, and conquest "doubtful." The bowling of Mr Aite and Mr Green was excellent, and also on the part of the Paragon that of Mr Lee and Mr Miller very good. Score:

PHŒNIX.	
C. Collson, Esq, c D. Innes, b Lee	17
R. Roberts, Esq, b Miller	17
F. G. Stoker, Esq, b Lee	11
C. Asprey, Esq, b Miller	1
H. Aite, Esq, c Fleming, b Lee	8
W. Houghton, Esq, b W. Miller	16
J. Prior, Esq, c Hastings, b Miller	12
H. Hare, Esq, b Miller	18
T. Pickford, Esq, b W. Miller	15
G. R. Burnett, Esq, not out	1
R. Green, Esq, b W. Miller	3
Byes 4, wide balls 16, no balls 2	22
Total	141

PARAGON.	
F. Miller, Esq, not out	5
G. Lee, Esq, b Green	19
G. Yates, Esq, b Aite	17
W. Baker, Esq, not out	57
W. Miller, Esq, b Aite	12
S. Hastings, Esq, c Pickford, b Aite	5
W. Fleming, Esq, b Aite	0
D. Innes, leg b.w, b Aite	2
I. H. Capper, Esq, run out	0
P. Noad, Esq, c Roberts, b Prior	0
Byes 14, wide balls 5	22
Total	119

With one wicket to go down.

SURREY CLUB v WALHAM GREEN.—Mr Editor: The return match between the above clubs was played on the ground of the latter, on Thursday, the 30th ult, when the W.G.C.C. was again victorious; but victory in this noble game, though always striven for to the utmost, is not the main object of true cricketers; and if a club like the Surrey can find no more than four gentlemen to attend a match, and bring only a team of eight (made up of players) instead of eleven, it would perhaps be better if such matches were not entertained by them. In the notice of the match, Surrey Club and Walham Green, in *Bell's Life* of August 26, it is stated that "the victory obtained by the W.G.C. may chiefly be attributed to the excellent score of Mr C. Coltson, who, although belonging to the Surrey corps, was, in this instance, allowed to be on the opposition side, in order to perfect the eleven." This is not the fact. Mr Collson is a member of the W.G.C. as well as of the Surrey, which was perfectly understood at the time the match was proposed, and moreover in the list of members given to the secretary of the Surrey Club, at least a month previous to the first match, Mr Coltson's name was inserted.—Yours, &c, A MEMBER.

Sep 9 1849

The South London Club seemed to be a comfortable tenant at Kennington Oval by now, and their matches feature regularly in *Bell's Life*. They seem to have stepped into the gap left by the Montpelier Club's vacation of the ground. There are noticeably fewer reports on "lesser" teams and the affection in which Montpelier matches were reported in the past has been lost too. There are also very few of the club's home matches reported on this season and this is also evident in *The Era*.

The Rosemary Branch Grounds

Just south of the Walworth Common, Montpelier Gardens and Beehive Gardens was the Rosemary Branch ground. Now part of the infamous North Peckham Estate covers the playing surface and there are a few clues left as to its previous life. There is no longer any sign of Rosemary Road.

The grounds were opened as a horse-racing course by James Smith on October 27th 1840. At this time it was described as "A race course on an extensive scale is in progress, adjoining the Rosemary branch, at Peckham, and is sufficiently advanced to admit of a days' sport on Tuesday next …. The course consists of two large meadows thrown into one, and the proprietor has been at great expense in forming it." It became the venue of the East Surrey Races (There is still an East Surrey Grove close by, see page 208), and was used for cricket as well.

The Parish of Camberwell by W.H. Blanch (1875) refers to the grounds as "The grounds surrounding it were most extensive and horse-racing, cricketing, pigeon-shooting and all kinds of outdoor sports and pastimes were carried on." The 1882 Ordnance Survey map refers to it as "Rosemary Branch Quoit and Cricket Ground" and there is an illustration of the *Rosemary Branch* public house facing page 369 of Blanch's book (see next page).

In Professor H.J. Dyos's *Victorian Suburb, a study of Camberwell* the ground is referred to as "the nineteen acres which lay between Peckham Grove and Cator Street … were sold to James Smith, landlord of the Rosemary Branch tavern, which stood on the south-western tip of the area, and in 1864 sold about seven acres to form Blake's road and Hornby road. The remaining land was kept for some years as a cricket field and place of amusement attached to the tavern."

The ground was auctioned in 1867 and ceased to be a cricket ground in 1874 and was developed for housing by Richard Strong. *The Rosemary Branch* was a public house and was sited on Southampton Way and the later version was demolished in 1971. Stephen Lawrence House now stands where it used to be.

In William Caffyn's biography, he refers to taking part in a shooting-match at the grounds, when it was run by a gentleman called Mr Chadband.

The Old Rosemary Branch.

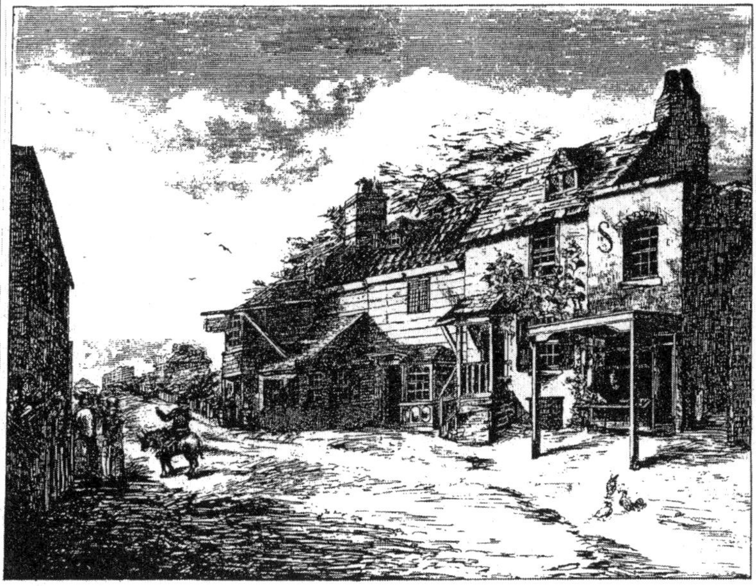

W Griggs. Photo-Lith

THE OLD ROSEMARY BRANCH.

This print is to be found in *Ye Parish of Camberwell* by W. H. Blanch, published in 1876. He writes "The Rosemary Branch, Peckham, although possessing but a local reputation at the present time, was a well-known metropolitan hostelrie half a century ago. Our illustration will convey some idea of the old house and its rustic surroundings. Tradition has it, that whenever the landlord of the old house tapped a barrel of beer, the inhabitants for some distance round were appraised of the fact by bell and proclamation! When the new house was erected it was decided in a print of the time as an "establishment which had no suburban rival." The grounds surrounding it were most extensive, and horse-racing, cricketing, pigeon-shooting, and all kinds of outdoor sports and pastimes were carried on."

1850

Scores and Biographies records a match between Montpelier and Islington Albion on August 22nd 1849 at Brixton. This is followed by another between the same clubs on August 5th 1850 at the Copenhagen Ground, Islington (neither though are mentioned in *Bell's Life*), and then the club is not mentioned again in Haygarth's work. George Smith searched old maps for this cricket ground in Coldharbour Lane, Brixton, but was unable to locate an area that gave any idea of it being so employed. Thus we are left to rue that perhaps it was just a patch of grass with no real infrastructure, or signs of permanence. I will presume that it disappeared as house-building carried on in a southerly direction.

This year sees the cricket reported in *The Era* mainly by way of full match reports; there are very few reports in the round-up section underneath these more detailed reports and very few with a local interest.

Apr 21st - "The South London Club will have their anniversary dinner on Wednesday next, on the commencement of the session, at their club house, Surrey Ground, Kennington Oval, when the members will be seeing many of their friendly opponents muster at the social board ..."

Apr 28th - There is nothing in the main body of cricket reports of a local interest but in the round-up the South London Club dinner is reported on "there was a strong muster of members and their friends, some of the latter entertaining the company with some excellent harmony, in the shape of duets & c. Numerous toasts were drunk, and a pleasant evening spent." This section contained more local news with "Union Club - This club will have a day's play and their opening dinner at the Surrey Ground, Kennington Oval on Wednesday next." And "Surrey Paragon Club - The annual dinner and first day's play of this club will take place at the Oval, Kennington, on Saturday next."

Jun 2nd - "The Kennington and West Hackney clubs play a match on the Surrey Ground, Kennington Oval on Tuesday next."

Does this indicate an upturn from Kennington Common for the Kennington Club who are now playing one of Montpelier's old opponents?

Jun 9th - In the round-up is mentioned that Kennington won the above match "by 16 runs on the first innings, time not admitting of it being played out. Score: Kennington 120 and 91-7, West Hackney 104."

Also in the columns is "The Montpelier and Peckham Rye clubs played a match at Peckham Rye on the 22nd ult when the latter won, with nine wickets to go down. Score: Peckham 86 and 10-1, total 96, Montpelier 74 and 21, total 95."

Jun 30th - "Islington and Montpelier Clubs - This match will be played on Thursdays at the Copenhagen. From the well known celebrity of both clubs, a first-rate match may be anticipated."

Jul 28th - "The Peckham and Montpelier clubs played a match on the 19th inst. on the ground of the latter at North Brixton, but owing to the unfavourable state of the weather, only one innings each was entered into. The Peckham scored 89 … Montpelier 33.."

Aug 18th - "Albion v Montpelier - These clubs played a match on Monday week on the Islington Ground. Scores: Albion 90 and 38-1, total 128 … Montpelier 87.." The newspaper continues "From the great pressure on our space this week we are unable to give this match at the length it deserves."

Aug 18th - *The Era* - Full match report on Wimbledon v South London played at Wimbledon on Thursday. The home team scored 63 and 52 and the guests from inner London 56. It was a return match as the newspaper reported "A new and improved team was brought out at Wimbledon and the same wore quite a new feature in consequence. The South London minus their most important characters who figured in the original match at the Oval on the 2nd inst…..". (I could find no report about this first match). At the bottom of the report are the scores, but the visitors are titled "Montpelier" - is this an error? As we know by now there were many players who played for both elevens, but this is a strange oversight by the newspaper. The team was listed as; Chapman, West, Plank, Edwards, Heath, Page, Hart, Houghton, Scott, Green and Winterflood.

Sep 15th - *The Era* - In a report on Twenty Gentlemen v Eleven Players of Surrey played on Monday and Tuesday at the Oval, C. Coltson scored 6 and 7 in the Gentlemen's scores of 48 and 122. The Players eleven scored 203. Coltson did not feature in any reports concerning matches played by the full Surrey team this season however.

This is the last copy of the newspaper for this season, the library are missing a binder which covers mid-September 1850 to mid-September 1851, thus most of next season is missing too.

St George's Church, Camberwell
c1850.

St GEORGE, CAMBERWELL, SURREY.

This impression of the church clearly shows the canal which was later filled in and is now part of Burgess Park. The best clue I found for the location of Hampton's (later Hall's) Ground is that it was located "near the Canal Church at Camberwell".

St George's Church, Camberwell
November 2007.

The church is no longer used at such and it has been divided into flats. Despite increased foliage and a tunnel being constructed, I was able to stand in a similar position to where the artist who etched the print on the previous page must have been located.

The Oval
1849.

This glorious print of which the original is in colour shows a match in progress with the bowler about to bowl in an under-arm fashion. It also shows St Mark's Church, the old pavilion, a thin line of spectators standing and seated (with a couple on horseback) and a large house which is most likely that where author and local historian H.H. Montgomery lived. It portrays the ground from a slightly different perspective to that on the next page, but from virtually the same place that Wanostrocht painted the ground (see page 194). The Montpelier Club left the ground the previous season, but this gives us a very good idea of what their players would have seen. Twenty-three years later the ground hosted the first ever football F.A. Final, and by that time Charles Alcock was making a big and positive impression as Secretary of Surrey C.C.C..

The Oval
c1850.

The Oval c1850

This postcard shows the ground from the Vauxhall end "circa 1850". On page 33 of *Old Cricket and Cricketers* by H.H. Montgomery is a print of The Oval "about 1854" from a similar perspective and below is written "Shows the old pavilion ….. which is still standing and the gallery is still to be seen … The present pavilion is built by the side and in front of the old house." This postcard therefore shows the same two pavilions; the old pavilion (with the balcony) on the left-hand side and the new one in front of St Mark's church. On page 203 is a painting of The Oval entrance dated "circa 1858". Accompanying text from *Scores and Biographies* states that a new pavilion was built in 1858, so it appears that the estimate shown on the postcard is about eight years out.

Dec 1st - "West Surrey Club - a new club has been formed under the above title, the club formerly bearing this name having ceased to exist for the last five or six years. This may be considered a revival, as one of the old members of that club, S. Bennett, a cricketer well known in Surrey, has succeeded in obtaining a field in the Wandsworth Road opposite the old cricket ground, a little beyond Forster's, the Three Goats' Head, where the first meeting will take place, on Tuesday evening next..."

Again this season witnessed less local matches being reported in the newspaper including the Montpelier Club.

1851

Montgomery's *The History of Kennington and its Neighbourhood* book contains this interesting tale relevant to this season; "One question is worth answering. Has the Oval been ever in danger of being built upon? Yes: about the year 1851, Mr. Driver, the solicitor to the Duchy was bringing a bill into parliament to enable the Duchy to built two and a half crescents, but the Prince Consort, who was administering the estate for the young Prince, was strongly in favour of keeping the Oval an open space. He argued that as the old Kennington Common had been taken for a public Park, so that cricketers could no longer use it, it was only right that another space should be found as near as possible, where South Londoners might enjoy the game; and he further declared that the Oval should be available for Cricket at a light rental so long as the people of South London wished to uphold cricket." We must therefore thank the Prince Consort for his wise decision and he would be pleased to know that cricket was being played on this space well over one-hundred-and-forty years later.

The Era for this year begins in the large bound volumes on September 21st with a full match report on Kennington v Kingston. Kennington scored 33 and 41 and the visitors 87, and the detailed match report is of interest as it tells of a new ground for Kennington and is written in an interesting style. "...The Kennington club has soared to no great altitude in the regions of popularity; we didn't enter into the question whether they were fixed with ambition to acquire it or not, but frequent successes gave them confidence and courage, and having contributed to an enclosed ground, they took a new position, and during the present season have tried manfully to maintain it ..... In the match on Tuesday at Bennett's ground, Wandsworth Road, there was striking proof of incompetency on the part of the Kennington to play the team shot up by rail from Kingston ... the batting of Kennington was puerile in the extreme." Instead of referring to them as ducks, the newspaper reports that "in their first essay at the wickets … five were honoured with "cockseys."" Kennington's poor first innings total of thirty-three included twenty-one extras made up of twelve byes, eight leg-byes and one wide.

Apr 27th - Although cricket reports have been sent in from around the world and feature in the newspaper in February and March, the first real reports of any interest are in today's newspaper. In the round-up is "Surrey Club - the members of this celebrated club meet on Tuesday next for a day's play, at their ground, The Oval, Kennington, on which occasion also their annual dinner takes place."

Below this report are consecutively;

"Surrey Union Club - the opening of the season for this club is fixed for Wednesday next, at the Surrey Ground, Kennington Oval, when a day's play among the members will take place, after which they will dine together."

"South London Club - this club commences operations for the season on Thursday next, at the Surrey Ground, Kennington Oval with a day's play. Their usual annual dinner also takes place."

"St George's (Surrey) Club - the members of this club meet tomorrow (Monday) for their opening day's play, at their ground, back of the Lord Nelson, Old Kent road."

Although the text is similar in each report and the words familiar; they do put teams at grounds and for that we must be grateful.

May 11th - Under "Further matches to come" there is nothing appertaining to the Montpelier Club to be found.

Jun 8th - Match report on Surrey Union v Hampstead match at The Oval. The home team scored 83-5 in reply to the visitors' 270.

Under "Future matches to come" is: "West Surrey - the first fixed day of the season of this club will take place on Whit Tuesday, on their new ground, Wandsworth road…." and "The Kennington and Epsom Club meet to play a match on Tuesday, the 17th inst, on Bennett's New Ground, in the Wandsworth road."

Jun 15th - "Kennington and Epsom Clubs - the first match of the season of these clubs of these clubs will be played on the West Surrey Ground, Wandsworth road, opposite Bradley Terrace, on Tuesday next."

We now have details of a new ground, its owner and exact location.

The print below of Kennington Oval in 1851 was painted by Nicholas Felix (Wanostrocht) who played at the ground for an England eleven. He painted many of the grounds that he played on with this team as they travelled the country and these paintings were re-discovered again in the latter part of the last century. The old pavilion with the balcony can be seen, but there is no trace of the new pavilion .

Jun 22nd - There is a match report on Kennington v Epsom which "….took place on the West Surrey (Bennett's) Ground, adjoining the Stag Inn, Wandsworth road. It being the first match played on this new ground, it attracted a goodly muster of spectators …. Kennington gained the victory, but only by 3 runs …"

In the round-up "West Surrey Club …. After a good game the members retired to their club house, the Three Goats Heads"

Jul 27th - Under "Other matches to come" - there are no Montpelier Club matches advertised up to the end of August.

Again there has been no mention of our club in the newspaper this season. Perhaps the team folded quickly or faded gradually away due to members joining other clubs?

1852

Again this season sees woeful coverage of local cricket in *The Era* although the Surrey eleven are often featured along with the Kennington Oval eleven, who also play at the Oval.

Apr 25th - On the front page of the newspaper in the fifth column is mention of the formation of another new club in the area; The Kennington Oval Cricket Club. It goes on to say "Prospectuses may be obtained upon application to Mr Houghton, Oval, Kennington."

May 9th - There is a list of fixtures for a variety of clubs, but again there is no mention of the Montpelier Club, even as an away club.

May 16th - "Surrey Ground, Oval, Kennington - the following clubs practice on this ground: - The County of Surrey Club: practice days Mondays, Tuesdays, Wednesdays and Saturdays; practice bowlers Brockwell, Lockyer, W. Mortlock, Sherman and Taylor. Union Club: practice days Wednesdays and Saturdays; bowler Plank. Kennington Oval Club: practice days Tuesday's and Wednesdays; practice bowlers F. Caesar and Hinkley.

Jun 27th - "Surrey Union v Hampstead - These clubs played a match at Kennington Oval on Tuesday … Union 74 and 91-4… Hampstead 171."

Aug 1st - *The Era* - Gentlemen of Surrey v Gentlemen of Sussex played at Horsham - but there is no Coltson or Hoare in the Surrey eleven however.

Aug 15th - Full match report on Kennington v Orpington at Bennett's Ground, Wandsworth Road. Kennington scored 54 (W. Mortlock, a Surrey player scored 29 and took 3 wickets) and Orpington 142.

Aug 29th - *The Era* - Full match report on Twickenham who scored 41 and 9-1 v The Oval Club who scored 39 and 9 which was played at Twickenham on Monday. Montpelier's William Denison played for the Oval Club and recorded a pair.

Sep 12th - Full match report on East Surrey v West Kent played at Coombe House, Croydon, which saw the team from Surrey lose by 37 runs over two innings. Cricket reports with a local interest end much earlier this season and there have been a lot less of them in the newspaper.

Sadly there has been no re-appearance of reports on the Montpelier Club, and as can be seen, reports on local clubs have faded rapidly too.

1853

Kennington Oval and the various Surrey club's matches were featured in the newspaper this season but not as frequently as in recent years. The total amount of local match reports in the newspaper is less, and yet again there are none that relate to the Montpelier Club. Despite this, the newspaper does manage a comprehensive section on cricket from around the country and abroad.

May 8th - A short report on the general meeting of the Oval Club, Kennington and the election of officers - Messrs S. Jones and W. Houghton were elected as President and Treasurer respectively.

May 22nd - The Surrey fixtures are listed for the early part of the season and they are shown to be playing, amongst others; M.C.C., West Wickham, Oxford University, Vine Club and Islington Albion in June and July.

Jun 12th - The fixtures of many prominent local clubs are listed viz: Clapton, Islington Albion, Blackheath Paragon and West Wickham, but none involve matches with the Montpelier Club.

Jul 10th - "The East Surrey and Peckham Independent Clubs play their return match on Thursday next on Bennett's Ground, Wandsworth road." This is another change of home venue for the team from Surrey, although close for both teams to reach.

Oct 23rd - "Kennington Oval Club - In order to keep membership united, during the winter season they will assemble, under the presidency of Mr S. Jones, at their club house, Surrey Ground, Kennington Oval, every Thursday evening, commencing next week, when business, friendship and harmony will be combined."

1854

Mar 12th - "Kennington Oval Club - a committee of members of this club was on Thursday evening last, at the club house, Kennington Oval, and a general meeting of the members of the club was appointed to take place on Thursday, the 23rd inst. to make arrangements for the ensuring season."

Mar 26th - Below a short report on the Second and Third Year (135) v Freshmen (74) on Parker's Piece, Cambridge, the first cricket report for the English season, is "Kennington Oval Club, Mr Editor, the president and officers of the club, at a meeting on Tuesday last, at the Oval, arranged for a general meeting of the meetings for Tuesday, 4th April, for the annual election of officers and other members, for the coming season. Members are requested to attend early. As several of the grounds in the environs have been destroyed, or otherwise appropriated than to cricketing purposes, many ardent cricketers will not know to enrol themselves…."

The comments about grounds vanishing in the previous report, may account for lesser local matches making it into the newspaper.

Apr 9th - At the Kennington Oval Club A.G.M. Mr W. Houghton was re-elected as Treasurer.

Jun 11th - "Kennington v Nelson House, Wimbledon - This match, played May 31, in which Kennington proved victorious by 76 runs should have been sent earlier."

At the bottom of the weekly round-up of lesser matches is: "Kennington Oval Club - During the temporary closing of the usual club house, the meeting of the above will be held at the Harrow Arms opposite Kennington Church. Consequently, for the purpose of carrying on the business of the club, it has been resolved by the committee that a general meeting of the members is held on Tuesday evening next, at eight o'clock when their attendance is earnestly requested."

Jul 30th - Full match report on Kennington Oval Club v Hackney - played at Oval Ground, Kennington which saw the home team win on first innings scores.

1855

By now five years have passed since the last mention of the Montpelier Club in the pages of *Bell's Life* and I had planned to draw the book to a close at the end of this season with the assumption that they had folded. However a surprise was looming in the newspaper, which now featured reports about the Crimean War amongst those of a sports nature.

Apr 1st - "Kennington Oval Cricket Club - This club will hold its annual meeting for the election of officers on Thursday next, at the Clayton Arms, Kennington Oval ..."

Apr 8th - Matches are listed for Marylebone, Surrey and "Matches in the Country" up to July 23rd yet not one of these features Montpelier. On August 12th another long list of fixtures for a large variety of teams are published up to the end of the summer, but again none involve our club.

In the round-up is a short report about Kennington Oval Cricket Club now being known as The Kennington Club. Unexpectedly eight paragraphs below this report under a sub-title of "The Old Montpelier Club" is; "We are glad to hear that this club has again been established, and will play its matches upon the Oval. They have a special meeting on the 18th instant to arrange matters for the approaching season."

Again it is a shame that there are no details regarding why the club vanished. It is interesting also to note that the club has not returned to their last ground in Brixton but had gone back to a ground that they left swiftly and after an argument. Perhaps like the Beehive ground, the Brixton one was also lost as London expanded?

Apr 22nd - "Kennington Park Club - this club which was formed last season, and played several good matches will play their opening match for the season, on Wormwood Scrubs on Tuesday next, April 24th."

Aug 26th - In the round-up is "Brixton v Peckham Rye Standard - This match was played on Saturday last on the 11th instant, on the ground of the Brixton Club, Cold Harbour-lane, Brixton in the presence of a very large assemblage. Scores: Peckham Rye 29 + 22, Brixton 50 + 2-0." We are left to guess whether this is the Royal Veteran ground where the Montpelier Club played having left The Oval.

Sep 16th - In the round-up is “Peckham Rye Standard v Brixton Club. Return match - This match was came off on Peckham Rye, on Wednesday week, the Standard being the victors on the first innings … Score: Brixton 79 + 43, Standard 88.” In the Brixton eleven is C. Whyting, no doubt the same player who first played for our club in 1837.

I was guided to the Surrey Historical Centre in Woking whilst doing my research for this book and it was they who referred me to the web-site of Chertsey Cricket Club in Surrey. Within the club history section is reference to a match at The Oval against The Montpelier Club on September 6th 1855, which I have not seen reported anywhere else.

1856

Apr 6th - “Kennington Club - The first committee meeting of the members of this club was held on weds last, and a general meeting is appointed for Wednesday, the 16th inst, at the Oval, Kennington, for the purpose of electing officers and making arrangements for the season. The club is in a very flourishing condition, several new members having joined …”

With the Montpelier Club having left The Oval nearly nine years ago, clearly the Kennington Club (ex-Kennington Oval Club) is now main team apart from the county team to be based at the ground.

May 4th - Again there are copious amounts of cricket fixtures for many teams listed in the newspaper and again none of them have the Montpelier Club as an opposition.

Jun 29th - Full match report on Kennington v Barnes Britannia played at The Oval on “the 25th instant”. Kennington scored 125 and the visitors 50 and 45-5. Again there is little of local interest in the newspaper and the amount contained in the round-up has also diminished considerably.

Jul 20th - Most unexpectedly there is a full match report for Surbiton v Montpelier which was played at The Oval, on July 9th and it is clearly our team (see next page). This is their first match report in the newspaper for nearly six years.

July 28th 1856

SURBITON v MONTPELIER.

This match was played at the Oval, July 9. Score:

MONTPELIER.		SURBITON.	
J. Seymour, c and b Chester	4	J. Chester, c Taylor, b Seymour	75
C. Pate, c Lipscomb, b Chester	3	J. Thompson, b Seymour	29
T. Winterflood, b Chester	8	E. Lipscomb, b Taylor	5
J. Ives, b Oliphant	2	A. W. Puck, c Hill, b Taylor	1
C. Whiting, b Oliphant	13	R. G. Currie, c Plews, b Taylor	21
W. Pyne, c Thompson, b Chester	9	T. A. Beard, b Taylor	2
P. Johnson, b Chester	0	H. L. Oliphant, c Ives, b Taylor	8
T. Hill, c Pressly, b Chester	1	G. T. Pressly, b Taylor	35
W. Taylor, not out	14	Weeding, c Winterflood, b Taylor	13
A. Plews, b Chester	12	R. Peel, b Taylor	12
W. Powell, absent	0	G. Arbuthnot, not out	0
B 2, l b 1, w b 2	5	B 18, l b 7, w b 8	33
Total	71	Total	23

Aug 24th - “Montpelier v Blackheath Dartmouth - These clubs played a friendly at The Oval, on Tuesday August 11th when the Montpelier came off victorious. Score: Montpelier 231 and Blackheath Dartmouth 37.” The Montpelier eleven and their respective scores (which do not add up) were shown as; A. Burbridge 5, J. Ives 26, R.H. Bushell 41, C. Whyting 8, T. Winterflood 41, E. Dowson 23, E. Garland 9, C. Cheney 24, T. Hill 2, G. Lambert 8 and W. Taylor 2. There were 21 byes and 18 wides in the total.

Sep 7th - Full match report on Surbiton v Montpelier played on Wednesday September 3rd (see below) which saw our team who still had E. Garland and C. Whyting playing for them, win by an innings. Also a full match report on Kennington v Mitcham United played at The Oval on Tuesday August 26th which saw the home team score 68 and 100-5 and the visitors 79.

Sep 7th 1856

SURBITON v MONTPELIER.

This match, which excited considerable interest, came off on Wednesday, and much to the astonishment of the Surbiton eleven, resulted in an easy victory for the Montpelier, they winning the match in one innings, with 15 runs to spare. Score:

SURBITON.	1st inn		2d inn
Thompson, b Taylor	2	J. Lipscomb (for Thompson, hurt)	0
F. W. Oliver, c Bushell	12	Pressly (for Oliver, absent)	0
E. W. Lipscomb, b Prior	2	run out	1
E. W. Vyse, c Prior, b Taylor	3	c and b Taylor	0
C. Lipscomb, b Prior	2	c Ives, b Taylor	1
J. Giffard, b Taylor	8	b Taylor	4
A. Street, not out	23	run out	3
J. A. Bland, c Garland, b Taylor	6	c Prior, b Taylor	2
Capt Lambert, c Ives, b Taylor	0	b Daly	3
S. Vyse, b Taylor	0	b Taylor	5
Ellis, b Taylor	5	not out	5
B 6, w b 1	7	B 2, w b 4	6
Total	—70	Total	—30

MONTPELIER.			
J. Ives, b Ellis	1	Dowson, b Street	4
E. Garland, b Ellis	1	Townsend, b Street	7
J. Seymour, c Thompson, b Street	23	Daly, b Street	1
H. Bushell, b Street	24	Taylor, not out	1
C. E. Waller, b Lipscomb	19	B 7, w b 6	13
C. Whyting, b Ellis	16		
T. Prior, b Ellis	5	Total	115

1857

May 10th - The customary comprehensive fixture list features this week and once again there is no mention of the Montpelier Club to be found amongst the many teams listed. There is another such list featured in the newspaper on June 28th which covers matches up to the end of the summer and again the club is absent.

Jul 12th - In the round-up "Kennington Park Club v Second Eleven University of London. This match was played at Lord's on Saturday July 11th and ended in defeat of the University of London by one innings and 216 run to spare, principally owing to the batting of Mr Seacombe (113), Moir (44) and Dodd (41). Kennington Park 311 and University of London 47 and 48."

It was interesting to note from this report that Kennington Park, who were only formed in 1854 now gets to play matches at Lord's.

Aug 23rd - In the round-up is a short mention of the match between Peckham Rye Albion and Camberwell Amicables who played at the Rosemary Branch ground. The scores were Peckham 113 and Camberwell 98.

Sep 27th - Full match report on Kennington v Dartford on September 16th, a match which was played at The Oval and which saw the home team win by 62 runs on first innings scores: Kennington 111 and Dartford 49.

1858

There are no mentions of our club in either newspaper this year, so we must speculate whether the comeback announced on April 8th 1855 was only short-lived. I have been able to find details of only four matches; three of which were played at The Oval - in 1855 versus Chertsey and in 1856, versus Surbiton (twice) and Blackheath Dartmouth. As no details of any club fixtures have come to light for 1857 or 1858, now seems an appropriate time to draw the research to a close.

As can be seen by the many match reports in previous years, they were not the only club to fold, although one must bear in mind that there was no consistency in what cricket reports featured in the two newspapers, if at all. Perhaps the editor considered that any matches that they did play were no longer worthy of inclusion?

By now Surrey County Cricket Club was growing in size and was no doubt the most powerful side in the area. Some ex-Montpelier players joined Surrey when it began in 1845, but by now they would probably have retired, so perhaps the drive to keep the Montpelier Club going was therefore lost? Sadly there is every chance that the real reason for our club's demise will never be known.

The Surrey Tavern and Entrance c1858.

This fine portrait of the Surrey Tavern and entrance to the ground (on the Harleyford Road) was painted by Harry Williams, about whom sadly little can be established. The Montpelier club had left The Oval about a decade prior, but may have seen this view as they arrived at the ground, as the building in the painting is not the new pavilion, but the rear of the original one. *Scores and Biographies* reports "In the year 1858, in consequence of the great increase in its members, a new and costly pavilion was erected, adding greatly to the comfort of the members…" and "In 1855 the Club did not muster more than 230 members, with an income of under £500; while in 1861, it had enrolled nearly 1,000 members with an income little short of £2,000…". Perhaps the painting was commissioned as a memory to the view prior to the completion of the new pavilion?

The Old Tavern.

The accuracy of the painting on the previous page can be gauged by this sadly undated photograph, entitled *The Old Tavern* which is currently displayed at the Vauxhall end of the ground beneath the new stand. "Surrey Cricket Ground" is visible and large displays of flowers adorn many of the window-boxes. This must have been an impressive sight for travellers approaching from the Camberwell end of the ground. Not one part of this beautiful building survives; the current pavilion would probably have necessitated its demolition at the end of the nineteenth century. A new tavern was built post-war, but thankfully in 2008 that was demolished and its demise opened up a view of the rear of the current pavilion from the road not seen for many years. Credit then to the current planners, who do not intend to obscure this view with another new building. The ground has been blessed with three very attractive pavilions; each bigger than its predecessor.

Map of the area in 1868.

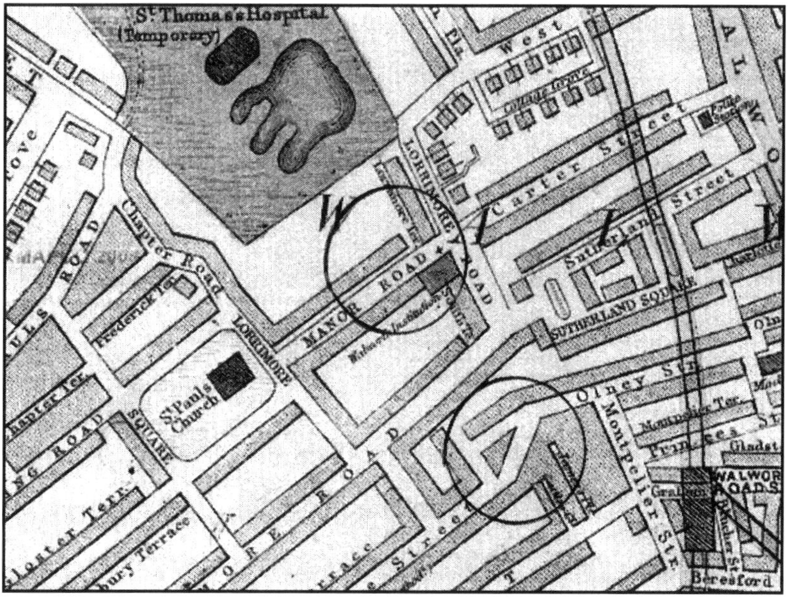

This map by Weller shows Manor Road built across the site of the Beehive ground (top circle) and housing upon the site of Montpelier Gardens ground (lower circle), on the left side of the northern end of Montpelier Street. Due to railway works at London Bridge, the local St. Thomas's Hospital re-located to the Surrey Music Hall in the Zoological Gardens for about thirteen years and this occupancy is shown on this map.

Kennington Oval Cricket Ground c1870.

There are very few early photographs of this famous ground, so although not precisely dated, this is a welcome find. The Montpelier Club vacated the ground about twenty-two years previously and it was now the ground of the county club. There are nine smartly attired figures on the playing surface; a fence can be seen on the right-hand side and the famous gas-holders too. In the centre a set of stumps are visible, perhaps the second set are obscured by the two figures standing together, left-of-centre? It appears that we are looking from a long-on position and if so, then the wicket has been turned by ninety degrees since. The figure in the foreground appears to have a cricket bat across their lap and there are a good number of supporters in the background and it would be very interesting to establish more details about the game in progress.

Map of the area in 1871.

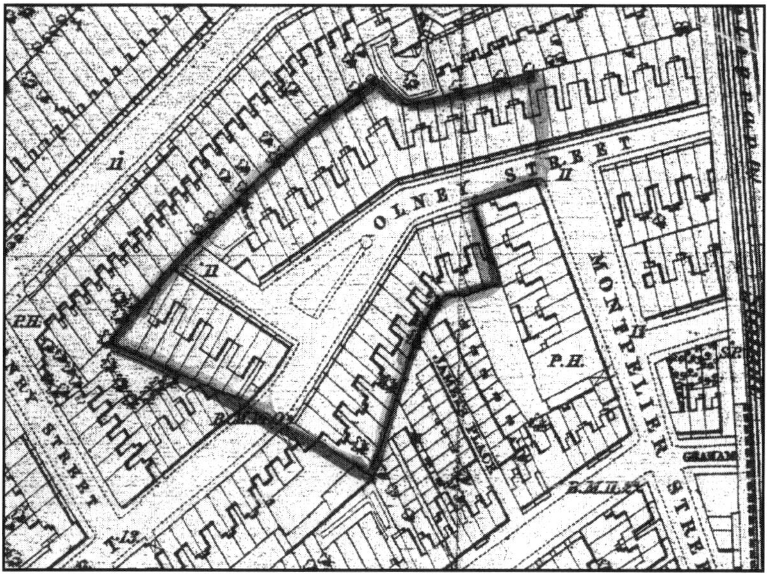

The map shows that there had been a considerable amount of building in the area over the previous forty years, so much so that so only a tiny area of greenery survived. Fielding Street now curves southeast from Penrose Street and joins Walworth Road, and covers some of Olney Street. There is a small island visible in the centre of Olney Street and if one goes back from this in each direction a boundary line at the rear of the various houses can be traversed which is virtually the same shape as the Montpelier Gardens (see map on page 71).

East Surrey Grove, Camberwell.

The site of the Rosemary Branch Grounds which hosted many different sports including cricket is now covered by the infamous North Peckham Estate where this sign is to be found. There is no similarity between the lay-out of the roads shown on an 1837 map which shows "Rosemary Branch" and "Rosemary Cotts" and the road lay-out today however. The sign is a tenuous link to cricket as although the venue hosted some of the East Surrey Cricket Club's matches (see match report on June 5th 1842) they were most famous for hosting the East Surrey Races.

Chapter Eight

A Treasured Find

To get this book into print has been a challenge, but worth every hour of research into it. Even at the end I sincerely believed that I was just collecting up loose ends and leaving a book which would be updated in the future by someone else who set out with the same intentions as myself.

In late 2005 I received a phone call from a gentleman in Sussex who had mentioned that one of his relatives had played for the Montpelier Club to Trevor Jones, the then Surrey C.C.C. librarian, whom I must thank for passing my phone number on.

He explained that a long-deceased relative, Mr Thomas Courtney Lewis had played for the club and also been secretary. Further Lewis had been awarded an ornate silver tankard which had been passed down the family and was still in safe keeping.

We arranged to meet at the annual cricket book fair at Hove cricket ground, so that I could see this historic and unique connection with the club whose history I was trying to trace, and for him to hand over some photographs of it.

Inscribed on the tankard which is about eight inches high is; "Thomas Lewis Esq. SecY to the Montpelier Cricket Club presented by his Brother Members on 2nd May 1843". Lewis was baptised in March 1816 so would have been just twenty-seven when this was awarded to him, although for what reason we do not know.

On the following pages are two photographs of this ornate and beautifully crafted tankard, still in immaculate condition and whose inscription is still crystal clear. I never envisaged locating or even touching something so close to the club when I started my research, and indeed something which many of the club's members may also have touched over one-hundred-and-sixty years ago. It predates nearly everything Surrey County Cricket Club have in their museum and archives and is a truly unique and priceless piece of cricket memorabilia.

The Montpelier Cricket Club Tankard.

This photograph clearly shows the ornate work on the tankard, whose lid still opens cleanly. It is unmarked and in immaculate condition, which, considering it is over one-hundred-and-sixty years old is outstanding.

The Montpelier Cricket Club Tankard.

This photograph of the tankard with its lid down, shows the inscription on the opposite side. My only regret is that the engraver has failed to state the reason for its award, which came at the start of the season. Perhaps it was awarded at an A.G.M., or club dinner to celebrate a successful season the previous year? Sadly it looks like we will never know.

Chapter Nine

Conclusion

Prior to compiling this research, I was concerned that little about the Montpelier C.C. appeared to have been put into print. Perhaps their establishment before newspapers were widespread has cost us considerable knowledge regarding their embryonic years?

It has taken three years of research and many visits to various libraries and museums to glean information, often but a snippet, with which to weave a vague history of this club. I am very grateful to Arthur Haygarth then for noting in his *Scores and Biographies* for June 28th 1837, that he was unable to find the scorebooks for the club. This shows that another, albeit over one-hundred-and-seventy years earlier than my own research, had problems compiling early records of the club. It adds to my belief that although they drifted out of the mainstream cricket media for a long period, they were probably playing lesser-level cricket matches for some of this apparent absence.

There is little doubt that they were a gentlemen's club; no playing on the local common for this outfit. It would however be interesting to know if playing for their Tuesday or Wednesday eleven, was evidence of a higher standing in the community, than an appearance for the Saturday eleven for example. It appears that between 1834-49 they played up to ten matches each summer. Some of the matches advertised in *Bell's Life* were perhaps never played, as I was unable to find a match report for them in the newspaper, or Denison's work gives a match report, but against a different opposition. There is some overlap in the works of Britcher, Buckley, Denison, Haygarth and Waghorn and although the dates of the matches differ occasionally and there is often no indication of whether they were one or two-day matches, I have used these to compile a master-list of matches played by the Montpelier Club, although it is too big to be included in the book.

Referring back to Charles Box's book of 1877 he asks "but what of them now?" in relation to both grounds. He then answers, "Aye, not a patch of green is left to mark out where once stood the wickets and the tents". This is not entirely true. With regard to the Montpelier Gardens ground, the aptly named Fielding Street now follows the boundary of the ground and adjoins a children's play area. Although the road sits just outside of the where the ground was located, the play area appears to be located within the boundary of the ground. Modern flats and houses that today make up part of the Pelier Estate now cover most of what was the playing area. The southern part of Montpelier Street is still in-situ, although it is now known as Pelier Street, but I wish that it had kept its original name. To have kept the previous name would have been a reminder of the area's historical past, and would have given this researcher a better clue as to where to start looking for the ground in the first place.

The site of the Beehive ground is covered by a mixture of quality Victorian terraced houses, a junior school and a modern, long block of flats behind which there is a large expanse of grass.

Opposite these is proudly located the well decorated and conspicuous *Beehive* pub, so it alone has stood defiant whilst the roads and parks in the vicinity have been redesigned at least twice. The building was placed in different places by different authors has in fact remained in-situ all along and outlasted all of what it overlooked.

Box continues "....there were gamblers too. Hence some of the matches belonging to the archives of Surrey had better perhaps be allowed to crumble and rot out of existence than be disturbed for the non-edification of the present generation". Ouch!

Today Walworth is a colourful, multi-cultural, throbbing and vibrant, and at times violent inner London suburb, located a short walk to the south of the Elephant and Castle roundabouts. Choking levels of traffic pass both ways most day-time hours along the Walworth Road, a vein into southeast London, and a route to the affluent suburb of Dulwich, renowned for its picture gallery, toll-gate and public school. The latter was a breeding ground for many cricketers, including England captain Monty Bowden.

Walworth still displays many architecturally beautiful and delightfully spacious houses from the Victorian era. However as a result of redevelopment and war-time enemy action, they are often overlooked by blocks of flats and have as neighbours, cheaply assembled council owned dwellings. During the period of the Montpelier Club's residence this area would have been one of affluence, due to its proximity to the city.

Despite the over population of the area, the flow of traffic and huge numbers of people seeking bargains in the famous East Lane market, there is an oasis of tranquillity around *The Beehive* pub, despite its proximity to the Walworth Road. Behind the pub are blocks of flats that cover a level area about the size of a cricket ground, where I first assumed the ground had been located.

Although the sites of both grounds are virtually covered by latter day buildings, small areas of greenery survive within both of their original boundaries. The immediate areas of both grounds are an eclectic mix of old and new although the masses of residents, passers-by and cricket lovers will all no doubt be oblivious to the history in their midst - a fact not helped by the re-naming of many of the local streets.

As for the club's third home which was also the one to which they occasionally returned after they left their fourth one; well, Kennington Oval as we all know is globally famous and still going strong, although it is now home only to the county club. As mentioned earlier, no trace has been found of the club's fourth ground; the Royal Veteran Ground in Coldharbour Lane. Perhaps if there was a pub by that name it has been demolished and the cricket ground built over. Or is there a chance that although houses now probably cover the site of the ground, there is a pub still standing that was once called *The Royal Veteran*?

A fair percentage of those associated with Surrey County Cricket Club are aware that the club has its roots in the Montpelier Club, although both the link and any knowledge of the earlier club will have faded over the passing years. In 2009 Surrey County Cricket Club decided to market "one of the most exclusive facilities in world cricket." Limited to seventy members and giving members personalised seating on their own terrace close to the player's entrance onto the field, luxury restaurant facilities and a bar service direct to the seats, it was called *The Montpelier Club* and I hope Surrey County Cricket Club will not mind me referring to their web-site as they pronounce "Those signing up for Montpelier Club seats will enjoy……an all inclusive food and drink package including a champagne reception, breakfast, a three course lunch with fine wine, afternoon tea, complimentary bar and an internationally renowned guest speaker…..The Club has been named after Montpelier CC, one of England's most prominent cricket clubs of the eighteenth and nineteenth century. …..On August 22nd 1845, when Montpelier CC was the leading Club in Surrey, its members gathered at Horn's Tavern to put in place plans to form Surrey County Cricket Club, and play on a cabbage patch and market garden leased to them by the Duchy of Cornwall. Just under two months later, on October 18th, Surrey C.C.C. was born with seventy Montpelier members forming the initial membership of the Club."

The members and players of the Montpelier Cricket Club would be very impressed to know that they were being remembered in such style over one-hundred-and-forty years later.

It has taken me many hours to convert the notes I took from the microfilm at the library into typed text and this brought with it, the problem of lay-out. I settled on a diary style; not my first choice of presentation, but one that would give me the chance to intersperse the notes taken from *Bell's Life* and *The Era* with other snippet's of information, short biographies of players, prints that I have found and photographs that I have taken. I hope that I have managed to break it up sufficiently well and that it does not read like a till-receipt.

I am very aware however that much of their history was never written down, or has been lost in time. I therefore join Charles Alcock and Arthur Haygarth in being frustrated at being unable to establish much about this club. However on the positive side we can trace the history of the club from 1796 to 1856, although this does include two breaks, and one was a long one.

Much of my research is inconclusive and there is much left to find, however I hope that what I have managed to unearth in three years from so many sources is interesting and gives others a good head start should they attempt to research this former club further.

Chapter Ten

Firsts, Lasts, Facts and Figures

To conclude the book I have included various lists appertaining to the Montpelier Club. From the many match reports that I have looked at, I have endeavoured to compile an accurate idea of the period of occupation for each of the four grounds that they called "home". These also include details of other matches that took place at these grounds if they were earlier or later.

I have also listed the Montpelier Club matches that feature in the individual works of Britcher, Buckley, Denison, Haygarth and Waghorn on subsequent pages.

<u>Montpelier Gardens</u>

<u>First reported match</u>:

Montpelier v Marylebone + Thursday on June 25th 1796
(*Scores and Biographies*)

<u>First reported Montpelier Club match</u>:

As above

<u>Last reported Montpelier Club match</u>:

v Homerton on June 12th 1806
(*Scores and Biographies*)

<u>Last reported match</u>:

Montpelier Tuesday v Marylebone Friday on July 7th 1808
(*Morning Post* but not in *Scores and Biographies*)

On the club's "second-coming" the match below appears to be their last:

Montpelier v Mile End New Globe <u>reported</u> on July 28th 1833
(*Bell's Life*)

Montpelier Club v Mile End New Globe 1835
(p 106 of *Annals of Cricket* by W.W. Read, but not in *Scores and Biographies*)
I believe the above venue to be an error, as by this time they were playing at the Beehive ground.)

The Beehive

First reported match:

Montpelier v Brompton on August 24th 1831
(*Bell's Life*)

(On June 19th 1831 a forthcoming match between Beehive Club v Blackheath is advertised in *Bell's Life*, yet to date I have not been able to find a report of it)

First reported Montpelier Club match:

As above

Last recorded Montpelier Club match:

v Clapton on July 23rd 1844
(*Bell's Life*)

The matches against South London on August 27th 1844 (reported in *Bell's Life* on Sept 1st) and on June 20th 1845 (reported in *Bell's Life* on June 29th 1844), were I believe home matches for the South London Club.

Last reported match:

Mr Monkhouse's X1 v Mr Houghton's X1 on October 1st 1846
(*Bell's Life*)

The Oval

First reported Montpelier Club match:

v Clapton on July 17th 1845
(*Scores and Biographies* and *Annals of Cricket* by W.W. Read)

Last reported Montpelier Club match:

v Carshalton on August 14th 1847
(*Scores and Biographies*)

Royal Veteran Ground, Coldharbour Lane

First reported Montpelier Club match:

v Croydon July 19th 1848
(*Scores and Biographies*)

Last reported Montpelier Club match:

v West Wickham August 22nd 1849
(*Scores and Biographies*)

A List of All the Principal Matches of Cricket That Have Been Played (1790-1805)

Samuel Britcher

Samuel Britcher's books cover matches between 1790-1805 and the Montpelier club's first mention is when they play M.C.C. on June 24th-25th 1796 at the Montpelier Gardens ground.

The book informs "The Montpelier Club was formed at a ground that had recently opened tea gardens, in Walworth, South London. By 1797, two years after this match, the gardens were home to at least three clubs - the Montpelier Monday, Wednesday, Saturdays - to which were added at least a Thursday club by 1800, and a Tuesday club by 1808 - what could be termed a working week."

We finally have a quotable article from the era which tells of the club's formation and also highlights that there were many other clubs playing under the Montpelier banner. As will be seen below, Britcher features some matches that are not to be found in Haygarth's tomes:

1796

Jul 6th-7th Montpelier v M.C.C. at Lord's - "M.C.C. won by 8 wickets".

Jul 13th-15th M.C.C. v Montpelier at Lord's - "M.C.C. won by 7 wickets".

Jul 25th Montpelier v Middlesex Club at Montpelier Gardens - no result shown.

Aug 15th-16th Montpelier v Highgate at Montpelier Gardens - "Highgate narrowly failed to win".

Aug 26th Montpelier and Kennington Clubs v Middlesex at Montpelier Gardens - "Postponed with home clubs needing 50 for victory".

1797

Jun 12th-13th Montpelier v M.C.C. at Montpelier Gardens - "MCC won by 42 runs".

Jun 22nd+24th Saturday's Club v Whitehall Club at Montpelier Gardens - no result shown.

Jun 26th-27th Montpelier v M.C.C. at Lord's - "MCC far too powerful for the South London club".

Aug 1st-2nd Montpelier v Fulham Club at Parson's Green - "Fulham won by an innings and 13 runs".

Aug 9th Montpelier v Parson's Green at Montpelier Gardens - "no result shown.

Sep 4th-6th Montpelier v M.C.C. at Montpelier Gardens - "As the game developed, Montpelier cruised past the MCC total".

1798

May 28th-29th M.C.C. v Montpelier at Lord's - Montpelier won by 55 runs.

Jun 13th-14th Montpelier v M.C.C. at Montpelier Gardens - MCC won by 155 runs.

Jun 25th-26th Saturday Club v Whitehall Club at Montpelier Gardens - "The weekend men did not have to bat for a second team".

Sep 3rd Montpelier v Woolwich at Blackheath - A single wicket match - "Woolwich won convincingly" Hampton and Tanner played for Montpelier and Stillman and Read for Woolwich.

Sep 26th Montpelier v Woolwich at Montpelier Gardens - no result shown.

Oct 8th-9th Woolwich v Montpelier at Barrack Field, Woolwich - "Game postponed with Woolwich needing 13 runs to win".

1799

Jun 17th-18th Montpelier v Richmond & Brentford at Montpelier Gardens - no result shown.

Jun 27th-28th Richmond & Brentford v Montpelier at Richmond Green -

Montpelier won by 48 runs.

Jul 4th-5th Saturday's Club v Homerton at Montpelier Gardens - Saturday won by 9 wickets.

Jul 19th-20th Homerton v Saturday's Club at Homerton - Homerton won by 5 wickets.

Sep 27th Hampton v Ray at Montpelier Gardens "Hampton was playing under Montpelier colours and Ray under the colours of those of the MCC. A single wicket match, which was won by the former.

The reports from now on are very abrupt.

1800

Jun 25th Homerton v Montpelier at Homerton - no result shown.

Jun 26th Montpelier v Richmond at Montpelier Gardens - Montpelier won by 52 runs.

Jul 2nd-3rd Richmond v Montpelier at Richmond - Richmond won by 69 runs.

Jul 3rd Homerton v Montpelier at Homerton - Homerton won by 4 wickets.

Jul 24th-25th Woolwich v Montpelier at Barrack Fields, Woolwich - Woolwich won by 8 wickets.

These matches show again the size of the club, as on July 3rd the club is shown playing two matches at different venues.

1801

Jun 11th Homerton v Montpelier at Homerton - Montpelier won by 3 wickets.

Jun 30th Montpelier v Homerton at Montpelier Gardens - "Montpelier won by 18 runs".

Aug 6th Montpelier v Deptford at Montpelier Gardens - Montpelier won by 25 runs.

Aug 22nd Deptford v Montpelier at Blackheath - Montpelier won by 7 wickets, with seven men".

Sep 3rd Montpelier v Kennington at Kennington Common - Montpelier won by 61 runs.

Sep 21st Woolwich v Montpelier at Woolwich Common - "Wet weather caused this match to be postponed until next season when the rain arrived. Montpelier were 55 runs ahead with 3 wickets down".

1802

Jul 12th Montpelier v Homerton at Montpelier Gardens - Homerton won by 5 wickets.

Jul 13th Montpelier v Woolwich at Montpelier Gardens - Woolwich won by 7 wickets.

Jul 19th Woolwich v Montpelier at Woolwich - no result shown.

Aug 2nd Montpelier v Richmond at Montpelier Gardens - Montpelier won by 13 runs.

Aug 12th Montpelier Saturday Club v Homerton at Montpelier Gardens - Montpelier won by an innings and 22 runs.

Sep 3rd Richmond v Montpelier at Richmond Green - A tie.

1803

Aug 29th Montpelier v Homerton at Montpelier Gardens - Homerton won by 30 runs.

On page 122 it is noted "At this point we bid farewell to Britcher's named involvement with the scores." There are no more Montpelier matches featured in the books although on Aug 12th and 21st 1805 their familiar rivals Homerton and Richmond play each other.

Unpublished Manuscript

George Buckley

I must thank Norman Epps and Roger Heavens for sending me a bundle of extra Montpelier Club matches which feature in the above manuscript (Padwick 800) and which to date has never been published. Most of these matches were played between 1801-03 and perhaps unexpectedly are covered in Britcher's *A List of All the Principal Matches of Cricket That Have Been Played (1790 to 1805).* Some are also covered in Buckley's own *Fresh Light on pre-Victorian Cricket* albeit with an occasional slight difference in date or venue. However some have not been published before, or were originally shown without results, so they are another welcome addition to the book.

1801

Jun 11th — Homerton v Montpelier at Homerton - Montpelier won by 3 wickets.

Aug 7th — Montpelier Thursday v Deptford at Montpelier Gardens - Montpelier Thursday won by 25 runs.

Aug 14th — Deptford v Montpelier Thursday at Blackheath - Montpelier Thursday won by 7 wickets.

Sep 3rd — Montpelier Thursday v Kennington at Montpelier Gardens - Kennington won by 5 wickets.

Sep 21st — Woolwich v Montpelier at Woolwich Common - no result shown.

1802

Jun 24th — Montpelier v Homerton at the new ground, Homerton - Montpelier won by 3 wickets.

Jul 13th — Montpelier v Woolwich at Montpelier Gardens - Woolwich won by 7 wickets.

Jul 26th — Woolwich v Montpelier at Woolwich - Montpelier won by 40 runs.

Aug 12th Montpelier Saturday v Homerton at Montpelier Gardens - Montpelier Saturday won by an innings and 22 runs.

Aug 18th Montpelier Saturday Club v Homerton and Richmond at Montpelier Gardens - Montpelier won by 13 runs.

Sep 3rd Richmond v Montpelier Saturday at Richmond Green - A tie.

1803

Aug 31st Montpelier v Homerton at Montpelier Gardens - Homerton won by 30 runs.

1842

Jul 4th Lingfield v Montpelier at Lingfield - no result shown.

1843

Sep 29th County of Essex v Montpelier at Abridge - no result is shown but County of Essex scored 115 and Montpelier 31 and 56-2 so the home team would have won by way of first innings scores.

Fresh Light on Pre-Victorian Cricket

George Buckley

I must thank Roger Packham for sending me details of these extra Montpelier Club matches which feature in the above book (on page 163) under the sub-title "JOHN NYREN'S scores which are unrecorded in S. & B." They are matches in which Nyren played for the club, although I have omitted his scores which are detailed in the book.

1801

Jun 11th Montpelier Saturday v Homerton away.

Sep 21st Montpelier v Woolwich away.

1802

Jun 24th Montpelier Saturday v Homerton away.

Jul 12th Montpelier v Woolwich away.

Aug 12th Montpelier v Homerton away.

Aug 18th Montpelier Saturday v Homerton & Richmond home.

Sep 3rd Montpelier v Richmond away.

1803

Aug 31st Homerton v Montpelier away.

Fresh Light on 18th Century Cricket

George Buckley

I must again thank Roger Packham for sending me details of these extra Montpelier Club matches to be found in the second of this compiler's works.

1797

Jun 22nd + 24th	Montpelier Saturday v Whitehall Club Montpelier Gardens.

1800

Jun 25th	Montpelier v Richmond Montpelier Gardens.
Jul 2nd	Richmond v Montpelier Richmond Green.

Cricketer's Companion

William Denison

Another series of early scorebooks were compiled by William Denison; of Montpelier Club and Surrey County Club fame. These records have recently been re-issued by David Ravern Allen who writes "William Denison is a natural successor to Samuel Britcher. One paved the way for the other" .... "Britcher, the first known scorer of M.C.C., gave his name to a series of fifteen annual productions which ran from 1790-1804/5, giving details of the ground matches of the period." Despite the results often being very brief, the compilations feature matches not found in Haygarth's works.

1843

Jun 19th Montpelier v Putney Clarence at Montpelier Gardens - Montpelier won by 32 runs (I believe this venue to be an error as by now they were playing at the Beehive Ground).

Jul 12th Montpelier v Chelsfield at Walworth - Montpelier won by 105 runs.

Jul 19th Montpelier v Clapton at Walworth - "At 8 o'clock Montpelier were 176 ahead with 5 wickets to go down".

1844

May 27th Putney Clarence v Montpelier at Finch's Ground - Montpelier won by 7 wickets.

Jun 12th Lingfield v Montpelier at Lingfield - Montpelier on first innings won by 75 runs.

Jun 20th Clapton v Montpelier at Clapton - Montpelier won by an innings and 63 runs.

Jun 26th Montpelier v Putney Clarence at Beehive Ground - Montpelier won on first innings by 66 runs.

Jul 3rd Montpelier v Lingfield at Beehive Ground - Montpelier won on first innings by 75 runs.

Jul 12th Montpelier v Bromley at Beehive Ground - "Bromley won by 4 wickets and 12 runs on first innings".

Jul 23rd Montpelier v Clapton at Beehive Ground - Montpelier won by 89 runs on first innings.

1845

Jun 27th Bromley v Montpelier at Bromley - Montpelier won by 95 runs.

Jul 11th Islington Albion v Montpelier at Copenhagen Ground - Islington 213 Montpelier 104-5.

Jul 28th Montpelier v Lingfield at Kennington Oval - Montpelier won by 84 runs.

Jul 30th Montpelier v South London at unknown - South London won by 35 runs.

Jul 31st Upper Clapton v Montpelier at Clapton - Clapton won by 10 runs.

Aug 8th Reading v Montpelier at Reading - Montpelier won by 87 runs.

Aug 18th Montpelier v Islington Albion at Kennington Oval - Islington won by 40 runs on first innings.

Aug 25th Lingfield v Montpelier at Kennington Oval - Montpelier won by 23 runs on first innings.

Sep 9th Montpelier v Reading at Kennington Oval - Drawn, Montpelier "had 3 wickets to go down for 18 runs.

1846

Jun 16th Clapton v Montpelier at Clapton - Clapton won by 40 runs.

Jun 24th South London v Montpelier at Kennington Oval - South London by 19 runs.

Jul 7th Hartley Row v Montpelier at Hartley Row - Montpelier won by 51 runs on first innings.

Jul 9th Montpelier v Upper Clapton at Kennington Oval - Clapton won by 12 runs on first innings.

Aug 17th Montpelier v Enfield at Kennington Oval - Montpelier won by 127 runs.

Aug 31st Islington Albion v Montpelier at Copenhagen Ground - Islington by 45 runs.

Scores and Biographies

Arthur Haygarth

Jun 24th 1796	Thursday and Montpelier v M.C.C. at Montpelier Gardens.
Jul 13th 1796	Thursday and Montpelier v M.C.C. at Lord's.
Aug 12th 1796	Thursday Club v Montpelier and Kennington at Lord's.
Aug 26th 1796	Montpelier and Kennington v Thursday Club at Montpelier Gardens.
Jun 12th 1797	Montpelier Wednesday v M.C.C. at Montpelier.
Jun 26th 1797	M.C.C. v Montpelier at Lord's.
Sep 4th 1797	Montpelier v M.C.C. at Aram's New Ground (Montpelier).
May 28th 1798	M.C.C. v Montpelier at Lord's.
Jun 13th 1798	Montpelier v M.C.C. at Aram's New Ground (Montpelier).
Jun 17th 1799	Montpelier v Richmond & Brentford at. Aram's New Ground (Montpelier).
Jul 4th 1799	Montpelier v Homerton at Aram's New Ground (Montpelier).
Jul 19th 1799	Montpelier Saturday v Homerton at Homerton.
Jun 25th 1800	Montpelier v Homerton at unknown venue.
Jul 3rd 1800	Homerton v Montpelier Thursday at Homerton.
Jun 30th 1801	Homerton v Montpelier at Homerton.
Jul 6th 1802	Montpelier v Homerton at Aram's New Ground (Montpelier).
Jun 29th 1803	M.C.C. v Montpelier at Lord's.

Jun 12th 1806	Montpelier v Homerton at Aram's New Ground (Montpelier).
Jul 21st 1813	M.C.C. v Montpelier at Lord's.
Jun 28th 1837	Montpelier v Mitcham at Beehive.
Jun 26th 1838	Chertsey v Montpelier at Chertsey.
Jul 19th 1838	Chertsey v Montpelier at Chertsey.
Jun 24th 1839	Montpelier v Lingfield at Beehive.
Jun 29th 1841	Montpelier v Islington Albion at Walworth.
Jun 29th 1843	Dartford v Montpelier at Dartford.
Jul 19th 1843	Montpelier v Upper Clapton at Beehive.
Jun 20th 1844	Clapton v Montpelier at Clapton.
Jul 23rd 1844	Clapton v Montpelier at Clapton.
Jul 17th 1845	Montpelier v Clapton at Oval.
Jul 28th 1845	Montpelier v Lingfield at Oval.
Jul 31st 1845	Upper Clapton v Montpelier at Clapton.
Aug 16th 1845	Montpelier v Islington Albion at Oval.
Jun 16th 1846	Clapton v Montpelier v Clapton.
Jul 2nd 1846	Montpelier v Surrey at Oval.
Jul 9th 1846	Montpelier v Upper Clapton at Oval.
Jul 15th 1846	Montpelier v Islington Albion at Oval.
Jul 27th 1846	Chertsey v Montpelier at Garratt's Field.
Aug 24th 1846	Montpelier v Chertsey at Oval.

Aug 31st 1846 Islington Albion v Montpelier at Copenhagen Ground.

Jun 6th 1847 Hartley Wintney v Montpelier at Hartley Row.

Jun 24th 1847 Montpelier v Harrow Town at Oval.

Aug 14th 1847 Montpelier v Carshalton at Oval.

Jun 26th 1848 Bramshill v Montpelier at Sir John Cope's Ground.

Jul 19th 1848 Montpelier v Croydon at Coldharbour Lane, Brixton.

Jul 12th 1849 Islington Albion v Montpelier at Copenhagen Gardens, Islington.

Aug 22nd 1849 Montpelier v Islington Albion at Coldharbour Lane, Brixton.

Aug 5th 1850 Islington Albion v Montpelier at Copenhagen Gardens, Islington.

No trace of the club for 1851-54 inclusive.

Two More Matches

I must thank Roger Packham for passing on brief details of two more Montpelier matches which he found in the *Sussex Agricultural Express* newspaper. Although there were no details of either opposition, the dates and venues of the matches are a welcome addition.

Jun 24th 1848 Montpelier v Unknown at New Cricket Ground (probably Royal Veteran Ground, Brixton).

Jun 16th 1849 Montpelier v Unknown (probably Dorking) at Dorking.

The Dawn of Cricket

Henry Waghorn

Two more early compilations were *The Dawn of Cricket* and *Cricket Scores: 1730-1770* by the above gentleman who worked at the British Museum. He used some of his spare time there to study old newspapers and periodicals and from them glean old cricket scores and reports. I must thank Ian Maun and Roger Packham for passing on details from the former of these works.

There may well be more examples of Montpelier matches listed in his works but the below are certainly to be found within the pages of his compilations.

1796

Jul 6th -7th Montpelier v Thursday at Lord's. He further states that this match took place on August 12th having been postponed from these dates. Thursday Club won by 8 wickets.

Jul 25th Montpelier v Highgate at Montpelier - Montpelier won by 6 runs.

1800

Jul 24th + 25th Woolwich v Montpelier at Barrack Field, Woolwich - Woolwich won by 8 wickets.

The author at The Oval in August 2009, taken by Surrey C.C.C. supporter John Banfield. He spent this season watching Surrey fail to ignite and disappoint in all four competitions. He saw them play at Bristol, Canterbury and Northampton, but did not attend any 20/20 "cricket". He has been a member of Surrey C.C.C. for thirty years and is a member of The Cricket Society, The Cricket Memorabilia Society and The Association of Cricket Statisticians.

I would like to thank John Banfield for allowing me to use this photograph.